ERNEST HEMINGWAY'S *A Moveable Feast*

Jacqueline Tavernier-Courbin

ERNEST HEMINGWAY'S
A Moveable Feast

THE MAKING OF MYTH

Northeastern University Press
BOSTON

Northeastern University Press

Library of Congress Cataloging-in-Publication Data

Tavernier-Courbin, Jacqueline.
   Ernest Hemingway's A Moveable Feast : The Making of Myth /
   Jacqueline Tavernier-Courbin.
      p. cm.
   Includes bibliographical references and index.
   ISBN 1-55553-103-2
      1. Hemingway, Ernest, 1899–1961—Biography. 2. Hemingway, Ernest,
   1899–1961. Moveable Feast. 3. Authors, American—20th century—Biography—History and criticism. 4. Paris (France) in literature. 5. Myth in
   literature. 6. Autobiography. I. Title. PS3515.E37Z8916   1991
   813'.52—dc20
   [B]   90-24537

Designed by Ann Twombly

Composed in Plantin by Graphic Composition, Inc., Athens, Georgia.
Printed and bound by Princeton University Press in Lawrenceville, N.J.
The paper is Glatfelter Writers Offset, an acid-free sheet.

MANUFACTURED IN THE UNITED STATES OF AMERICA
96 95 94 93 92 91   5 4 3 2 1

TO MY FATHER

CONTENTS

PREFACE

> Memory has idealized life, shedding it into literature. As a
> trained reporter I have to distrust the whole process. I remember
> the sound Hemingway formula—write it down on the spot. Or
> can emotion be recollected in tranquility? My foot! Reconsti-
> tuted, yes. Recollected as it was? Never. "True feeling," said
> Stendhal, "leaves no memory." Which is the fact of the matter? I,
> a man reborn without a memory, wish to believe that feeling is
> like the rain that seeps into the earth, lies there invisibly feeding
> the life that grows above it. Call it memory, knowledge,
> experience, what matters so long as it lives, sways in the winds,
> gives life to others.
> —Sean O'Faolain, *And Again?*

A Moveable Feast is clearly a reconstruction of the past rather than
a recollection of it. As Hemingway well knew, no one can write
"true facts in reminiscences," especially thirty years after the fact, when
the mind has had more than enough time to rewrite history, change, forget, distort, and remember selectively experiences which, even at the
time, had been perceived and lived subjectively, as must necessarily be
the case. Moreover, at the time of creation, the writer necessarily takes
artistic liberties, even in the writing of autobiography. As Diderot indicated clearly in "Le paradoxe sur le comédien" (1830), it is not when one
has just lost a friend or a lover that one can compose a poem on his death.
It is only when acute suffering has been dulled, when extreme sensitive-
ness has been deadened, when the catastrophe is a thing of the past and
the soul is quiet, that one can recall lost happiness and appreciate one's
loss, that memory and imagination can work together to recall the sweet-
ness of the past, and that, self-possessed, one can write well. When one
is hunting for the right word, the expression that will translate pain effectively, one is not suffering. When tears are flowing, one can no longer
write.

Artistic creation usually involves three major and very broad stages:
the experience, marked as it usually is by emotion and passion; the dis-
tancing, which can take any length of time and which is marked by a slow
decanting of emotions, and a psychological reordering of experiences ac-

cording to a preferential rather than a chronological order; and finally the artistic phase, when the creator's personality is split three ways: the one who recalls, the one who writes, and the one who becomes the reader and evaluates the effectiveness of the description. For Hemingway the first stage took place between 1921 and 1926, during his marriage to Hadley Richardson and his life in Paris; the third stage, between 1956 and 1961; and the second stage involved the thirty intervening years which were marked by, among other things, his three other marriages, his participation in World War II, his many adventures, successes, and failures, and eventually his serious physical and psychological illness. The material, which was highly subjective to start with, had therefore had much time to settle, decant, and become transformed.

Autobiographical theory, the complex critical issues involved in the writing of autobiography versus fiction, and the complex problems of creativity, even as they relate to *A Moveable Feast,* would require an entire book, and such is not the aim of this one. My purpose, instead, is to show how *A Moveable Feast* came into being, trace its conceptualization and the myth surrounding it, and examine the periods of time Hemingway actually devoted to the writing of it, the various stages of is composition, and the many posthumous alterations made by his editors and by Mary Hemingway. I also examine its origins in Hemingway's verifiable personal experience, his steady and complex combination of facts and fiction, and the admixture of legend about lost manuscripts, poverty, and fidelity, as well as his descriptions of the places he loved so much. Since some scholars believe that major parts of the book were written in the 1920s, I also examine early manuscripts that he could have used either as reminders of events or as models for some scenes. Naturally, this led me to look at chapters he had written for *A Moveable Feast* but eventually decided not to include in the book.

The first five chapters of this book are devoted to a critical study of the development and verity of the myth concerning the book's creation, of the last years of Hemingway's life while he was reminiscing, of the respective amounts of fact and fiction contained in the book, of the accuracy of his description of the setting, and to an analysis of his technique of self-portrayal through his portrayal of others. The last three chapters are devoted to a study of the manuscripts.

Theories of autobiography are changing, and many now believe that autobiography need not be factually verifiable—that, in fact, it may be just as fictional as fiction—and that even the background need not be accurate since one is always dealing with an imaginary world, whether it be Paris or an imaginary city on an imaginary planet. I have refrained from discussing such issues as the fictionality of all writing—whether it be ostensibly presented as fiction, biography, or autobiography—or the subjectivity of all fiction. Such issues are not new or about to be resolved. For centuries philosophers and writers have been aware of them and have debated them. We all know that our physical and mental machinery is not perfect, that it perceives and remembers selectively, that our perceptions are colored and distorted by our likes, dislikes, fears, dreams, and everything else that makes up our individualities. We are also aware that the act of creation is intimately linked to the personality of the creator, that imagination has its roots in the self and in personal experience, that there can be no such thing as perfect realism, that the "real" in fiction and in life are not the same thing, that fiction is what *seems* real, not what *is* real, and that the novelist may often have to correct actual facts for the sake of verisimilitude and to the detriment of accuracy. The lines separating the genres are in fact very shaky, and apparently opposite literary schools are far from incompatible. Schools or genres are nothing but labels which by their very nature simplify and therefore distort human experience. Whether literary or critical, they often do little more than reinvent and relabel tendencies which have existed since the very beginnings of literature, and autobiography, despite its avowed aim, can never possibly be objective self-appraisal or objective narration of the past. Like all issues involving the way the mind functions, the problem of artistic creation will not be solved until psychology has become an exact science, which is a most unlikely occurrence.

Aside from artistic achievement itself, and granted the limitations of the human mind and eye, we are still left with the problem of personal honesty when dealing with a work of art that purports to be autobiographical, or which has been advertised as such. As will be seen in "The Mystery of the Ritz Hotel Papers," Hemingway went to great lengths to advertise *A Moveable Feast* as an autobiography of his early years in Paris, written long after the fact but based solidly on documentary evidence and on an excellent memory. He thus opened the door to what is the focus of my book: an objective examination, at least to the extent that my own "weak mental machinery will allow," of the book as an autobiography narrating events that are supposed to have taken place in the very real settings of France and Austria—the very type of critical detective work he disliked. After the book was written, Hemingway had serious qualms about its accuracy and the distortions it contained, and he kept repeating in the manuscripts that it was fiction and could not be anything else. But he had already carefully set the stage for it to be read as autobiography, and I am reading it as such in "Fact and Fiction" and in "Hemingway's Paris, Lyon, and Schruns." In presenting the evidence I have found, I do not really argue whether the book should be read as fiction or as autobiography. For me it is both to a large extent, as all autobiography must be at least to some extent. What interests me is the complex proportion of fact and fiction, what can be determined and what may never be, and what it reveals about the author.

That Hemingway's editors were concerned, just as he himself was, with the problem of accuracy is revealed in a letter from Mary Hemingway to Hadley, in which she asks Hadley to do whatever she thinks best about "Papa's early years": "I know next to nothing about them, naturally, and could not pretend to judge the accuracy of anyone else's recollections. Maybe you and Bumby together might wish to do something sometime" (20 July 1961). Assuming that Hemingway would have wanted it to be, the book might have been more true to the facts had it been written in the 1920s, but then it would not have had the emotional impact the book written at the close of his life has, for he would have been too close to the experience. The years separating his lost happiness from its narration allowed him to appreciate his loss, allowed his memory to unite with his imagination to recreate past events, exaggerate the lost happiness, and surround even the most minor occurrence with a halo of significance. The book combines the best of Hemingway's style with the perspective necessary to unify the various experiences into a myth of himself—a myth which he had started many years before and which he attempts to consecrate in his autobiography.

A Moveable Feast is beautifully written and truly vintage Hemingway. For me, Hemingway's greatest achievement has always been in the descriptions of places he loved, such as Paris, Spain, Italy, and Africa. They have been the saving grace of books such as *The Garden of Eden* and *Across the River and into the Trees*. Paradoxically, unlike F. Scott Fitzgerald in *Tender Is the Night*, Hemingway was unable to capture the atmosphere of the French Riviera in *The Garden of Eden*. It just does not come to life, while Paris does come to life in *A Moveable Feast*. Some of the descriptions of life in Paris are as vivid as any in *The Sun Also Rises*, and they are far more numerous, for the focus of the book is as much Paris as those who lived there. Moreover, *A Moveable Feast* is pervaded by a strong feeling of nostalgia—the nostalgia of an old man looking back on his youth, his first, and some might say his only great love, and his years of apprenticeship in a city not only very beautiful but also perhaps the most romantic and artistic in the world. This very nostalgia adds a new dimension to Hemingway's descriptions of Paris that is not present in *The Sun Also Rises,* and it may well be the greatest quality of Hemingway's autobiography. Without the wonderful prose and the emotional undertones constantly present, the commentary about other writers and the descriptions of often minor incidents would be far less exciting or amusing. What makes the book poignant is the fact that Hemingway was afraid of no longer being able to write, while he was in fact writing so well. The subtext that is always present and constantly telling us "I loved and I lost; I was a writer and I can no longer write" makes every description of Paris and of life with Hadley a deeply moving experience which, in the final analysis, transcends the gossip and the pettiness often present in the book. It is the quality of the writing that makes us read *A Moveable Feast,* enjoy the anecdotes, and bear with the self-glorification of Hemingway. While some scholars still find it hard to believe that Hemingway actually wrote the book at the end of his life, I have found no evidence to even suggest that he had written it in earlier years. To me, *A Moveable Feast* is indeed his last great achievement.

Some of my early and partial findings were presented in a number of articles, including "The Mystery of the Ritz Hotel Papers" (*College Literature,* 1980, reprinted in *Ernest Hemingway: Papers of a Writer,* ed. Bernard Oldsey [New York: Garland, 1981]), "The Manuscripts of *A Moveable Feast*" (*Hemingway Notes,* 1981), "The Paris Notebooks" (*Hemingway Review,* 1981), and "Fiction and Reality in Ernest Hemingway's *A Moveable Feast*" (*Hemingway Review,* 1985). I am grateful to these journals for allowing me to reuse some of the material here. However, it has been expanded, put in a broader context, developed much more fully, and sometimes, as is often the result of more comprehensive and detailed work, the conclusions have been revised. Furthermore, new research based on manuscripts and letters now available at the John F. Kennedy Library yielded interesting new documents.

Some of the research was carried out with the help of a Leave Fellowship in 1979–80 and two Time Research Stipends from the Social Sciences and Humanities Research Council of Canada in 1983 and 1987–88, which allowed me to spend several periods of time at the John F. Kennedy Library in Boston, which houses the main Hemingway manuscript collection, at the Beinecke Library at Yale University, and at the Princeton University Library. I also read the Hemingway family letters at the Humanities Research Center at the University of Texas in Austin.

I refer extensively to unpublished manuscripts, which are identified by their file numbers in the Kennedy Library collection, and to unpublished letters. However, I have refrained from quoting at any length from unpublished manuscripts and letters because of the still uncertain copyright situation of the Hemingway estate. Long quotations from the manuscripts and from Hemingway's letters were either published previously or authorized by the Hemingway Foundation. An effort has been made to preserve Hemingway's spelling in these quotations. I have departed from the traditional French practice of not capitalizing the word *rue* and have capitalized it throughout for the sake of visual emphasis.

I want to thank Jo August and her successors at the Kennedy Library for the help they gave me during my work there, as well as the librarians at the Bibliothèque de l'Hôtel de Ville de Paris, who were not only very helpful but also very patient with the "weird" topics I was researching, in particular, the presence of goats in the streets of Paris in the 1920s and the points of access to the sewers of Paris. They did look a little incredulous at first when I explained what I was after, but without their help, I might never have found the answers. I also want to thank a librarian at the Bibliothèque du Musée du Luxembourg who helped me in my research concerning the paintings present at the Luxembourg in the 1920s by bringing relevant books down to me so that I could read them in the gardens, since that library is a parliamentary library closed to the general public and scholars like myself. He certainly went beyond the call of duty.

Hemingway's Life with Hadley

3 September 1921: Marriage of Ernest Hemingway and Hadley Richardson in Horton Bay, Michigan. They honeymoon for two weeks at Windemere, Ernest's parents' chalet near Lake Michigan.

December: They cross over to Europe aboard the *Leopoldina* and arrive in Paris shortly before Christmas. They move into the Hôtel Jacob, 44 Rue Jacob, and, after the holidays, into an apartment at 74 Rue du Cardinal-Lemoine, near the Place de la Contrescarpe.

January 1922: Two-week holiday at the Gangwischs' pension in Chamby, near Montreux.

March: Hemingway meets Gertrude Stein.

Mid-May: Hemingway and Hadley set out for a month-long trip. Chink Dorman-Smith joins them in Chamby. They do a lot of hiking.

1 June: They climb through knee-deep snow up the pass of the Saint Bernard and spend the night in a monastery. Then they move on to Aosta, Milan, and Schio. They rent a car and keep traveling, eventually visiting Fossalta-di-Piave, where Ernest had been wounded during World War I.

Mid-June: They resettle in Paris until mid-August, when they leave on a fishing trip to Germany with some friends.

25 September: They have been back for a week when Ernest leaves for Constantinople to cover the war between Greece and Turkey.

21 October: Ernest returns to Paris.

22 November: Ernest arrives in Lausanne to cover the Peace Conference. Hadley's plans to join him are delayed by a bad cold.

December: When Hadley finally joins him, she takes with her all his manuscripts in a suitcase which is stolen on the train.

16 December: They settle at the Gangwischs' pension.

February 1923: They go to Italy to visit Ezra Pound in Rapallo, where they meet Edward O'Brien and Robert McAlmon. Then they move to Cortina d'Ampezzo.

Late March: Hemingway is asked to go to Germany to cover Franco-German relations in the Ruhr. He leaves Hadley in Cortina and takes the train to Paris and on to Germany.

Mid-April: Hemingway returns to Cortina, where he and Hadley stay for a while before returning to Paris.

Late May/Early June: Hemingway takes a trip to Spain with Robert McAlmon and Bill Bird.

July: He returns to Spain, this time with Hadley.

17 August: They sail for Canada.

August 1923 to January 1924: The Hemingways have a disappointing stay in Toronto. John Hadley Nicador Hemingway (nicknamed Bumby) is born on 10 October.

19–29 January: They return to France on board the *Antonia*.

February: They move into a new apartment at 113 Rue Notre-Dame-des-Champs.

July: Trip to Spain with Hadley. They are joined there by Chink Dorman-Smith, Bill and Sally Bird, John Dos Passos, Robert McAlmon, Don Stewart, and young George O'Neil. At the end of the Feria (14 July), they go to Burgete, where they rejoin their friends.

Late July: Return to Paris.

19 December: They leave for Schruns in the Vorarlberg, where they stay at the Hôtel Taube until March 1925.

March 1925: The Hemingways meet Pauline Pfeiffer.

May: Hemingway meets F. Scott Fitzgerald. Trip to Lyon to pick up Scott's car.

25 June: Departure for a week of fishing in Burgete with Bill Smith, prior to attending the Pamplona Fiesta with Don Stewart, Harold Loeb, and Lady Duff Twysden. The events that took place during the Fiesta provided the inspiration for *The Sun Also Rises*. After the Fiesta, Hemingway and Hadley move to Madrid. After eight days there, the Hemingways move down to Valencia to escape the cold and be present for Antonio Ordoñez's next engagement, beginning 24 July. Hemingway works on *The Sun Also Rises*.

August: They return to Madrid early in August, then on to San Sebastian, and, later, Hendaye. On 12 August Hadley takes the train back to Paris, while Hemingway stays for another week.

21 September: Hemingway finishes the first draft of *The Sun Also Rises*.

12 December: Arrival in Schruns for their winter stay. Pauline joins them for Christmas and New Year's.

1 January 1926: Hemingway receives a cable from Liveright rejecting *The Torrents of Spring*.

3 February: Hemingway sails for New York on the *Mauretania* to change publishers and sign with Scribner's.

End of February: He returns to Paris and shortly afterwards Schruns.

March: Dos Passos and the Murphys visit the Hemingways in Schruns. The Hemingways return to Paris at the end of the month.

May: Bumby has whooping cough. On 12 May Hemingway leaves for Madrid, and Hadley takes Bumby to Cap d'Antibes. After three weeks in Spain, Ernest joins Hadley at Cap d'Antibes.

June: Hemingway shows *The Sun Also Rises* to Fitzgerald, who recommends major cuts at the beginning. Pauline joins the Hemingways.

July: The Hemingways take Pauline and the Murphys to the Fiesta in Pamplona.

Early August: Stopover at the Villa America; the Hemingways have decided to set up separate residences. They return to Paris. Hemingway moves into Gerald Murphy's studio.

27 January 1927: Hadley and Ernest's divorce becomes final while he and Pauline are skiing in Gstaad, in the Alps.

CHRONOLOGY 1956–1961

The Writing of the Book

17 November 1956: Hemingway leaves Spain and drives back to Paris to settle at the Ritz. Purported discovery of the trunks.

Late January 1957: Mary and Ernest return to the United States on board the *Ile de France*. Mary leaves the ship in New York to go to Minneapolis; Ernest stays on board until Cuba.

Spring 1957: Ernest is depressed; the *Atlantic* requests a sketch on F. Scott Fitzgerald; the sketch is completed by June. But Hemingway sends instead "A Man of the World," written between mid-May and mid-June, and "Get Yourself a Seeing-Eyed Dog," composed in 1956.

July: Hemingway begins writing *A Moveable Feast*.

September/October: Trip to New York.

December: Between three and fourteen sketches are written.

Spring 1958: Ernest keeps on working on *A Moveable Feast* and works on rewriting *The Garden of Eden*.

18 April: The charges against Ezra Pound are dismissed.

31 July: Ernest claims *A Moveable Feast* is virtually finished.

Early October: Trip to Ketchum, Idaho.

November: Bronislaw Zielinski, Aaron Hotchner, and Gary Cooper visit the Hemingways in Ketchum. Hemingway works on *A Moveable Feast*, which he wants to finish before going back to the Finca. He also revises three chapters of *The Garden of Eden*.

20 December: The Hemingways move houses in Ketchum.

February 1959: Hemingway makes arrangements to spend the next summer in Spain.

Mid-March: The Hemingways leave Ketchum by car, with Hotchner driving with them as far as New Orleans. In Key West, they leave the car and fly over to Cuba, arriving on Easter Sunday. Ernest meets Tennessee Williams.

Early May: They arrive at La Consula, the residence of Bill Davis, near Málaga, Spain. Ernest has the manuscript of *A Moveable Feast* with him.

13 May: He has roughed out a draft of a preface for a new school edition of his short stories. He goes to Madrid.

26–30 May: Hemingway follows Antonio Ordoñez's fights in Córdoba, Seville, and Aranjuez. Ordoñez is gored on the 30th and a week later flies down to Málaga to recuperate with Ernest.

May/June: Ernest revises his Preface. When Ordoñez resumes fighting, Ernest follows him once more. By 6 July he has seen twenty bullfights.

28 June: Hotchner catches up with Ernest in Alicante. Ernest meets Valerie Danby-Smith, a nineteen-year-old who introduces herself as a journalist and whom he adopts as his secretary.

21 July: Sixtieth birthday party for Ernest.

Mid-August: In Bilbao, the *mano a mano* between Ordoñez and Dominguín comes to an end with Dominguín's being seriously gored. Shortly afterwards, Ordoñez is also gored again, this time in Dax.

10 October: Hemingway gets down to working on the bullfight article for *Life*. Except for the short-stories preface, he has written nothing all summer.

15 October: 5000 words done on the *mano a mano* piece.

Mid-October: The Hemingways leave Spain for Paris, where they stay until the end of the month, when they board the *Liberté* back to New York.

31 October: Hemingway meets Andrew Turnbull in the ship's bar.

3 November: He delivers the manuscript of *A Moveable Feast* to Scribner's. One chapter is missing.

November: A short stay in Cuba, then a trip to Ketchum with Antonio and Carmen Ordoñez. On November 27 Mary has a shooting accident and shatters her left elbow.

January 1960: They return to Cuba by train, via Miami, in mid-January. He resumes working on the bullfight article; by the end of the month he brings Valerie over as his secretary.

1 April: More than 63,000 words done on "The Dangerous Summer."

28 May: Has 120,000 words completed. By 1 June Ernest shows the first signs of losing his reason.

End of June: He summons Hotchner to help him cut the manuscript.

July: Late in the month, Hemingway goes to Key West because he is overly worried by Valerie's alien status in the U.S. He then flies to New York, while the women come up by train.

21 July: Quiet birthday in New York.

4 August: Ernest flies to Madrid alone. At the end of two weeks, he fears a complete nervous breakdown; he experiences symptoms of extreme nervous depression.

September: Mary sends Valerie over to help him with his mail.

October: Hotchner joins him in Madrid. At last, his friends manage to get him aboard a plane to get back home. He reaches New York on 9 October. After a few days, Mary manages to get him on a train to Idaho, where she hopes he can rest. He arrives on 22 October, still haunted by fears and delusions of persecution.

30 November: He is flown to Rochester, Minnesota, and hospitalized at the Mayo Clinic, St. Mary's Hospital, under an assumed name— George Saviers, the name of his own physician who accompanied him to the hospital.

12 January 1961: Hemingway is invited to the inauguration of John F. Kennedy on 19 and 20 January, but cannot go.

22 January: He is discharged from St. Mary's Hospital and returns to Ketchum. He resumes work on the Paris book, mostly rearranging the sketches in proper sequence.

February: Ernest finds writing difficult and becomes more and more of a recluse. He is unable to write a sentence for a presentation volume to President Kennedy.

March: Return of paranoia and delusions of persecution. Hemingway is very much concerned about the possibility of being sued because of the Paris book. He makes a phone call to Hadley.

21 April: He attempts suicide. Mary manages to buy time by talking to him until the arrival of Dr. Saviers. He is taken to Sun Valley Hospital and put under sedation. Second suicide attempt on 23 April while at home before being flown to the Mayo Clinic, where he is readmitted on 25 April. More difficulties during the flight.

26 June: Ernest is discharged from the Mayo Clinic against Mary's better judgment. They set off for Ketchum with George Brown at the wheel. Ernest's delusions return on the 27th.

30 June: They arrive in Ketchum.

2 July: Suicide of Ernest Hemingway.

ERNEST HEMINGWAY'S *A Moveable Feast*

CHAPTER ONE

The Mystery of the Ritz Hotel Papers

A Moveable Feast is a series of reminiscences written by Hemingway during the last years of his life about the years he spent in Paris with his first wife, Hadley, between 1922 and 1926. Much has been made of the story that, in November 1956, Hemingway supposedly retrieved from the basement of the Ritz Hotel in Paris two trunks which he had left there in 1927. Mary Hemingway, the writer's last wife, and apparently Hemingway himself claimed that it was the discovery of the old papers and manuscripts contained in those trunks that gave him the idea of writing his memoirs of the old days in Paris, and that he used that material of thirty years past in the composition of the book.

This is a very nice story, very much in the same vein as that of the discovery of James Boswell's journals, and there seems to be little reason to doubt it. However, the various accounts of the discovery are often conflicting, and, so far, I have not found a direct statement by Hemingway himself concerning the discovery of the trunks. Moreover, he is reported to have claimed that he found in these trunks manuscripts that could not, in fact, have been there. It is, therefore, important to attempt to determine three things: whether these trunks really existed and, if so, at what time they were left at the Ritz; which papers were in them; and what use Hemingway made of these papers in writing *A Moveable Feast*.

There were various reports concerning the discovery of the trunks even before Mary Hemingway's description of them in the *New York Times Book Review* of 10 May 1964. In fact, the story seems to have originated with Leonard Lyons who, in his column "The Lyons Den" in the *New York Post* of 11 December 1957, mentions the discovery and reports that Hemingway told him that the manuscript of *A Farewell to Arms* was in the trunks, which could hardly have been the case since Hemingway had

3

given that manuscript to Gus Pfeiffer in 1931. Lyons mentions again the discovery of the trunks in his column of 5 January 1964, after Mary Hemingway's press conference of 9 December.[1] However, it seems that Mary had not talked about that discovery in her press conference, since none of the other responses to it refer to the trunks. The story came out in force in April 1964 with George P. Hunt's review in *Life* and, on May 10, with both Mary Hemingway's and Lewis Galantière's in the *New York Times Book Review*, Mildred Carr's in the *Greensboro Daily News*, and Reece Stuart's in the *Des Moines Register*.[2] Mary describes the trunks as follows:

> They were two small, fabric-covered, rectangular boxes, both opening at the seams. . . . The baggage men easily pried open the rusted locks, and Ernest was confronted with the blue-and-yellow-covered penciled notebooks and sheaves of typed papers, ancient newspaper cuttings, bad water colors done by old friends, a few cracked and faded books, some musty sweat shirts and withered sandals. *Ernest had not seen the stuff since 1927, when he packed it and left it at the hotel before going to Key West.* (Italics added)

Mildred Carr is very cautious and, although she gives various details concerning the composition of the book, which she probably obtained from Mary Hemingway or from Hadley (such as the fact that Hemingway telephoned Hadley to ask her to refresh his memory about certain people), she begins her mention of the trunks with "It is said that." Other, less careful, reviewers used their imagination to fill in the details and even transformed the notebooks contained in the trunks into diaries.[3] But all the reviewers clearly linked the discovery of the old manuscripts and the writing of the book. Lewis Galantière, for instance, writes that *A Moveable Feast* is composed of twenty sketches rewritten from Hemingway's notebooks of the years 1921–26; and Mildred Carr asserts that, discovering the notes in 1956, Hemingway began piecing the reminiscences together and in 1960 delivered the manuscript to Scribner's.

In her description of the event, Mary Hemingway first mentions that Ernest had left these trunks at the Ritz in 1927 before going to Key West, which is clearly an error since he did not go to Key West until late March 1928.[4] Similarly, elsewhere in her article, she indicates that the baggage men at the Ritz had asked Hemingway to remove his trunks since 1936, when he had been on his way home from Spain. Again, it is not until 9 to

13 May 1937 that Hemingway was in Paris on his way home from Spain. Mary Hemingway's own report, therefore, contains some inaccuracies.

Of course, after the so-called description of the Ritz Hotel papers by Mary Hemingway and other early reviewers, many scholars and critics described these papers with some assurance and assumed their importance for the composition of *A Moveable Feast*.[5] What is important is not only the fact that everyone took the existence of the trunks and the papers for granted but also the fact that it has been widely held that Hemingway wrote the better parts of *A Moveable Feast* in the early 1920s and the rest—the inferior parts—before his death. Some have even believed that the whole book was written in the 1920s. In fact, the purported use in the writing of the book of the old manuscripts discovered in the trunks has often been seen as evidence that Hemingway had lost his talent and was reduced to plagiarizing his past. That Hemingway found it very hard to write in 1960 and 1961 has been well documented. But, as we shall see, although Hemingway did indeed use some of his earlier writings in the book, he used far less than one might imagine.

A. E. Hotchner's account of his last visit with Hemingway in 1961 enhanced the theory that Hemingway had written the book earlier. Hotchner quoted Hemingway as saying, "The best of that [*A Moveable Feast*] I wrote before. And now I can't finish it."[6] What Hemingway probably meant is that he had written the book in 1956–57. Indeed, he had considered it finished in 1960 when he sent it to Scribner's. He withdrew the manuscript, however, for at least two reasons: officially, because he wanted to improve it (as evidenced by his letter to Charles Scribner of 31 March 1960),[7] and also, probably, because he was afraid of libel suits, as shown by the many drafts he wrote of the preface to the book.

It is interesting to notice that what probably started out as inaccurate reporting on Lyons's part, or even as a distortion of the truth on Hemingway's part, became an accepted fact after Mary Hemingway's review of the book and was generally seen as Hemingway's major motivation for writing his memoirs. Mary Hemingway contradicts herself somewhat in her later description of the event in *How It Was*,[8] and the details that she gives concerning the discovery of the trunks are quite different from those of her earlier account. The progression in her accounts from a rather casual incident to a much more formal occurrence reflects the increasing importance given with time to those trunks and their manuscript contents in the composition of *A Moveable Feast*.

The evidence supporting the story that Hemingway had left trunks of old manuscripts somewhere in Paris—if not necessarily at the Ritz—in the late 1920s, apart from Mary Hemingway's claim, and the evidence suggesting that the discovery of the Ritz Hotel papers was part of Hemingway's myth-making are almost evenly balanced.

Apart from Hemingway's reported claim and Mary's direct claim that he found two trunks of old manuscripts in the basement of the Ritz, there are in Hemingway's correspondence various references to old papers, manuscripts, and letters stored in Paris. Probably the most reliable piece of evidence is found in a letter to Gus Pfeiffer dated 16 March 1928. Gus had asked Hemingway for the manuscripts of "Fifty Grand" and "The Undefeated," and Hemingway wrote back to him:

> I have hunted through all my old trunks here at the apartment to find the manuscripts of Fifty Grand and The Undefeated so I could send them to you. But have found 8 or 10 other mss. but not those. Evidently they are in storage with my 4 trunks of old letters and mss.
>
> So I am enclosing the manuscript of The Killers, the first typescript of The Undefeated and the only part I have found of Fifty Grand. The part I eliminated in publishing it. I hope you will hold these as hostages—they are for you too—until I can find the manuscripts you want when we return in the fall. I put in 6 hours or so going through old stuff in order to "make delivery" but havent found them yet (I never placed any value on them and so did not keep . . . track of them in all my very varied stuff) and am sure they are in storage.

Hemingway was by that time already very fond of Gus Pfeiffer, who had been very good to him and Pauline, and there seems to be no reason why he should lie to him. "When we return in the fall" has to mean "when we return to Paris," for Hemingway had not yet settled in Key West, and the apartment he refers to is the Rue Férou apartment. However, he mentions four trunks and not two, and certainly makes no mention of the Ritz Hotel. Although the date of this letter coincides closely with the time at which Hemingway is supposed to have left his trunks at the Ritz, it does not seem, by the contents of it, that he was doing any such thing.

In a letter to Julien Cornell concerning Ezra Pound's release from prison, Hemingway writes on 11 December 1945: "I do not have any of Ezra Pound's letters here, since I do not believe he has written me since 1935 or 1936. It is very probable that I have some of his old letters stored in Paris." In a handwritten draft of that same letter, he had written: "or, possibly in Key West." Again, this suggests the possibility of papers stored in Paris, although there is no certainty that Pound's letters were among them. However, Hemingway may have used this as an excuse for not taking the trouble to search for Pound's letters in order to send them to Cornell. Pound's letters would, in fact, have added little fuel to Hemingway's claim that he was crazy.

A third and final, although least reliable, reference to papers stored in Paris can be found in a letter from Hemingway to Arnold Gingrich dated 16 November 1934, in which he writes:

> Like [Gilbert] Seldes, I've had him worried about that letter for a very long time now and I'm going to keep him worried. Don't say I mentioned it anymore. I've got it locked up with my papers in Paris and no matter how his critical career comes out this makes a bum of him in the end. I've written all the facts about Gertrude so they'll be on tap if anything happens to me but I don't like to slam the old bitch around when she's here having a wonderful time.

This is probably mostly bluster, for I have not yet been able to locate any such letter from Gilbert Seldes, and Seldes himself strongly denies its existence.[9] Although there are several rather cruel references to Gertrude Stein among Hemingway's papers, there does not seem to be any manuscript such as the one he refers to here. Only "The Autobiography of Alice B. Hemingway"—a six-page typescript titled "complete sketch" and subtitled "or who Taught the Fifth Grade Then?" or "Finally She bit on her nail again, a Little" (File 265a)—might qualify. Although there is no date on this typescript, it probably dates back to 1933 since Pound and Hemingway discuss it in correspondence. In a letter of 22 September 1933 Pound writes Hemingway: "The Stein piece sounds superb. Can't wait to see it. Hope it is funny"; Hemingway himself writes Pound in a letter dated about September 1933 that he has written six typed pages titled "The Autobiography of Alice B. Hemingway," that he thinks Pound will like it, that it is very good and for the *New Yorker.* In a letter to Pauline written at the same time Hemingway again refers to it: "it's you as though I were married to you in temps de Gertrude. 6 pages typed. Think you'll like it. esta muy bien. For the Newyorker." What seems to have prompted this piece is Hemingway's reading, while he was in Spain in 1933, of *The Autobiography of Alice B. Toklas* and James Thurber's *My Life and Hard Times.* It could therefore well be this story Hemingway refers to in his November 1934 letter. However, the Stein piece is obviously fictional and it could hardly have any value as objective proof. Indeed, the papers supposedly stored in Paris were a rather handy weapon for Hemingway, who seems to have had an obsession with claiming that he had concrete evidence to damn his contemporaries.

Thus, at various times in his life, Hemingway claimed that he had papers stored in Paris. However, not all of his old papers were stored there, as evidenced by the draft of his letter to Cornell, as well as by a letter to Arthur Mizener, dated 6 July 1949, in which he claims that he had Fitzgerald's old letters in Key West for a time:

> I had everything filed in a cabinet and in pretty good order, but while I was away at one of the wars someone decided to use the cabinet to keep their files while setting up a small antique business and as a consequence, *much of my early manuscripts, Scott's letters and more or less valuable documents became rat and roach food*. (Italics added)[10]

One might have some doubts as to the accuracy of this statement (since Hemingway is once more apologizing for not sending something of a personal nature to an outsider) were it not for the fact that fourteen years earlier, on 16 December 1935, he had written to Fitzgerald from Key West that he had just found Fitzgerald's long letter to him in which he advised him about the ending of *A Farewell to Arms*. This clearly corroborates the fact that Hemingway had some of his early manuscripts and letters in Key West.

Other evidence of trunks stored in Paris can be found in the correspondence between Hemingway and Gerald Murphy, between Mary Hemingway and Mr. Mourelet, concierge at the Ritz, and between Mary and Hadley. On 20 September 1937 Gerald Murphy wrote to Hemingway that he had left at the Elysée Park Hôtel, where he was staying, three pieces of luggage belonging to Hemingway to be kept in storage. Attached to the letter was a receipt for the luggage from the concierge of the hotel. What these pieces of luggage were is difficult to determine. There is, of course, a slim chance that they might have been pieces of luggage left by Hemingway in Murphy's studio in the Rue Froidevaux ten years earlier. Correspondence between the Hemingways and Mr. Mourelet dates back to 1950 and involves a trunk of old clothes and manuscripts, two boxes of books, and one box of china, which were to be shipped to Cuba. When these had been left at the Ritz is unclear and it seems that the trunk belonged to Mary: "I think we should insure the books for $200.00 and the

China for $100.00. If *my trunk* [italics added] has also been held up, would you insure that and its contents (which are simply personal belongings, old clothes, letters, and manuscripts) for $200.00."[11] One would expect that, if the trunk had contained Hemingway's early manuscripts, it would have been insured for much more than $200. But, then, Hemingway hated paying customs as much as he disliked paying income tax! In any case, the description of the contents of that trunk comes disturbingly close to the description of Hemingway's forgotten trunks at the Ritz.

The last pieces of evidence are provided by Mary Hemingway's letters to Hadley from Ketchum, Idaho, while she was still sorting out Hemingway's papers after his death. On 12 October and 21 November 1961 she writes:

> We are only beginning to go through 3 big Vuiton trunks full of papers Ernest shipped out here 2 years ago and which seem to contain smatterings of everything from fishing licences from Navarra, 1924, to requests for autographs, 1959. (12 October)

> In July 1960 Ernest shipped out here from Cuba three Vuiton trunks full of papers which a couple of years before he had shipped to Cuba from the Ritz Hotel's storeroom somewhere outside Paris. Ever since I got back from Cuba I have been going through these papers with the help of a young Irish girl who was Ernest's secretary in Cuba early in 1960. . . .

> Now we have almost finished with these old papers and the letters here are all of yours that we encountered in these trunks.

This seems to verify Mary's and Hemingway's claim that he had left trunks of papers stored at the Ritz for some time. However, the details of these letters contradict in several respects the information given earlier to Lyons and, later, provided in Mary's own accounts. It is also noteworthy that she makes no mention of manuscripts contained in these Vuitton trunks, or of their contents having been stored at the Ritz for thirty years. In fact, she suggests that the items contained in these trunks date from 1924 to 1959, which could hardly have been the case if the papers transferred to them had been the ones left at the Ritz for thirty years. In this last letter and in an earlier one, dated 31 July 1961, Mary indicates clearly that she is saving Hadley's letters and those of Ernest's old friends, and that she hopes to return them eventually. Surprisingly (if one considers the extensiveness of the Hemingway manuscript and letter collection available), she also indicates that she has been burning Ernest's letters "along with mountains of other papers since he left instructions that they were not to be published." Faithful to her word, though, Mary returned letters to Hadley on 27 April and 2 May 1962.

Outside of Mary's and Ernest's claims, there is therefore no direct evidence in favor of Hemingway's having left trunks of old manuscripts at the Ritz for some thirty years, although there is evidence in favor of his having stored papers, letters, and manuscripts in Paris, perhaps at the Murphys' and at the Elysée Park Hôtel in the 1920s and 1930s and at the Ritz in the 1950s. However, there is valid evidence—if basically negative evidence—that suggests that the discovery of these trunks may have been a myth added to Hemingway's already legendary life.

The most tangible evidence against the discovery of the trunks as Mary described it is the fact that the old employees at the Ritz Hotel who remember Hemingway clearly, and who remember that he often left things at the Ritz from one year to the next, *do not remember* that he left anything for thirty years.[12] Another factor militating against the story as told by Hemingway and Mary is the fact that Ernest apparently never mentioned the discovery of these papers in his private correspondence, even in his letters to close friends like General Lanham and Harvey Breit.

For instance, Hemingway writes to Harvey Breit from the Ritz in Paris, in December 1956, shortly after the papers have supposedly been discovered, and he does not mention that discovery at all; neither does he mention it in any subsequent letter to him. Nor does he mention it to Lanham, to whom he wrote very long letters full of details about his personal life. In his letter to Lanham of 8 April 1957 he talks about the past summer and fall in Spain and Paris, gives many details about his health but does not mention the trunks or the papers. Mary, who wrote to Patrick Hemingway and his wife on 27 December 1956 from the Ritz, makes no mention of the trunks in her long and chatty letter; neither does Hemingway mention them to "Mouse" in any of his letters of that period. As a matter of fact, there does not seem to be one single mention of the trunks in the Hemingway correspondence at the Kennedy, Princeton University, Beinecke, and Houghton Libraries.

Finally, it seems somewhat unlikely that Hemingway would have left two trunks in the Ritz basement before moving to Key West in 1928 instead of shipping them with the rest of his baggage, especially if he considered them important enough to instruct the baggage men at the Ritz to take good care of them, as they contained important papers. Although

Hemingway admittedly had a tendency to leave manuscripts in various places, such as a barn which burned down in Piggott or Sloppy Joe's Bar in Key West, it just does not seem quite logical that he would have left these trunks in a hotel where he and Pauline did not stay even after they had given up the apartment in the Rue Férou. Of course, Hemingway may have been a customer of the Ritz bar as early as the mid-1920s; at least he suggests as much in a short story on World War II, involving his being court-martialed (File 356a):

> I had known him [Georges] when he was seventeen and the wisest
> boy of seventeen I had ever known and the fastest and most skillful.
> He had known me when I had come in with only the money for two
> drinks, coming in no oftener than once a month and happy to see the
> stainless steel beau monde before there was such a thing as stainless
> steel.

However, according to the management of the Ritz, Georges Sheuer was not employed there until 1947. Clearly, by that time, Hemingway could afford to come in more than once a month and have more than two drinks. Again, contradictions abound; but Hemingway may still have been a customer of the Ritz bar in the 1920s, since he was not a fraction as poor as he claimed to be, and friendships with bartenders or baggage men may perhaps have led to trunks being stored at the hotel.

Should there have been no trunks full of old manuscripts stored in the Ritz basement for some thirty years, Hemingway's self-dramatization and myth-making would have served several practical purposes. They would have served as a justification for his writing the same sort of thing, and much worse, that he had violently attacked Mizener for writing; for destroying in print people whom he had never liked and some he had professed to like; and finally for writing a book he had always claimed that he would write only when he could not write about anything else.

Hemingway had been extremely angered by Mizener's article on Fitzgerald published on 15 January 1951,[13] as evidenced by the letters he wrote to Harvey Breit, Malcolm Cowley, and Mizener himself. For instance, on 17 January 1951 he wrote to Breit:

> Just read the piece in *Life*. I wrote him that he was an undertaker;
> but that piece is straight grave robbing and he sells the body. I will
> have to see him some time to see who can do such things. . . .
> Maybe he's a nice guy. But the *Life* piece is not nice and it has his
> name on it.

> . . . I'd kill a guy for money if times were bad enough, I guess.
> But I don't think I could do that.[14]

Hemingway kept harping on Mizener's article for a long time in his correspondence with various people. To Mizener himself he wrote, on 18 January 1951: "For your information I would gladly clean sewers for a living, every day, or bounce in a bad whore house or pimp for a living than to sign such an article."

However, when he himself wrote about Fitzgerald, barely five or six years after this exhibition of outrage, he was probably more destructive than Mizener, for he made a fool of Fitzgerald and presented him as a total failure as a man and close to one as a writer. He was clearly aware of it, too, for, in 1957, when the *Atlantic Monthly* asked him for an article for their hundredth anniversary issue, he wrote a piece on how he had met Scott, but had qualms about sending it once it was done:

> I started to write about Scott and how I first met him and how he was; writing it all true and it was tough to write and easy to remember and I thought it was very interesting. But when I read it over I remembered that character writing about his friend Mr. Dylan Thomas and thought people would think I was doing that to Scott and him dead. So I had worked a month on it and finished it good and then put it away and wrote them a story.[15]

Since there are two completely different manuscripts of his meeting with Scott, one is at a loss to know which one may have been the one written for the *Atlantic*; there is, of course, the manuscript which became with few revisions the first chapter on Scott in *A Moveable Feast*, and there is another manuscript that gives a rather different account of his first meeting with him. This second account (File 486) begins with a two-and-a-half-page explanation of why he writes about Scott which is written on a completely different type of paper from the manuscript of *A Moveable Feast*, suggesting that this more friendly account was the one Hemingway wrote first. One might thus hazard a guess that it is also the more accurate one. It is interesting to notice that he was still hesitant about these chapters in the fall of 1958, for he contradicts himself in two letters written within three days of each other—of course, it could also be that, depending on his audience, he was assuming a different attitude. On 18 September 1958 he wrote to Buck Lanham that he had done "a book, very good, about early earliest days in Paris, Austria, etc.—the true gen on what everyone has written about and no one knows but me." Three days later, he wrote to Harvey Breit that the long thing about Scott he had written before he came up north last fall and then two more he wrote after coming back were "unreadable" and that he would probably throw "it" in the wastebasket. Hemingway thus clearly knew the impact of what he had written, and claiming that he had written it after he had unexpectedly discovered notes taken during his early years in Paris could have been, consciously or not, a way of shirking full responsibility for his merciless portrait of Fitzgerald.

In any case, the purported discovery of the Ritz Hotel papers gave Hemingway an ideal excuse for writing about his former friends—writing things he had often said in his private correspondence but which he had never made public. The discovery of the papers and the claim that they gave him the idea of writing the book lent authenticity to what he wrote and established the purity of his motives. It thus appeared that it was not Hemingway, the bitter and somewhat paranoiac writer who was stabbing at Gertrude Stein, Ford Madox Ford, Fitzgerald, Ernest Walsh, Cheever Dunning, and others, but the older Hemingway reporting accurately on what the young Hemingway had seen and felt. It had the strength of documentary evidence; thus no one could question the accuracy of the anecdotes he related, and no one could say, for example, that he was revenging himself for what Gertrude Stein had written about him in *The Autobiography of Alice B. Toklas*. His phone call to Hadley, though, certainly establishes the fact that his intentions were not entirely pure.[16] Clearly forgetting his own earlier baiting of Gertrude Stein, he had often claimed, in private correspondence, that he had never attacked her or retaliated after *The Autobiography*. For instance, he wrote to Gingrich on 16 November 1934:

> . . . it goes against my digestion to take shots at anyone who's ever been a friend no matter how lousey they get to be finally. Besides, I've got the gun and it's loaded and I know where the vital spots are and friendship aside there's a certain damned fine feeling of superiority in knowing you can finish anybody off whenever you want to and still not doing it.[17]

Finally, the discovery of the papers gave him the perfect excuse for writing the book he had often said he would write when he had nothing else to write about, that is, when his genius had dwindled. Without such an excuse, the mere writing of the book would have been an admission to himself and his friends that he had indeed reached the end of his rope as a writer. Angry as ever about critics who wanted to write his biography, he wrote to Malcolm Cowley on 13 May 1951:

> Did it ever occur to any of these premature grave robbers that *when I was through writing books* I might wish to write the story of my life myself if the people concerned were dead so that they would be hurt no more than I would? *Writing it with the evidence to back it up and telling the part few people know about it.* (Italics added)

Much earlier, just after the publication of Gertrude Stein's memoirs, he had written to Janet Flanner on 8 April 1933 that he would write his own memoirs when he could not write anything else, and that they would be funny and accurate and not out to prove a bloody thing. On 22 July he wrote to Ezra Pound: "Well gents it will be a big day when write my own bloody memoirs because Papa isn't jealous of anyone (yet) and have a damned rat trap memory and nothing to prove. Also the documents—Il faut toujours garder les paperasses." And to Maxwell Perkins, on 26 July, he wrote in the same vein that he would write "damned good memoirs" because he was jealous of no one, had a "rat trap memory and the documents"; but that he had plenty to write first.[18]

One should note that, even before Gertrude Stein had attacked him, Hemingway had intended to use his memoirs as a weapon against those he did not like. For instance, he wrote to Pound on 2 February 1932:

> Listen—did Walsh ever promise you that $2500 prize in writing or only verbally—I saved the letter in which he promised it to me and will use it when I write my own fuckin memoirs which will strive for accuracy. . . . Am not going to write these memoirs until commenced over a period of years that unable to write anything else. Hope will be some time yet.[19]

That, in 1961, he still meant his memoirs to be an attack on some people is made clear by his phone call to Hadley shortly before his death.

Thus, the idea of writing his autobiography certainly did not come to Hemingway as an *epiphany* after the discovery of the Ritz Hotel papers. It was in fact an idea that he had entertained for a very long time, in particular since the publication of *The Autobiography of Alice B. Toklas*. Moreover, by 1956, many of his contemporaries had published their memoirs of the early days in Paris, which gave him an added reason for writing his own. Whether or not he truly discovered trunks of old manuscripts in the basement of the Ritz, he could not have found a more convenient reason for writing his memoirs at a time when his creative genius was escaping him. His memories of the old days in Paris, old manuscripts that he had either found in the famed trunks or had always had in his possession, added to his resentments and loyalties, would provide the inspiration he was lacking. Moreover, claiming that these trunks had given him the idea of writing his memoirs would exonerate him from accusations of resentment, or so he probably subconsciously hoped.

If one assumes that Hemingway left trunks in storage at the Ritz in the late 1920s, it is of course important to attempt to determine at what time he might have done so, as this would influence the possible contents of these trunks. If Hemingway did indeed leave two trunks stored at the Ritz, the most unlikely time for him to have done so, despite Mary's statement, was in 1928 before going to Key West, for he was at that time comfortably settled in an apartment at 6 Rue Férou. Moreover, according to Ernest's letter to Gus Pfeiffer, he already had four trunks stored somewhere in Paris in 1928. This leaves two periods of time when Hemingway would have been likely to store things: after his breakup with Hadley and when he and Pauline had to give up the apartment at the Rue Férou.

When Ernest and Hadley separated, he moved into Gerald Murphy's studio in the Rue Froidevaux, and she found a room at the Hôtel Beauvoir and later an apartment at 35 Rue de Fleurus. It is from that apartment that she wrote him on 19 November 1926 that he could "take over [his] suitcase, etc. They are all piled up in the dining room." However, Ernest kept the apartment in the Rue Notre-Dame-des-Champs until early June 1927 and left a part of his belongings there until he married Pauline. In a tiny notebook in which he had made a list of the things he needed to do before his marriage to Pauline, he had indicated:

> Sunday
> go to church
> pack letters etc. at 113 ND
> dinner at 6 rue Férou
> tell Marie to arrive with Tonton for 113 packing
> p. m. move things with Tonton and Marie

It seems that Hadley had left Ernest and Pauline her share of the contents of 113 Notre-Dame-des-Champs, as suggested by her letter of 2 January 1927, written at the time she was giving up her apartment before returning to America for a visit. She also offered them the use of all her household things and requested only that her steamer trunk be returned to her, as she needed it for her trip. She was unsure, however, where he kept it, whether at 113, or in Murphy's studio, or elsewhere. In 1926 and 1927, therefore, Hemingway's belongings were spread out among four apartments, and it would be a little surprising that he should also have stored things at the Ritz. Moreover, at that time, his connection with the Ritz could only have been slight.

Ernest and Pauline clearly left the apartment in the Rue Férou very unwillingly in late December 1929 or early January 1930,[20] after the owner had terminated their lease, as evidenced by Hemingway's letter to Maxwell Perkins of 27 September 1929:

> We haven't heard yet if we can stay in this apartment. (Put 3000 dollars into fixing it and improvements on strength of supposedly valid lease). If we are kicked out will store some things and bring others over, probably landing in Cuba and Key West as before sometime in December.

Hemingway had known for a long time that their lease for the apartment might not be renewed and he had even tried to ingratiate himself with the owner by giving him one of his books, as evidenced by a letter to Sylvia Beach dated 24 September 1928:

> Also I would like to send a copy to Monsieur René Pottier my landlord hoping that he would thus think of me kindly and perhaps renew my lease which runs out next Jan—not this Jan but December 1929. Consult with the highest authorities y compris Monnier or surtout Adrienne and send me a dedication to Monsieur Pottier. . . . Send me something to write that will make M. Pottier not congé me when my bail is up.

I have not been able to determine where they stored their furniture and belongings between December 1929 and September 1931, when they probably shipped everything to Key West and returned there to settle in the new house.[21] Therefore, the most likely time for Hemingway to have stored trunks at the Ritz would have been in December 1929 or early January 1930; but why would he have done so instead of putting these trunks in storage with the rest of his belongings, of which he had made a cautious inventory with estimated values, probably for insurance purposes, in another small notebook? Moreover, it appears that Hemingway and Pauline did not stay at the Ritz after they had given up the Rue Férou apartment, or before they settled into it, for that matter.[22]

There is, therefore, a good chance that Hemingway did leave trunks stored in Paris for a time, but it seems unlikely that he left them at the Ritz in the late 1920s as he and Mary later claimed. He possibly left them elsewhere, and they might have been transferred to the Ritz later. Whether they stayed at the Ritz until 1956 is also doubtful. Mary's emphasis on the discovery of these trunks in her review of *A Moveable Feast* could well have been intended to exonerate Hemingway from accusations of spitefulness in his treatment of fellow authors.

At this time, it seems virtually impossible to identify specifically the manuscripts that could have been in the trunks. It is well known that Hemingway gave his manuscripts to his friends rather easily; even if one could track down every early manuscript that he gave away, it would still be impossible to determine which ones could have been left in the trunks, for, as we also know, he had taken some of these early manuscripts to Key West. Actually, it is more than likely that he had some of them with him as early as January 1930, when he was working on *Death in the Afternoon* at the Nordquist Ranch in Wyoming. At least one passage of that book— the story of the quarrel between two homosexuals in chapter 16—is clearly rewritten from an earlier manuscript entitled "There's One In Every Town" (File 743), which describes the way young Americans become homosexuals in Paris. Thus, if the trunks did exist, they might have contained "some" of Ernest's manuscripts written prior to 1930, letters from friends and from Hadley, sketches of his contemporaries, drafts of letters to his landlord, old bullfight tickets, programs of exhibitions and races, and the like. They might have contained, too, the "blue-and-yellow-covered notebooks" first described by Mary Hemingway, or at least some of them, with the exception of the three notebooks in which the ending of *A Farewell to Arms* was drafted.[23] If they contained the manuscript of one novel, it had to be the manuscript of *The Sun Also Rises* and not that of *A Farewell to Arms* (however improbable it might seem that Hemingway should have left unattended the manuscript of his first and very successful novel). Had this and other manuscripts been at the Ritz, as he later claimed, one would expect that rescuing them would have been one of his preoccupations when he "freed" the Ritz just before the liberation of Paris in 1944. Actually, as will be seen in "Borrowings from Early Manuscripts and Discarded Material," Hemingway made relatively small use of his early manuscripts in the writing of *A Moveable Feast*.

An attempt at determining whether the story told by Hemingway and

Mary about the trunks of old manuscripts left at the Ritz Hotel in Paris in the 1920s is accurate and at identifying specifically the manuscripts that were in these trunks is a frustrating enterprise. Further information on this matter will probably come mostly from personal testimonies; those, however, are unfortunately more and more difficult to gather since most of the people involved are now dead (Pauline, Charles Ritz, Leonard Lyons, Hadley, and so on). At this point, the evidence in favor of the story as told by Hemingway and, especially, Mary is not overwhelmingly convincing, and there is a possibility that the whole thing was a figment of Hemingway's imagination. In any case, whether Hemingway discovered some of his old manuscripts at the Ritz in 1956, or whether he had had them in his possession for a long time before that, he made relatively small use of them in the composition of *A Moveable Feast*. A study of the manuscripts reveals, with little chance of error, that the book was written late in Hemingway's life, and that no major or even minor portion of the book was written in the 1920s. Thus, its "stylistic felicities" were not achieved during his youth but were Hemingway's last achievement. If he actually did discover trunks of old manuscripts, they only served to remind him of details he might have forgotten. A study of Hemingway's letters, though, shows that he remembered occurrences rather well, or, at least, that he was faithful to his own version of things to the end. A study of the letters is, in fact, more rewarding from the point of view of trying to separate fact from fiction in *A Moveable Feast* than a study of the old manuscripts, as it is relatively easy to find in them the origin of many of the episodes he relates in the book. At times, his memoirs even appear to be a combination of the gossip and anecdotes he wrote to such friends and acquaintances as Ezra Pound, Charles Scribner, Donald Gallup, Edmund Wilson, and others, with the exception, of course, of the beautiful and evocative descriptions of Paris, which are the true strength of the book. In any case, "a good story is a good story is a good story . . . ," and it does not have to be true, at least in fiction. Indeed, for Hemingway,

> It is not unnatural that the best writers are liars. A major part of their trade is to lie or invent and they will lie when they are drunk, or to themselves, or to strangers. They often lie unconsciously and then remember their lies with deep remorse. If they knew all other writers were liars too it would cheer them up.
>
> Sometimes two of them will lie to a stranger and then they enjoy

it without remorse. If they would realize that no stranger is entitled to the truth and that no one knows the truth anyway they would be spared much remorse. . . . Not having done penance I will prepare to write again. [handwritten on the back of that same page:] To start new again I will try to write truly about the early days in Paris. (File 845)

CHAPTER TWO

The Composition of A Moveable Feast

*I*T IS DIFFICULT to determine exactly what Hemingway was working on, when, and where, as he was generally very close-mouthed
about his work, never saying much that was specific in his letters to family and friends. Moreover, both Hemingway and his correspondents occasionally became confused as to what had happened, and when. For
instance, Buck Lanham expressed surprise on 9 March 1961 at Hemingway's mention of his new Paris book:

> In your last letter you refer to "the Paris book" and say you have put
> aside Dangerous Summer pending completion of this. Here again
> my curiosity is aroused for this is the first mention you have made to
> me of a "Paris Book." Is it Paris in World War II, Paris after World
> War II, or Paris in Hemingway's Salad days?[1]

He inquired again on 5 June: "I am curious to know what Lenny Lyons
meant when he referred to your new book as 'the Paris book,' also when
it is coming out." Lanham's memory was thus clearly at fault since Hemingway had written him on 18 September 1958 that he had written "a
book, very good, about early earliest days in Paris, Austria. . . ." It is
perhaps not entirely surprising that Lanham had forgotten Hemingway's
more than two-year-old remark, since Hemingway usually wrote to him,
as to almost everyone else, in the vaguest of terms, referring to his work
in progress as "this that I am writing," or "god-damned book." On the
other hand, his correspondence with A. E. Hotchner, Harvey Breit of the
New York Times, and Ed Thompson of *Life,* who were not only friends
but also business associates, tends to provide more specific and reliable
information. Consequently, Hemingway's progress in writing *A Moveable Feast* can be determined only by piecing together the various refer-

ences he makes to "the Paris book" in his letters—references which are occasionally contradictory and generally unclear. The task is also made difficult by the fact that Hemingway was also writing *The Garden of Eden*, *The Dangerous Summer*, and a preface to a new school edition of his short stories during the last five years of his life. Moreover, Mary followed her husband's policy of not giving much specific information to friends concerning his writing. She seldom gave a title to what he was working on and would write, for instance, that he had "done a full-sized 'thing'" or that he had "started on a new thing." Moreover, Hemingway's letters to Harry Brague, his editor at Scribner's, which might prove more enlightening, are not available to scholars, except for the few that were published by Carlos Baker.[2]

When Hemingway settled down to writing *A Moveable Feast* is never made clear by Mary Hemingway either in her review of the book or in *How It Was*. Her review suggests that it might have been in either February or October 1957:

> Soon after we returned from New York, he gave me a manuscript on which he had been working, a novel set in southern France in the Twenties, to put into one of our safe deposit boxes in Havana.
>
> He was going to do something about Paris in the early days, he said. Mostly on his typewriter, partly by pencil as he sat at our 10-foot-long library table, he began *A Moveable Feast*.[3]

Baker believes that it was October 1957;[4] however, it seems that neither month is correct and that Hemingway began writing the book in July. The novel Hemingway asked Mary to put away was most likely *The Garden of Eden*, which he had begun in early 1946.[5] If this is true, the manuscript of *The Garden of Eden* did not stay for long in the vault, since Hemingway started working on it again around Christmas 1957. In fact, it seems that Hemingway worked mainly on *A Moveable Feast* between July and December 1957, then on both books between January 1958 and March 1959. From May 1959 to October 1960, he devoted himself essentially to *The Dangerous Summer*, eventually resuming work on *A Moveable Feast* in January 1961, less than six months before his death.

Most evidence suggests that Hemingway began by writing the first Fitzgerald chapter. When the *Atlantic Monthly* asked him to write something for their centenary number, he decided that he didn't want "to take a chunk out of a book nor give them stories [he] was doubtful about" or that were not suitable for the *Atlantic,* so he decided to write something "that would be worthwhile and good for them," and he started to write about Fitzgerald and how he first met him. But, as he wrote further in his letter to Breit of 16 June 1957, he had qualms about sending this portrait of Fitzgerald and wrote them a good story about "out west." [6] If one gives credence to what Hemingway wrote to Breit—and one probably should since Breit was one of the few people Hemingway wrote to rather openly about his own writing and that of others—then one must accept that Hemingway had not yet begun *A Moveable Feast* as a book, for he stated clearly that he didn't want to take a chunk out of a book for the *Atlantic.* Thus the Fitzgerald portrait may well have been the seed of the book. Indeed, the feeling of guilt evidenced by his comment that he remembered what had been done to Dylan Thomas and didn't want to do that to Scott, "and him dead," suggests that he was not yet involved in the writing of a book that was in many ways a series of such betrayals. It is also possible that he decided not to give this sketch to the *Atlantic* because he had realized that, together with other sketches of the same nature, he would have a book. That he did not start writing *A Moveable Feast* until after the first Fitzgerald sketch and the *Atlantic* story is verified by his letter to Lanham of 18 September 1958, in which he wrote that he worked from "last July until now and did a book about . . . Paris." [7]

According to his letter to Breit, it took him a month to write the first Fitzgerald sketch, and it seems that he finished it by mid-May, for he wrote to Breit on 17 May that he had been "writing every day until [that] morning" and that he had finished what he was working on the day before. [8] The writing seems to have been painful, as he wrote to Hotchner on 28 May that, not having had a glass of hard liquor since 5 March, writing was "about as much fun as driving a racing motor car without lubrication for a while." This, of course, contradicts Mary's statement in her review of the book. Another factor militates against Hemingway's having started work on *A Moveable Feast* in February: when he came back to Finca Vigía, he apparently found "over 400 letters that . . . hadn't [been] forwarded nor even sorted except as to size!" Moreover, he also had to do his income tax, and thus complained to George Plimpton that, like a fool, he had expected to sit down and go right to work on a book. [9] Clearly, these trivial tasks had kept him from doing so, and, eager to get back to work, he asked Plimpton not to come and visit, as he would be too busy to entertain. This suggests that he did not get to the Fitzgerald chapter until late March or possibly early April. On the other hand, Mary's comment that he wrote mainly on the typewriter seems to verify that he started with the Fitzgerald chapter, since it is the only one typewritten by Hemingway. With the exception of "With Pascin at the Dôme," which was partly typed and partly drafted in pencil, all the other chapters were first handwritten.

Hemingway went back to the sketches after finishing the *Atlantic* story. According to both Mary Hemingway and Leonard Lyons, he had several sketches done by December 1957. Mary claims that he had written the opening chapter and the Gertrude Stein and Ford Madox Ford chapters, while Lyons writes in his column of 11 December 1957 that Hemingway read to him the pieces he had just finished on Fitzgerald, Ford, and Stein. Thus, Hemingway had written up to eight chapters, since neither Mary nor Lyons specifies how many chapters he had written on each writer. In any case, he had written at least the three Fitzgerald chapters, since he wrote to Harvey Breit on 21 September 1958 that, before he had come up north the previous fall, he had written "a long thing about Scott and then . . . two more when [he] came back." This suggests that after the first Fitzgerald sketch he moved to portrayals of others before going to New York in September 1957, and only returned to Fitzgerald sometime in October. In fact, it is possible that he had written up to fourteen sketches by December, as he wrote to Lanham on December 16 that he had been working every day as hard as when he was a hungry writer (and he was "a hungry writer O.K. made so by Gvt. and that lawyer"[10]), that he had been going well and had fourteen chapters done on "this that" he was writing. His having fourteen chapters done as early as December 1957 would tally with his claim that the book was finished seven months later, when he wrote to Brague on 31 July 1958 that the book was virtually finished, but that he was still trying to figure out the best way to handle it, by which he probably meant that he still did not know how to organize the sketches.[11]

By 1958 the references to *A Moveable Feast* in the correspondence are more numerous and explicit. In January, he was hard at work again,[12] and he seems to have worked regularly until October, when he went to Ketchum, Idaho. He apparently did not leave the Finca, except for the odd day of fishing, which was unusually poor that year,[13] and did not even find time to write his friends. He apologized to Breit on 21 September for not having written, saying that he had given up writing letters entirely while in a stretch of working that ran from when he had seen Breit in New York (the preceding fall) until then. It had been like a fever, and he had written only to his children and the most necessary business letters. Apparently, he first started working on *A Moveable Feast* and then resumed work on *The Garden of Eden*. According to Mary's letter to Bill Seward of 22 August, he had done a full-sized "thing" in the autumn and winter and early that spring had started on a new thing that grew and grew and enslaved him to the point where he had postponed writing even his oldest friends; he tore himself away only as far as the telephone when their "idiot lawyer in New York made a big ugly untrue manoever, creating publicity for himself out of a minor technical point."[14] Hemingway's postscript—"Have written over 100,000 words on a novel since we were on the train together . . ."—verifies Mary's statement that he had been working like a fiend but does not specify on which book; neither does his letter of 23 August to Layhmond Robinson of the *New York Times*, in which he wrote that the "Rice-Esquire business" had caught him while he was writing the last chapters of a novel.[15] On the other hand, his letter of 26 June to Juanito Quintana suggests that he had been working on *The Garden of Eden*, as he indicated that he still had at least six chapters to finish, although twenty-eight were done on the book he was working on. He also emphasized that he had been working "mañana, tarde, y noche," which all verifies Mary's letter to Bill Seward.

According to Carlos Baker, by July 1958 the number of sketches had swelled to eighteen, including two more on Gertrude Stein and one apiece on the esthete Harold Acton, the poet Ralph Cheever Dunning, and the editor Ernest Walsh.[16] If he had fourteen sketches done by December 1957, he would then have had nineteen done, which suggests that even the first draft of the book was not quite finished, since, on top of the twenty chapters eventually published, he had also written six chapters which remained unpublished: one on "writing in the first person," one on Ford, one on Fitzgerald, one on a boxer, Larry Gains, one about living in Paris with his son Bumby, and a much later one on Evan Shipman about a visit which took place in 1956 or 1957.[17] He had shown some of the sketches to Plimpton when the latter came to visit him at the Finca to work on the *Paris Review* Interview which was published in the spring of 1958.[18] In fact, Plimpton wrote Hemingway on 27 April 1958 that he remembered the sketches with such pleasure that he found it hard to keep his mouth shut about them. He also hoped that the new book pleased Hemingway. Later, on 4 March 1961, he recalled reading the chapters at the Finca:

> I'm delighted to hear you're back on the Paris book. There are few days I remember as distinctly, and with such pleasure, as that after-noon sitting in the long room at the Finca, reading the chapters you were kind enough to show me. I remember laughing there (particu-larly at the Ford Madox Ford) not only because of the humor and warmth of the pieces, but also out of sheer excitement of discovery: I don't think many people had read it at that stage. It came as a complete surprise and it was such wonderful material.

Plimpton may in fact have been the third person to see them after Leon-ard Lyons and, of course, Mary Hemingway.

Thus, it seems that Hemingway worked on both books from the spring to October—and that he worked hard, although one is never quite sure which book he was working on at any specific time. As he wrote to his son Patrick on 14 July 1958, he was trying to finish "a book. Jamming awfully hard." [19] By the end of June, it seems that he had revised twenty-eight chapters of *The Garden of Eden*, and, at the end of July, he predicted that it would be finished in three weeks' time. By 18 September, he wrote to Lanham that he had 160,000 words done and was close to the end. According to this same letter, he had not taken twenty days off in eight months to fish or anything else, and he had the Paris book "done and copied by Mary and ready to give final go-over." This letter to Lanham reveals not only that he had consciously begun working on *A Moveable Feast* in July 1957 and that it was basically finished by September 1958, but also that he had worked on both books for a while. [20] When he would lay off each day, it was because he was empty. When he wrote a book, he felt that there was nothing left of him "except the god-damned book" and that it was "more difficult all the time."

In any case, he seems to have enjoyed the writing, despite the fact that he got to working so hard that he took to writing on Sundays too. [21] As he wrote to Breit on 21 September 1958, he was appalled at how things were in the world and figured that the only positive thing he could do was to write something worth reading, something that would give him pleasure to read, since almost nothing published did. He loved to read and couldn't get anything worth reading, so he thought that he had better write it himself. It had been fun despite the overwork, since he had some-thing worth reading "every god-damned day."

Hemingway took both the manuscript of *A Moveable Feast* and that of *The Garden of Eden* to Idaho in October 1958. The hot, sticky weather of Cuba had been getting him down, and, as he had not taken any time out from working since the end of October 1957,[22] he felt entitled to a break. It would be nice to see the country in the fall; so he and Otto Bruce drove up to Ketchum from Key West via Chicago, where they picked up Mary and Betty Bruce.[23] Although he was in no hurry to get to work at first, he eventually settled down to a good writing schedule: writing from four to five days a week, keeping in shape, and hunting three days a week and sometimes afternoons too. He worked each day until he was "dead pooped" and then forced himself to walk and climb in order to keep in shape, be healthy, and sleep.[24] Characteristically, his letters are very unclear as to which book he was working on: he wrote to Patrick Hemingway on 24 November that he wanted to finish "book," and to Gianfranco Ivancich on 7 January 1959 that he had to go to bed so that he might write well on the book, and that he would not go out again until the book was done.[25] Upon arrival in Idaho, he had written that he still had a month to go on "this book."[26] It seems, though, that he worked on both books, rewriting parts of the Paris sketchbook and revising three chapters of *The Garden of Eden*.[27] Chapters 25, 26, and 27 of *The Garden of Eden* bear the annotations in Hemingway's hand "Rewrote, 19/11/58," and a notation beside chapter 25 reads, "very good."

On 22 February 1959 he wrote to Harry Brague that he had worked four days out of the week but had no heart to work that day, that he had hoped to finish the first draft in Ketchum (he was on chapter 45), but had lost ground badly during the week; he would probably finish it in Cuba or in Spain. Clearly, he can have been speaking only of *The Garden of Eden,* of which, the two previous weeks, he had written respectively 4000 and 2950 words. Moreover, he wrote in the same letter that the next book to publish would probably be the Paris stuff he had showed Plimpton. It was typed and he would take it to Europe with him, go over it, and perhaps write a couple more chapters. "It is a hell of a good book."[28] In fact, Hemingway would neither revise the manuscript nor write more pieces while in Europe, and the manuscript was delivered to Scribner's on 3 November in essentially the same state it left Ketchum in mid-March 1959. The remainder of the spring, the summer and the fall were devoted to following Luis Miguel Dominguín and Antonio Ordoñez from bullfight to bullfight, writing a preface to a school edition of his short stories, and beginning to write the *mano a mano* article for *Life.*

The Hemingways left Ketchum in mid-March, driving as far as New Orleans with Aaron Hotchner, then to Key West, and, flying out to Cuba, arrived in Havana on Easter Sunday.[29] By early May they were at La Consula, the estate of a wealthy American expatriate, Nathan (Bill) Davis. By 13 May, Hemingway had roughed out a first draft of the preface, but he put it aside in order to attend his first bullfights of the season. On 30 May, Ordoñez was gored, and, while he recovered, Hemingway returned to his preface, working mornings but finding it hard to concentrate. When Antonio resumed fighting late in June, Ernest followed him once more. The *mano a mano* contest between Antonio and Luis Miguel fascinated Hemingway, and he was keeping notes for the piece he had contracted to do for *Life* magazine. By 27 August, though, he was surfeited with spectator sports and felt that being involved with Antonio's fortunes was like being married to an alcoholic.[30] Earlier, on 5 August, he had written to Patrick that being around Antonio was like being with him or with Bum, "except for having to sweat him out all the time."[31] Hemingway was in residence again at La Consula at the end of August, but it was 10 October before he got back to work and began writing the bullfighting article for *Life*. Except for the short-story preface, he had written nothing all summer. The 6000-word preface, which Hemingway had written between 1 May and mid-June, was mailed to Scribner's by the end of June but rejected in July.[32] On 10 October he wrote 541 words, on the 11th, 845 words, and on 14 October he wrote to Bill Seward that he was hard at work "on that Death in the Afternoon business you read about." If he got it right, the piece would give Seward some idea of what they had been doing. He felt it had been a marvelous summer, one of the best he'd ever had. Despite Hemingway's belief, it had not been a really good summer for him, for his sixtieth birthday had been marked by some early signs of the paranoia and nervous imbalance that would lead to his suicide.[33]

By 15 October, he had 5000 words done on the *mano a mano* article, and he was only beginning. *The Dangerous Summer* was going to develop far past his expectations of 20 September, when he wrote to Hotchner that he wanted to get it wrapped up quickly, so that he would be free to go back and finish the novel, and then let it rest for a while. "It is all done but the end & I should have the advantage of coming to that from a long way away." He was most probably referring to *The Garden of Eden*, for he carried with him the typescript of *A Moveable Feast* which he delivered to Scribner's shortly after his arrival in New York on 3 November, with instructions to forward it to Ketchum. His cover note to Charlie Scribner mentioned that one chapter was missing—a very good one—but that Hotchner had a photostat of it and would send it in.[34] In fact, it seems that he had loaned the typescript to Hotchner, for Hotchner mailed it back to Hemingway on 11 September 1959, writing:

> Have had the Paris chapters copied and am returning all to you under separate cover. Now that I have had a good chance to read and re-read them, think they are absolutely wonderful. The funny is deep-down funny and the sad things are unexpected and very moving. The more I spend time thinking about the material as a possible stage venture the more attractive it becomes. But if it must be ready by the winter of 1960–61, it must be put into motion quite soon.[35]

Hotchner was doing some preliminary work on television productions of *The 5th Column* and "The Snows of Kilimanjaro" and wanted to broach the topic of a similar production for the Paris book. The chapter missing from the typescript given to Scribner's was probably "Ford Madox Ford and the Devil's Disciple," as it is the only photostat in the manuscript collection at the Kennedy Library.

Hemingway flew down to Havana shortly afterwards and stayed there only a few days before driving to Ketchum with Antonio and Carmen Ordóñez, to whom he wanted to show the American landscape. Mary was already in Ketchum, preparing the house for their arrival. Hemingway was "bone tired and very beat up emotionally," as he wrote to Hotchner on 11 November. He wanted to get back in shape out west, but what he wanted to do most was get back to writing. However, it seems that his determination to work was a source of friction with Mary, for he wrote in that same letter to Hotchner that one of the big issues was that he expected other people to subordinate themselves to his writing and thus made them lead the lives of drudges. His desire to work was thwarted on 27 November, when Mary fell down in a shooting accident and shattered her left elbow. The operation took an hour and a half, and afterwards he had to take her to the hospital every morning, look after her back at the house, and do the errands—none of which was much to his taste, as is suggested in his letter to Seward of 11 January 1960. However, he concluded bravely: "This is not a complaining letter but things have been a little rough."[36] He was no longer sure that he could be back in Cuba by 9 January, "the 16th at the latest—to finish work" that he wanted to do "no matter what." In fact, they started the train trip back on 16 January.[37]

By 25 January he was already at work on the bullfight piece. By 18

February he had added 17,000 words to what he had already written before getting back to Cuba, and on the 18th itself had written 1536 words, which was above his usual writing average.[38] He was indeed working like a steam engine: by 1 April, he had 63,562 words written, and by 1 May, 92,000.[39] But he was tired of "skinning all those dead horses" and felt that they could "take bull fighting . . . and put it where they found it."[40] By 28 May he had reached 108,746 words and declared the piece finished. But it was far too long, and he summoned Hotchner to help him cut the typescript. *Life* had contracted for only 5000 words, and Hemingway had to renegotiate the deal. On 31 March 1960 he wrote to Thompson, enclosing the box score showing 63,562 words written at La Consula and Finca Vigia. He felt that he could work hard and finish it by 14 April, but that "it would be unfair to Life, Literature and the Pursuit of Happiness." A month's more solid work was needed, and then typing, correcting, retyping, for it to be what he wanted. He really was not eager to finish it "under such forced draft" and offered to return *Life*'s advance of funds. The story was a difficult one to write, as he had explained to Will Lang,[41] which would have been simple if either Dominguín or Ordóñez had been killed. Dominguín was pretty well destroyed but still functioning, which made it more difficult to write a story with permanent value. Hemingway offered *Life* another 40,000 words for an extra $10,000, which was the minimum price he had been paid per word "since before the Spanish Civil War." He closed by suggesting that he and Thompson could talk about *Life*'s using some of the Paris book later. This was a good bait, and Thompson cabled his acceptance of Hemingway's conditions on 14 April, indicating his interest in the Paris book.

Despite Hemingway's and Hotchner's hard work, they managed only to cut the typescript down to some 70,000 words, that is 25,000 words more than *Life* had accepted. Finally, Thompson agreed to pay $90,000, plus $10,000 for reprint rights in Spanish for "The Dangerous Summer."[42] Of course, with his compulsive work on "The Dangerous Summer," Hemingway had had no time even to look at *A Moveable Feast*. When Hotchner wrote to him on 30 January 1960 and asked what he should tell the magazines ("Sat Eve Post, McCall's, etc") who had inquired concerning the Paris book and wanted to know whether they would have a chance to read it and submit proposals on the price, and whether Hemingway had made a decision on "the Broadway thing," he replied on 8 February that he had to do one thing at a time and was not even thinking about the Paris book. He had no plans for serialization, but

"*Life* would have first call since George Plimpton mentioned it to them first," and since they would have been glad to give him an advance on it if he had wanted them to. Hotchner wrote back on 13 February:

> Have sent words to the magazines that inquired about Paris book that all is tabled for now and to drop further inquiry. As you know, never intend to press; sorry if it came in at work time and interrupted. Always please disregard that which should be disregarded. One thing I got, as fellow sufferer, is understanding. End Paris inquiries.

With his usual humor, Hotchner also commented on "Astute Alfred" being gloomy about not getting his 10 percent "squeeze" on the new show—probably the television play of "The Snows of Kilimanjaro."[43]

Because of his time-consuming work on "The Dangerous Summer," Hemingway had scratched *A Moveable Feast* from Scribner's 1960 fall list and wrote to Scribner on 31 March:

> . . . the Paris book should be good whenever it comes out but I am very sorry not to have it for this fall as we had planned. But tomorrow is the first of April and I could not possibly get into it before the end of May or middle of June and it is stupid to work yourself to death. . . .
>
> Plenty of people will probably think that we have no book and that it is like all the outlines that Scott had borrowed money on that he could never have finished but you know that if I did not want the chance to make it even better it could be published exactly as you saw it with a few corrections of Mary's typing.[44]

But by 6 July he was a little sorry, for he had spent a week with Hotchner trying to cut "The Dangerous Summer" down to 30,000 or 40,000 words unsuccessfully and was not sure *Life* would accept it for publication. Moreover, he had reread *A Moveable Feast* and arranged the chapters in their proper order and felt they read very well. He had tried to write some more, but felt "stale from over-work" and wanted to "get some juice back in before writing any others" so as not to lower the quality. In any case, he felt the Paris book should be published first.[45] He had not had a day off from work nor been out fishing in the Pilar from 19 May to 4 July. Perhaps he had not missed much, unless fish had returned to the Gulf since 12 March when he wrote to Hotchner that he had been cleaning the Pilar up for when things started running again. They had had some good cock fighting, swimming, and walking, though.

Moreover, the spring of 1960 had not been altogether free from minor annoyances. News of the Paris book had reached the papers and Hemingway had received inquiries from friends such as Bill Seward and Bron Zielinski.[46] And the news published had not always been accurate. Leonard Lyons made some fanciful statements in a column in the *New York Post*, which prompted Hemingway to write Hotchner on 31 March 1960 concerning Lyons's piece "about the Paris book being used in the stage (thing) (project)." He knew that he and Hotchner had agreed that it was not to be done, so he figured the news was as "balled up as other pieces that have been published recently." Another piece said that Lauren Bacall was to be in the stage show. Hemingway was annoyed and felt that if she was a client of theirs, "her picture should hang in Alfred's office" and not in his book. In his reply of 20 April 1960, Hotchner confirmed that there had been a variety of errors in Lyons's reporting:

> Sorry that honest Lennie Lyons, boy reporter, keeps feeding out these gin-crazed items. Don't know anything about his source other than it ain't me. Any rate, am not now, nor have ever, nor will ever use or attempt to use any material from the Paris Sketch book. Also about Bacall, had a drink with her one evening and we discussed project, but that's all. Have no idea, this point, who cast will be, and when I have information on any of these things, you can be sure that you will get the true gen, when it's formed, before Mr. Lyons.

It is interesting to know that Leonard Lyons's gossip column was not always reliable, especially if one recalls that he was the one who first spread the rumor of the Ritz Hotel manuscripts. Moreover, Hemingway was not above using Lyons deliberately to spread rumor himself, as evidenced by his letter to Buck Lanham concerning his having been misquoted in the *Havana Post*. He acknowledged that he had sent a message to Lyons, who was publishing rumors, and had expected that his message would be published and would straighten things out, so that his friends to whom he had been unable to write would have the true story.[47]

Late in July 1960 Hemingway started making his way to Spain, via Key West and New York. He wanted to gather up loose ends and stand by his friend Antonio for what remained of his fighting summer. Only afterwards could he return to the Paris book. As he wrote to Thompson on 2 June, he wanted to do his income tax, then get the bullfight manuscript in shape. "Then must get what I need for the end and then get to work on the Scribner Paris book for 1961." He spent his sixty-first birthday seldom leaving his New York apartment. While in New York he consulted with Scribner's as to which book should be published first. After changing their minds twice, Scribner's finally decided to publish *The Dangerous Summer* as a book first. Flying out to Madrid on 4 August, Hemingway cabled his arrival to Mary on the 5th. It was to be an ill-fated trip, as he showed immediately the symptoms of extreme nervous depression: fear, loneliness, boredom, insomnia, guilt, remorse, failure of memory, and, especially, suspiciousness and delusions of persecution. For instance, he was convinced that his old friend Bill Davis had tried to kill him. Two weeks later, he acknowledged that he feared a "complete physical and nervous crack up from deadly overwork," strangely echoing Fitzgerald's phrase of 1936.[48] After his friends had sent him back to the United States in early October and Mary had convinced him to return to Idaho with her, where they arrived on 22 October, he was still haunted by fears and unable to work. Hospitalized on 30 November at the Mayo Clinic at St. Mary's Hospital in Rochester, Minnesota, he was discharged on 22 January 1961 and returned west.

He tried to get back to work on *A Moveable Feast* as soon as he was back in Ketchum but found it difficult. Finishing the book had been uppermost in his mind for some time, and he had asked Harry Brague on 8 January for a deadline to work toward as soon as he could resume work, acknowledging that he had had to stop working on the Paris book the previous November.[49] What energies he had left would be devoted to completing the book, and he made a show of optimism in his letters to family and friends; he wrote to Patrick on 16 January that he didn't think the *Life* pieces were very good, but that they were part of a long book which might be, and that he was working on another book about early days in Paris which he thought or hoped was very good. He wanted to finish it and had plenty of other projects ahead.[50] On the same day he wrote to Carlos Baker that he had "to bite on the nail now to get the Paris book finished for [the] fall." To Thomas Shevlin on 17 January and to Peter Barret on the 20th, he wrote respectively that the books would go all right as soon as he could get back to them, after the hospital nonsense; the Paris book was scheduled for that fall and he would work on it as soon as he could get back somewhere where people would leave him alone and let him work—and that he had much work that he was anxious to get back to, which made all else secondary. Confident that he would have no trouble resuming work, he asked Peter Briggs on 19 January not to come and visit, since he would be very busy working when he got back west. This did not turn out to be the case.

Although he cabled Patrick three days after his arrival in Ketchum that he was working hard again and that he had his blood pressure licked,[51] and although he would get up every morning at seven and begin work at eight-thirty, stopping at about one, he found it hard to concentrate. According to Mary, he stayed for hours in the back bedroom, standing at his high desk before the window, shifting papers and hardly looking at the magnificent panorama of mountains below his eyes. He was also feeling insecure about the factual aspects of the book. The typescript bears repeated notes to the effect that he must check into the spelling of the names of people, places, and streets, as well as into dates. Finding it hard to work without his library and source books,[52] he asked Harry Brague for some books, including *Paris in the Twenties* and *Paris fin de siècle*.[53] On 6 February 1961 he reported to Brague on his progress on the book:

> Here's gen to date: Have material arranged as chapters—they come to 18—and am working on the last one—No 19—also working on title. This is very difficult. (Have my usual long list—something wrong with all of them but am working toward it—Paris has been used so often it blights anything.) In pages typed they run 7, 14, 5, 6, 9½, 6, 11, 9, 8, 9, 4½, 3½, 8, 10½, 14½, 38½, 10, 3, 3: 177 pages + 5½ pages + 1¼ pages.[54]

This letter is interesting in many respects. First of all, Hemingway referred to eighteen chapters but gave page counts for nineteen, plus two other page counts. By the number of pages mentioned, it is clear that he was still revising the first typescript which he had given Scribner's in November 1959. As a matter of fact, he mentioned later in the same letter that he was trying out a new secretary who was doing an experimental chapter, which he expected back the next day, and that he hoped that she would be able to read his handwriting. It is likely that this new secretary is the "Betty" he gave instructions to in the margin of some of his chapters, in particular "A False Spring," "The End of an Avocation," "Scott Fitzgerald," and "There Is Never Any End to Paris." If this is indeed the case, Betty is the one who typed the complete manuscript of *A Moveable Feast* which can be found at the Kennedy Library (Files 188–89). Finally, and most importantly, the page count Hemingway gave Scribner's is somewhat confusing, and it seems that, by 6 February 1961, he wanted to include chapters that, eventually, would not find their way into the last typescript. The page count he gave seems to correspond to the following chapters:

7 pp. :	"A Good Café on the Place St.-Michel"
14 pp. :	"Miss Stein Instructs"
5 pp. :	"Shakespeare and Company"
6 pp. :	"People of the Seine"
	"The End of an Avocation"
9½ pp. :	"A False Spring"
11 pp. :	"Ford Madox Ford and the Devil's Disciple"
9 pp. :	"Une Génération Perdue"
	"With Pascin at the Dôme"
	"The Man Who Was Marked for Death"
8 pp. :	"Hunger Was a Good Discipline"
	?
4½ pp. :	"Ezra Pound and His Bel Esprit"—part 1, up to "Ezra was the most generous writer"
3½ pp. :	"A Strange Enough Ending"
10½ pp. :	"Evan Shipman at the Lilas"
14½ pp. :	"There Is Never Any End to Paris"—part 1, up to "During our last year in the mountains"
38½ pp. :	"Scott Fitzgerald"
10 pp. :	"Hawks Do Not Share"
3 pp. :	"On Writing in the First Person" (unpublished chapter)
	"Ford" (unpublished chapter)
5½ pp. :	"Larry Gains" (unpublished chapter)
1¼ pp. :	?

This raises some obvious questions. 1) What were Hemingway's plans for the chapters that were not typed—that is, "An Agent of Evil" (eight pages) and "A Matter of Measurements" (seven pages)? 2) What did he intend to do with "Birth of a New School," for which there was a six-page typescript as well as an alternative ending of three typed pages? 3) What was the second eight-page typescript? 4) Why did he indicate eighteen chapters and give the count for nineteen, with an inaccurate sum of 177 pages instead of 180—or, to ask the question differently, was there an error in Carlos Baker's transcription of that letter, which, for instance, might have added one three-page chapter too many? 5) Which two of the three nine-page chapters did he want to publish?

During the three months that preceded his readmission to the Mayo Clinic, Hemingway was indeed desperately trying to revise *A Moveable Feast*,[55] in particular four chapters that bear repeated annotations of his attempts. Although the year is not always mentioned in these notes, one may assume that most were made in 1961, since many dates revolve around the same months, and even the same days. One typescript of "A False Spring" bears the following annotations: "Question if put in after D"; "Must decide"; "Re-did Jan 27th"; "D Bis"; "Reworked 28th, 29th, 30th." One typescript of "The End of an Avocation" is annotated: "Question if use after D Bis i.e. D 2"; "Must Decide"; "No D 3"; "Reworked Jan 27, 61, 28, 29, 30." "Evan Shipman at the Lilas" bears the following comments, showing that Hemingway was still unsure about it: "K bis"; "(if include)"; "If it is included necessary changes must be made in the Scott story as indicated." Although he had decided not to use it ("Believe better not use"), he changed his mind on 25 January: "Jan 25 O.K. to use"; "Chapter 14." He had also been unsure as to where to use "The Man Who Was Marked for Death," since one of its typescripts is labeled "H" (crossed out), then "J" (crossed out), then "K" and "Go over again"; "Went over Jan 25, 61"; "Check again"; "March 18"; "Chapter Thirteen." The chapter that gave Hemingway the most trouble was "There Is Never Any End to Paris," as abundantly evidenced by the many rewrites and by the various dates that many pages of the manuscript and of the first typescript bear. Here are a few: "Dec. 16, 17"; "Still work on it Feb. 26"; "March 26"; "March 28, 29, 30"; "April 1"; "Continued March 27" on the drafts of the manuscript, and "Go over E. H. Jan 26" on the typescript beginning "The first year in the Voralberg." The typescript beginning "When there were the three of us" is annotated, "Last version March 15."

There is no doubt that Hemingway was at war with himself over these chapters. Neither "A False Spring" nor "The End of an Avocation" actually raised problems of conscience, but "The Man Who Was Marked for Death" did, since, even after it had been retyped by Betty, Hemingway wrote on this final typescript: "This is too dangerous and libelous to publish. Absolutely." As is well known, Hemingway was at that time terrified of being sued and spied upon, and he knew that his portrait of Ernest Walsh was both merciless and unfair. Why use "Evan Shipman at the Lilas," since he had summarized the contents of that chapter in the "Scott Fitzgerald" chapter and may have been working on a final chapter focused mainly on Evan? Finally, he was intensely worried about having been unfair to Hadley and not having portrayed her effectively enough as the true heroine of the book. Since he did "not want to hurt Hadley nor Pauline alive or dead nor the children,"[56] he decided not to use the portion of "There Is Never Any End to Paris" starting "The First year in the Voralberg," as evidenced by another annotation next to the 26 January date: "Don't use until I'm dead. Maybe not then! Not in Hadley's lifetime." It may be because of these qualms of conscience that he repeatedly pushed back the publication of the book, delving deeper and deeper into *The Dangerous Summer,* a book in which he was not personally involved and which therefore made no claim on his unresolved feelings toward the past. Indeed, it was a hard task to recall the happiness without recalling at the same time his role in its destruction, to settle scores with those who had hurt him without feeling guilt for having hurt others who loved him. Looking at one side of the coin necessarily entailed looking at the other side, too.

Although Hemingway devoted nearly five hours a day to revising *A Moveable Feast,* he achieved but little between January and April 1961. He was exhausted and found it almost impossible to write. In February he was unable to write a coherent sentence for a presentation volume to President Kennedy. He would often sit with his physician, Dr. George Saviers, tears coursing down his cheeks, complaining that he could no longer write. Aaron Hotchner recalled a similar episode in *Papa Hemingway.* But more important than the fact that he could no longer write was the fact that he had lost the belief that he would ever be able to write again. It is thus likely that the revisions amounted to little more than rereading the chapters, putting them in order, and attempting to come to grips with the preface and a last chapter. It may well have been on a day when he was struggling with the preface that he called Hadley, who was wintering with her husband in Arizona, in the hope that she could remind him of the names of the man and woman who had exploited young writers in Paris in 1925, for he wrote between drafts of sentences: "Hearing someone's voice over the telephone you know they still are and that they deserve it." Clearly, talking to Hadley had brought back some old emotions.[57]

His feeling insecure about the beginning and the ending is also evidenced by his desire to quote from the interview published by Plimpton, to whom he wrote on 25 February that, the night before, he had come across that number of the *Paris Review* and had seen some "stuff" he might want to quote directly from in the book about his early days in

Paris.[58] The next morning, he wrote to Brague that he was not sure which parts of the interview he would want to quote, but that they would not be extensive and that he would probably use them in the "forward matter" or at the end.[59]

The last chapter with which Hemingway was struggling, and which he never completed to his satisfaction, underwent several rewrites in March but without any obvious improvements. It was intended to conclude on what Hemingway had written and outline what he might also have written about. Finally, he gave up on it, and on 1, 2, and 3 April he seems to have written a different closing chapter (File 124a), which incorporated some of the material contained in earlier drafts (Files 123 and 124) that he had worked on throughout March and which continued with a narration of Evan Shipman's last visit to the Hemingways in Cuba. Somewhat sadly and with a pathetic appropriateness, this manuscript, which may well have been Hemingway's last work, deals with Evan Shipman dying of pancreatic cancer in atrocious pain, but holding tight in true Hemingway-hero fashion, proclaiming his admiration for Hemingway's work and urging him to write about Paris: "You have to put in the fun and the other that only we know who have been at some strange places in some strange times. Please do it even when you want to never think about it. And you have to put [it] in now." The feeling of urgency is great, and with good reason: Shipman was dying at the time when this narrative took place, and Hemingway killed himself perhaps three months after having written it. Hemingway was taken back to the Mayo Clinic at the end of April. On 26 June he was released. He reached Ketchum on June 30, and shot himself on 2 July 1961. He would never finish the book that contained "certain material from the remises of [his] memory and of [his] heart." Writing "was what [he] was born to do and had done and would [never] do again."[60]

CHAPTER THREE

Hemingway's Paris, Lyon, and Schruns

*H*EMINGWAY'S PRESENTATION of Paris, Lyon, and Schruns is fascinating not only because of its evocative power, which is undeniable, but perhaps most of all, for the scholar, because of its contradictory characteristics. The descriptions and background information provided are often accurate but, at the same time, extremely limited. In fact, much of what Hemingway describes could have been provided by the maps and books he had at his disposal, and his descriptions of Paris could have been written with either little knowledge of the city or with an imprecise memory. Similarly, while Hemingway describes the walks he used to take with reasonable precision and with an obvious concern to identify the various streets by name or by some physical characteristic, suggesting that he either had an excellent memory or was making good use of his maps of the city, his spelling of street and place names is surprisingly haphazard and generally so inaccurate that one is tempted to think that he had not seen those names for a long time. The misspelling of these names suggests that Hemingway did not really know what they meant or referred to historically. Some of these misspellings have survived despite the intensive copy editing done at various levels by the two main typists—Mary Hemingway and Betty—and, after Hemingway's death, by Mary Hemingway and the editors at Scribner's. One is therefore rather taken aback to read in Mary Hemingway's review of *A Moveable Feast* that she flew over to Paris and "retraced all the steps Ernest wrote that he took, first by [herself] and then with [her] friend, Gordon Parks, the photographer and writer." She states that "Ernest had made two mistakes in the spelling of street names. Otherwise his memory had been perfect." There remain in fact far more than two errors in the spelling of street names in the published text, even after Mary's and Parks's "careful verification." Twenty recurring errors would be a truer count. As for Hemingway himself, there are few French names he had not misspelt and, in some cases, distorted almost completely.[1] It is not surprising that Hemingway made spelling errors, since his French was never very good to start with. In fact, he had seldom written a correct French sentence in previous books. He was, moreover, writing *A Moveable Feast* not long after being involved in a plane crash in Africa, after which he was never completely well. He also suffered from deep and disturbing depressions and was on several medications, the side effects of which could only have made writing more difficult. What *is* surprising is that his editors did such a poor job of correcting simple spelling errors, while at the same time not only claiming that he had made virtually none but also that they had checked his spelling carefully. In fact, they even occasionally added errors.

I propose to follow Hemingway's steps through Paris, discussing the information he provides from the points of view of accuracy and thoroughness, filling in some missing information of interest, while mentioning some of the most glaring misspellings and their significance.

In "A Good Café on the Place St.-Michel," Hemingway describes his walk down from the Rue du Cardinal-Lemoine to the Place St. Michel:

> I walked down past the Lycée Henri Quatre and the ancient church of St.-Etienne-du-Mont and the windswept Place du Panthéon and cut in for shelter to the right and finally came out on the lee side of the Boulevard St.-Michel and worked on down it past the Cluny and the Boulevard St.-Germain until I came to a good café that I knew on the Place St.-Michel. (4–5)

His walking past the Lyçée Henri IV and the church of St. Etienne-du-Mont suggests that Hemingway took the Rue Clovis, with the church on his right and the lyçée on his left. Then, still on the Rue Clovis, he would have reached the Place du Panthéon, passing the Panthéon on his left, and continuing down the Rue Cujas. The original manuscript reads at this point: ". . . and cut in for shelter behind the Sorbonne and to the finally right and finally came out . . ." (File 128). The crossing out on the manuscript of "behind the Sorbonne" and of the first "finally" suggests that Hemingway preferred not to give too many details, which could be motivated by any number of reasons—from a desire not to overburden the reader with details to a reluctance to check a particular detail at a particular time. In any case, the original manuscript sentence indicates that he intended a right-hand turn on the Rue St. Jacques, then a left-hand turn on either the Rue des Ecoles or the Rue du Sommerard, the only two streets that could have allowed him to come out on the Boulevard St. Michel above the Café de Cluny—the Cluny being situated at the intersection of the Boulevard St. Michel and the Boulevard St. Germain, on the side opposite the Sorbonne and closest to the Seine. Hemingway then keeps walking down toward the Seine to an undetermined café on the Place St. Michel. The description is accurate. All that is missing is most of the street names, but, with the details he provides, there are few alternatives, especially when taking into account the original manuscript sentence. The return trip to the Rue du Cardinal-Lemoine is made by the "shortest way back up the Montagne Ste. Geneviève," which is extremely imprecise, since it is bound to involve several among many possible narrow streets.

The facts Hemingway stresses concerning his neighborhood are both accurate and inaccurate, skimpy, and oriented toward a presumably North American reader unacquainted with the rich history of that section of Paris. He emphasizes things that any Frenchman would take for granted, such as the "strangely named apéritifs" (which are strange only to a foreigner) and the "squat toilets . . . with the two cleated cement shoe-shaped elevations on each side of the aperture" (3). Here Hemingway is clearly writing for readers who have never been to France or, if they have, were insulated from the life of the French by luxury. At the same time, he indicates his own surprise at the unfamiliar.

There was indeed a bus stop, whether or not a terminal, at the Place de la Contrescarpe. In *The Sun Also Rises* Hemingway had identified it as an "S" bus,[2] and Richard Le Gallienne, in his excellent and most entertaining *From a Paris Garret*, describes the "S" bus as "one of the most useful and conspicuous of Paris motor buses . . . which, after we have explored this ancient quarter, will take us back to . . . the neighborhood of the Rue Royale or the Rue de la Paix."[3] The Rue Mouffetard was indeed a crowded market street, and much more. Le Gallienne, among others, describes its colorfulness in more detail than Hemingway:

> . . . the Rue Mouffetard, where perhaps more than any other street in Paris the old Paris of the people, Paris of the eighteenth and seventeenth centuries and earlier, is most swarmingly and vociferously alive. It runs downhill between rows of tall old houses, a narrow "wynd," as it might be called in Scotland, cluttered up with stalls and foodshops, until it ends near the Avenue des Gobelins, with a

sad old time-worn church, Saint-Médard, at the corner. This is first
and last a church of market women.[4]

This description of the Rue Mouffetard is still valid today in almost every
respect, in particular on weekdays. Actually, this very quality has turned
it into a modern tourist attraction and it is now developing a fashionable
arty side.

The Café des Amateurs, which Hemingway describes as "the cesspool
of the Rue Mouffetard," has disappeared, but it was probably situated at
2–4 Place de la Contrescarpe, at the intersection with the Rue Mouffetard
at No. 9.[5] There are now two main cafés on the Place de la Contrescarpe:
La Chope, located where the Café des Amateurs probably was, and La
Contrescarpe, on the opposite side of the Place, at the intersection with
the Rue Mouffetard.

It seems worthwhile to mention here one of the most curious features
of the Rue Mouffetard where it frames the Place de la Contrescarpe: until
recently there was above No. 14 a sign reading, "Au Nègre Joyeux," and
a painting representing Madame du Barry sitting at a table and being
served coffee by the black page Zamor.[6] The old residents are very proud
of this painting, and they are always willing to attract the newcomer's
attention to it and tell the story of the figures it represents, a story which
goes way back in French history. The Comtesse du Barry, born Jeanne
Bécu, was a notorious *courtisane* who was, for many years, the all-
powerful mistress of Louis XV. Zamor, a native of Bengal, who borrowed
his name from Voltaire's *Alzire* and his fortune from Louis XV's pocket,
had been given to Madame du Barry as a very young page and was raised
by her in unbelievable luxury. It appears that he became her lover, and
that she gave him a *Hôtel particulier* in Paris. But, when the French Revolution broke out, he denounced her to the vengeance of the people—
accusing her of wanton extravagance with state funds—and, nominated
to the Comité de Surveillance of the district of Versailles, he testified
against her at the Tribunal Révolutionnaire and secured her execution.
Madame du Barry was beheaded on 8 December 1793. Zamor, however,
did not profit from his betrayal as he had expected and did not obtain the
coveted "Brevet de Citoyen de Saint Domingue," which would have allowed him to leave France. Himself arrested but set free again, he eventually died in utter poverty and bitter resentment on 7 February 1820 in
a hovel at 13 Rue Maître-Albert, a narrow street which Hemingway must
have walked many times on his way down to the Seine from the Rue

Descartes or the Rue du Cardinal-Lemoine.[7] Although Hemingway does not mention the Nègre Joyeux in *A Moveable Feast*, he does in *The Sun Also Rises*, when he writes that "Music came out of the door of the Nègre Joyeux."[8] However, he does not identify the place. Robert Gajdusek, however, in his *Hemingway's Paris* identifies the Nègre Joyeux as a restaurant, which is probably inaccurate, since for the years 1921, 1922, and 1923—the years Hemingway spent in that quarter—No. 14 is listed in *Didot-Botin* as being a grocery store.[9] In any case, whether the place was a restaurant, a café, or a grocery store, the sign and the painting clearly referred to Zamor's "coffee" color.

More intriguing is the fact that Le Gallienne does not mention this painting either when he carefully reminds us, for example, that at No. 1 Place de la Contrescarpe once stood the Cabaret de la Pomme de Pin, immortalized by Rabelais and Ronsard, and that in a neighboring street, at No. 2 Rue Rollin, Pascal died in 1662.[10] But, unlike Le Gallienne, Hemingway was no historian and seemed generally little interested in French life and history when it did not involve eating or drinking, although Hadley mentioned that, in February 1922, he was "deeply engrossed in Hilaire Belloc's 'Paris' which tells much about this old Quarter, built by the Romans."[11] This, of course, did not prevent him from enjoying fully the delights of Paris. Hemingway, however, does tell us in *A Moveable Feast* that he had a room in the hotel where Verlaine had died, which would have been at 39 Rue Descartes—with the reservation that there was no hotel at that number.[12] What Hemingway probably had, if indeed he had a room there, was a maid's room—the top floor of most Paris buildings was devoted in the past to servants' quarters—on the sixth floor rather than the eighth. However, whether he really had a workroom there or not, he could of course hardly have been unaware that Verlaine had died there, for next to the door of 39 Rue Descartes is a plaque reading, "Dans cette maison est mort le 8 janvier 1896 le poète Paul Verlaine né à Metz le 30 mars 1844. Hommage des amis de Verlaine. 29 Juin 1919." What may have confused Hemingway, in his recollection of the past, is that in 1923 there apparently was the Select Hôtel situated next door at No. 41, and also that there was across the street, at No. 42, the Hôtel Descartes.[13] Of course, it may not have been confusion on his part but an early example of the self-romanticizing which pervades the book.

Hemingway is probably right when he describes the horse-drawn tank-wagons emptying the cesspools at night. There was a law in France dating back to 1818 that made it compulsory to empty those cesspools at night so that the inhabitants would not be bothered by pestilential odors.[14] Although a law dated 18 July 1894 adopted the principle of the "tout à l'égout" (modern sewage system) for the city of Paris, the enormous work involved in expanding the sewers of Paris would take many years, and it is likely that the inhabitants of the Montagne Sainte Geneviève, a poor quarter, would not have been among the first to be served by the new system. Moreover, participation in the plan was neither compulsory nor free. Each owner had a choice and had to apply for the privilege and pay an annual fee which, in 1921, was 90 francs.[15] It is therefore more than likely that the owners of Hemingway's flat had not applied. The emptying of these cesspools would therefore have taken place between 10:30 P.M. and 8 A.M. during the winter, and between 10:30 P.M. and 7 A.M. during the summer.

In "Miss Stein Instructs," Hemingway tells us only that he would have liked to take the shortest way back to the Rue du Cardinal-Lemoine from the Rue de Fleurus, which would definitely have involved crossing the Luxembourg Gardens. But, indeed, as the gates, or at least some of them, are closed at night, the logical way would have been around the lower end of the park—that is, left on Guynemer, right on the Rue de Vaugirard (the longest street in Paris), and right again on the Rue de Médicis. After that, he could again have taken a variety of streets back to his flat.

In this chapter, Hemingway talks about his going to the Musée du Luxembourg, "where the great paintings were that have now mostly been transferred to the Louvre and the Jeu de Paume. [He] went there nearly every day for the Cézannes and to see the Manets and the Monets and the other Impressionists . . ." (13). There would indeed have been no impediments to Hemingway's having seen those paintings on numerous occasions, as the collection of the artist Gustave Caillebotte, containing sixty-seven impressionist paintings, had been given to the state in 1883. This collection included four Manets, sixteen Monets, eight Renoirs, thirteen Pissarros, eight Degas, eight Sisleys, five Cézannes, one F. J. Millet, and one Caillebotte. Only the thirty-eight paintings judged the best from this collection were shown at the Musée du Luxembourg, among which were nine Monets (including "Le Déjeuner," "L'église de Vétheuil," "La Gare Saint-Lazare," "Les Rochers de Belle-Isle," "Régates d'Argenteuil," "le Givre," "Les Tuileries," and "Un coin d'appartement"), two Manets ("le Balcon" and "Angélina"), two Cézannes ("L'Estaque" and "Cour de village à Anvers"), six Renoirs ("Champrosay," "Le Moulin de la Galette," "la Balançoire," "Torse de jeune femme au soleil," "le Pont de Chemin de fer à Chatou," and "Liseuse"), seven Pissarros ("les Toits rouges," "la Moisson," "La brouette," "Le lavoir," "Chemin sous bois en été," "Chemin montant à travers champs," and "Potager: arbres en fleurs"), and six Sisleys (among which was "Bords de la Seine"). In addition to this collection, one could also see at the Luxembourg impressionist paintings donated by Moreau-Nélaton (1906) and Count Isaac de Camondo (1908), as well as a few paintings which had been donated by smaller estates, and some which had been purchased by the French government. The collection of impressionist paintings at the Luxembourg in the early 1920s was therefore very rich. Most of these paintings were removed from the Luxembourg in 1929 in order to make room for the paintings of more contemporary artists. However, in order not to break the continuity between living artists and their forbears, the Luxembourg retained at that time Manet's "Angélina," Renoir's "Liseuse," one Cézanne, one Fantin-Latour, one Monet, one Pissarro, and a few others. Most of these paintings were moved in 1947 to the Musée du Jeu de Paume and can now be seen at the Musée d'Orsay.[16]

In "Une Génération Perdue," Hemingway gives us few details about Paris, aside from mentioning that, walking home from Gertrude Stein's apartment at 27 Rue de Fleurus, he stopped at the Closerie des Lilas to keep company with the statue of Marshal Ney (30). Hemingway must have been in a wandering mood that evening, for the Closerie was hardly the shortest way to 113 Rue Notre-Dame-des-Champs from Stein's place. Instead of walking up the Rue d'Assas and cutting to the right either through the Rue Joseph-Bara or the Rue Le-Verrier, which would have brought him respectively to 97 or to 101 Rue Notre-Dame-des-Champs, a few numbers below his own, he walked all the way up the Rue d'Assas to the Closerie, and then down his own street. Again, of course, Hemingway does not indicate which streets he used, but the alternatives are few, short of increasing the distance significantly. In any case, the extra walk to the Closerie was a short one.

Rude's statue of Marshal Michel Ney is still standing in front of the Closerie des Lilas, as it has been since 7 December 1853, when it was erected to commemorate the "bravest of the brave," who was executed for treason on 7 December 1815. Hemingway's comments about Ney are basically accurate. Ney commanded the rear guard during the retreat of the Grande Armée after the burning of Moscow and virtually singlehandedly protected this disastrous operation with remarkable heroism and levelheadedness. While Napoléon, and later Murat, shamefully abandoned the Grande Armée, Ney kept the pieces together by sheer personal strength and brought its remnants back to France. Later on, though, his catastrophic tactical error partly brought about the defeat of Waterloo and Napoléon's final downfall. After the second return of the Bourbons, Ney was arrested after a halfhearted attempt to flee the country, condemned, and shot in front of No. 43 Avenue de l'Observatoire.

The comment concerning Apollinaire's death, however, is inaccurate. But, since Hemingway indicates that he heard the story from Gertrude Stein, it is difficult to know whose memory is at fault. Apollinaire did not die on the day of the Armistice, but on 9 November 1918 at five in the afternoon. The story is that Apollinaire's friends who were watching by his corpse heard the overjoyed crowd on 11 November shouting in the streets, "A bas Guillaume, conspuez Guillaume." The allusion was to the defeated emperor. During Apollinaire's funeral, the march was also interrupted by similar popular outcries.[17]

In "Shakespeare and Company," Hemingway writes almost nothing about Paris, apart from the well-known fact that Sylvia Beach's bookshop was situated at 12 Rue de l'Odéon. Sylvia Beach moved to that address in 1921, after having first opened in 1919 in the Rue Dupuytren.[18] On the other hand, "People of the Seine" is probably the chapter that is the most packed with information about Paris—information that is both accurate and erroneous.

> There were many ways of walking down to the river from the top of the rue Cardinal Lemoine. The shortest one was straight down the street but it was steep and it brought you out, after you hit the flat part and crossed the busy traffic of the beginning of the Boulevard St.-Germain, onto a dull part where there was a bleak, windy stretch of river bank with the Halle aux Vins on your right. This was not like any other Paris market but was a sort of bonded warehouse where wines were stored against the payment of taxes and was as cheerless from the outside as a military depot or prison camp. (41)

Walking straight down the Rue du Cardinal-Lemoine is truly the shortest way down to the Seine from Hemingway's apartment on that street. The street is reasonably steep, but not uncomfortably so. However, the Halle aux Vins was not immediately on the right when one reached the river bank, but was separated from the intersection of the Rue du Cardinal-Lemoine and the Quai de la Tournelle by a whole block of buildings six to eight stories high. Only after one had turned right on the Quai de la Tournelle, walked one block, and crossed the Rue des Fossés-St-Bernard did one reach the Halle aux Vins. The buildings of the Halle aux Vins have now disappeared and been replaced by the modern buildings of the Université de Paris VI and Paris VII Pierre et Marie Curie.

Hemingway's description of the role played by the Halle aux Vins is somewhat incorrect. The Halle aux Vins was not a bonded warehouse where wine was stored against the payment of taxes. Completed in 1814, it was built to free wholesalers and retail merchants who set up business there from having to pay tax on the wines and other alcoholic beverages they had in stock. Only the bottles that were sold were taxed upon leaving the Halle. It was also as of 1811–12 a tax-free warehouse for all the drinks exported outside the "Mur des Fermiers Généraux." In fact, the Halle aux Vins was a traditional French market that offered tax advantages to the merchants who operated there.[19] As for the appearance of the building, it was generally considered rather attractive, but of course tastes differ. In *Promenades dans les Rues de Paris*, Rochegude-Clébert writes, "La Halle aux Vins garde un aspect campagnard fort agréable, avec ses rues grossièrement pavées et ses murs de ferme."[20] Le Gallienne also finds it attractive and describes it as a picturesque institution that connoisseurs of wine would wish to visit, "a huge iron-railed enclosure, a town in itself, rustling with trees and intersected by roadways bearing such significant names as Rue de Bordeaux, Rue de Champagne, and Rue de Bourgogne. . . . If one lacks time to enter it, one gets pleasant glimpses of this city of Bacchus through the railings as one walks along the riverside boundary."[21] It is the very boundary that Hemingway finds "as cheerless . . . as a military depot or a prison camp. "

Later, in "People of the Seine," Hemingway writes: "I knew several of the men who fished the fruitful part of the Seine between the Ile St.-Louis and the Place du Verte Galente" (44).[22] There is no *Place du Verte Galente*, nor a *Verte Galente*. There are, however, a Vert Galant and a Square du Vert Galant. Clearly, Hemingway did not know what *Vert Galant* meant or that it was a nickname given to Henry IV because of his lively interest in women. As one might guess, a *vert galant* is a passionate lover, however inadequate this translation may sound for all the implications of courtesy, gallantry, and passion suggested by the expression. Giving this name to the little square overlooked by the statue was a way of commemorating one of the weaknesses of the most beloved king of France.

The confusion between *square* and *place* on Hemingway's part, which occurs on other occasions in the book, is interesting. In French, a *square* is a small garden. *Place*, on the other hand, indicates an open area where streets intersect, and translates as "square" in English—for example, Place de la Concorde and Trafalgar Square. Hemingway's inaccurate terminology is therefore revealing on two levels: the linguistic and the historical.

Hemingway's statement about the bookstalls on the Quai de la Tournelle, the Quai des Grands Augustins, and the Quai Voltaire is probably accurate, although difficult to verify one way or the other. The Tour d'Argent is situated at the intersection of the Rue du Cardinal-Lemoine and the Quai de la Tournelle, and was also a hotel. But Hemingway's emphasis on the total ignorance of the French booksellers concerning the books they sold is hardly believable, even if his opinion was shared by others such as George and Pearl Adam. On the other hand, Pierre MacOrlan feels that the booksellers of the quais know their business:

> Good English books, however, command fair prices, and bargains among them are not as easy to find. In cases when he is at a loss, the second-hand dealer asks the expert advice of one of his wealthier *confrères* established close at hand, in order to avoid those unpleasant surprises that fall to the lot of the tradesmen who deal with merchandize with whose exact value they are not familiar.[23]

This is indeed different from Hemingway's description of the booksellers as knowing a good French book from the pictures, and a good English book from whether it had been bound properly for a ship's library (41–43). It is, of course, always dangerous to generalize, and both opinions could have been based on personal experiences; however, Hemingway's problem may well have been one of communication.

On another level, Hemingway's reference to the restaurant La Pêche Miraculeuse at Bas Meudon is accurate but leaves the reader of Maupassant and the admirer of Sisley to fill in the details for himself (43–44). An inquiry into the *Guide du gourmand à Paris* yields an attractive description of that restaurant, in particular this passage which adds specific details to Hemingway's:

> Devant l'harmonieux paysage de la Seine, le sage s'assied à la terrasse du premier étage: le soleil se couche sur la rivière: la ville s'estompe dans la brume. La *matelotte d'anguilles*, les *barbillons*, les *fritures de goujons* y sont un délice. Et un petit vin léger délie les

langues, adoucit les caractères et répand partout le plus aimable optimisme.*[24]

In "A False Spring," Hemingway and Hadley's walk back from Pruniers to the Rue du Cardinal-Lemoine is accurate in its physical details. Pruniers is and was situated at 9 Rue Duphot. Therefore, from Pruniers to the Tuileries, they probably walked down the Rue Duphot, crossed the Rue St. Honoré to the Rue Cambon, then continued down the Rue Cambon to the Rue de Rivoli, and probably entered the garden of the Tuileries by the gate situated near the Jeu de Paume, across from where the Rue Cambon and the Rue de Rivoli intersect. They would then have walked through the garden of the Tuileries to the Place du Carrousel with the Arc de Triomphe du Carrousel. Indeed, if one stands under the Arc de Triomphe du Carrousel, with one's back to the Palais and the Musée du Louvre, one can see through the gardens in a straight line the Obélisque of the Place de la Concorde, then the Avenue des Champs-Elysées, and finally the Arc de Triomphe (53). The gateway through which they would have exited would be the closest one to where they were standing, which would lead them straight to the Pont du Carrousel, and still in an almost straight line up the Rue des Saints-Pères to Michaud (54, 56). From Michaud they could have walked back home through a variety of streets, but nothing in the text suggests a particular itinerary. The comment that they were "hungry again from walking" when they reached Michaud is amusing, since the distance between Pruniers and Michaud is hardly sufficient to justify two dinners in a row. (It can be walked at a normal pace in half an hour.) But, of course, as Hemingway makes clear later in the chapter, the source of their hunger had little to do with walking or with food.

Michaud, about which Hemingway ruefully commented that he could afford to eat there at most once a week, when Joyce and his family ate there every day,[25] is described in *Le Guide du gourmand à Paris* as a modest restaurant (*un restaurant simple*) largely frequented by literary people: "Beaucoup de monde. Gens de lettres. Cuisine excellente. Certains *pieds de mouton*, des *filets de soles*, un *canard au sang*, arrosés de *vins du Rhône*,

---

*The wise customer sits at the tables on the second-floor terrace, overlooking the beautiful scenery of the Seine: the sun sets on the river; the city becomes blurred in the mist. The *matelotte d'anguilles*, the *barbillons*, and the *friture de goujons* are delicious. A light wine makes people chatty, softens their moods, and prompts in everyone the most pleasant optimism.

satisferont les plus difficiles."*[26] Pruniers, on the other hand, is listed as a good average restaurant (*un restaurant moyen*), and the ground-floor bar where Hemingway and Hadley ate is described as a "bar amusant où l'on peut agréablement déjeuner de quelques *huitres*, d'une *bouillabaisse*, d'un petit *homard*, de *crabes à l'indienne*, de *clauvisses*, arrosé d'un *Pouilly* et surtout d'un *Anjou* tout à fait remarquable.**[27] There may also well have been the *"Crabe Mexicaine"*—or rather either the "crabe mexicain" or the "crabe à la mexicaine"—and the Sancerre which Hemingway mentions, although it does not seem to have struck the gourmet and gourmand Robert. One might regret that Hemingway did not mention, as he had in *The Sun Also Rises*, Madame Leconte's restaurant Le Rendez-vous des Mariniers, which, according to a gourmet friend of Le Gallienne, was the best place in Paris for roast chicken—so much so that Le Gallienne's friend would announce his arrival by telegram so that he might be sure to have some "superlative" chicken.[28]

While on first consideration it is somewhat surprising, there were indeed goats led by goatherds walking the streets of Paris in the early 1920s. Le Gallienne describes these goats in 1931 very much as Hemingway would describe them in *A Moveable Feast* in the late 1950s (49):

> Suddenly in the most crowded avenue one would hear a charming piping, the veritable pipes of Pan, and there was a bronzed Southern man . . . leading a herd of the wildest-looking goats across the stream of cars.
>
> No one seemed to resent this Virgilian "disturber of traffic." On the contrary, delighted curiosity was on every face as they watched the uncanny creatures, with their long black hair and yellow eyes, and formidable twisted horns, some with swollen udders, for the satisfaction of infant Parisians, whose mothers, as soon as the herd had debouched into some medieval side street, came around them with pails, into which presently one heard the milk go hissing. . . .[29]

Le Gallienne, however, deplores the disappearance of these two or three goatherds in the late 1920s,[30] blaming it on Mr. Jean Chiappe. He is in-

---

*Many people. "Gens de lettres." Excellent food. The *pieds de mouton*, the *filets de soles*, the *canard au sang*, washed down with a *vin du Rhône*, will please the most discriminating.

**An entertaining bar where one can lunch most pleasantly with a few oysters, a *bouillabaisse*, a small lobster, some *crabes à l'indienne*, or a plate of clams, washed down with a *Pouilly*, and especially a very remarkable *Anjou*.

deed right, for Chiappe, who was at the time prefect of police of Paris and who, in Le Gallienne's opinion, had a "drill sergeant bent," passed on 10 June 1929 an ordinance forbidding the circulation of cattle in the streets of Paris in all but a very few streets. He even had the heart to forbid on 20 February 1931 the use of musical instruments and street calls by itinerant craftsmen and vendors.[31] If the ordinance on traffic had not already taken care of the goats, the second one on street cries would have taken care of the goatherds, thus spelling the disappearance of what Le Gallienne describes as one of the quaintest anachronisms of the Paris streets. And one cannot help smiling at his outraged comment that "anyone who would silence this joyous pandemonium is a sickly, anaemic soul, who should have been born with ear-clips and is not properly to be called a human being." Hemingway describes these goats very much in the same romantic vein:

> The goatherd came up the street blowing his pipes and a woman who lived on the floor above us came out onto the sidewalk with a big pot. The goatherd chose one of the heavy-bagged, black milk-goats and milked her into the pot while his dog pushed the others onto the sidewalk. The goats looked around turning their necks like sightseers. The goatherd . . . went on up the street piping and the dog herded the goats on ahead, their horns bobbing. (49)

However, he does not mention their demise; nor does he tell us anything about the bees which were also one of the country touches that charmed Le Gallienne: "Bees in the heart of Paris! Could there be a more delightful surprise?"

Henry Miller's description of these same goats both contrasts with and echoes Hemingway's and Le Gallienne's:

> A little farther along we stumbled on a flock of goats picking their way erratically down the precipitous slope; behind them a fully-blown cretin followed leisurely, blowing a few strange notes now and then. The atmosphere was one of utter tranquility, utter peace; it might have been a morning of the fourteenth century.[32]

Hemingway could indeed have bought a paper in the Rue Descartes since there was a *papeterie* at No. 49, although not at the corner of the Place de la Contrescarpe.[33] Hemingway's reference to the "public bathhouse down at the foot of the street by the river" (51) is also partially accurate. *Didot-Botin* lists for the early 1920s Les Bains du Cardinal-Lemoine at 33 Rue du Cardinal-Lemoine and 42 Rue des Fossés St. Bernard. If it was not actually by the river, it was only a short block away from the river. These bathhouses offered baths, showers, steam baths, and other amenities; but they had a questionable reputation. However, they did serve their purpose. Hemingway and Hadley might also have used later on the one that was situated almost across the street from their second Paris flat on the Rue Notre-Dame-des-Champs: the Bains de l'Observatoire at 169 Boulevard du Montparnasse and 126 Rue Notre-Dame-des-Champs.[34] As Hemingway's bakery did, this bathhouse opened on both streets.

"The End of an Avocation" provides little information about Paris, except for some details regarding bicycle racing and horse racing. What few physical details Hemingway gives about Paris are correct. The Guaranty Trust, where Hemingway went to see Mike Ward, was located at 1 Rue des Italiens, which would indeed have been at the intersection with the Boulevard des Italiens. The Bibliothèque Nationale faces the Square Louvois across the Rue de Richelieu. The most detailed sections of this chapter deal with horse and bicycle races, particularly the latter.

The three stadiums Hemingway mentions, the Vélodrome d'Hiver, the Stade Buffalo, and the Stade du Parc des Princes—not the "Parc du Prince"—existed in the 1920s and 1930s. The six-day races used to take place in March at the Vélodrome d'Hiver, which was destroyed in 1959. The Stade Buffalo near Montrouge, which Hemingway refers to, was in fact the second Stade Buffalo, replacing the one at Neuilly which had been inaugurated in 1892 and whose director had been Tristan Bernard. The track at the Stade Buffalo was not five hundred meters, as Hemingway indicates, but one third of a kilometer (333.33 meters). The "courses de demi-fond" as well as the one-hundred-kilometer races took place on all the vélodromes. The stadium of the Parc des Princes is indeed the one where Ganay fell in August 1926 during a "match de demi-fond" against Léon Didier. Ganay's front tire burst as he was racing behind his trainer and he fell on the 666-meter cement track. He died at the Clinique de Vaugirard shortly after the accident. It appears that over the years several riders fell and died at the same spot Ganay fell. Finally, Linart was not only the "great Belgian champion," but also the world champion in 1924, 1926, and 1927. His first championship was won at the Stade du Parc des Princes behind Léon Didier. I have not been able to verify, however, that Linart was nicknamed "the Sioux."[35] What Hemingway has to say about bicycle races is therefore generally accurate, if not totally so. However, as the dates given indicate, his acquaintanceship with these races did not come "at another time in Paris" (65). If he saw Ganay fall, he was already acquainted with these races in 1926, at the time of his breakup with Hadley. Of course, he may be talking of emotional time rather than calendar time—namely, that the bicycle races remind him of Pauline rather than of Hadley. In fact, in the original manuscript, he had made it clear that he was with Pauline when he saw Ganay fall.[36]

"Hunger Was a Good Discipline" describes Hemingway's wanderings through the Latin Quarter, avoiding restaurants because he is skipping lunch, after his return from Canada. His itinerary is easy to follow, as it obviously starts from the Rue Notre-Dame-des-Champs, where he was living at that time, continues through the Square de l'Observatoire and the gardens of the Luxembourg, on to Sylvia Beach's bookstore. One finds here the same misunderstanding seen previously in "People of the Seine" concerning the meaning of the words "place" and "square" in French (69). There is no Place de l'Observatoire, but there is a Square de l'Observatoire, a long and comparatively narrow garden stretching between the Carrefour de l'Observatoire and the gates of the Luxembourg and occupying the central section of the Avenue d l'Observatoire. It is a lovely garden with long rows of huge chestnut trees, beds of flowers, and Carpeaux's famous fountain, not far from Marshal Ney's statue. From 113 Rue Notre-Dame-des-Champs it is a very short walk to the Square de l'Observatoire. After having crossed the garden lengthwise, one need only cross the Rue Auguste Comte to enter the Luxembourg gardens, then walk through the length of the garden and cross the Rue de Vaugirard to enter the narrow Rue Férou. If one avoids looking to the right when emerging from the Rue Notre-Dame-des-Champs (if one did glance that way, one would of course see the Closerie des Lilas), one will indeed encounter no restaurant all the way to the Place St. Sulpice. This would clearly be a good walk for someone wanting to skip lunch, except that there would probably be people having a picnic in the Luxembourg gardens.

In the first draft of that chapter, Hemingway had described the fountain on the Place St. Sulpice as being ornamented with statues of "scholars" (File 148). He corrected himself when he revised the first typescript and replaced "scholars" with "bishops." The change was well advised, for the statues are those of F. S. Fénelon (archbishop of Cambray), J. Bossuet (bishop of Meaux), E. Fléchier (bishop of Nîmes), and J. B. Massillon (bishop of Clermont). The remainder of Hemingway's walk is described accurately, if in general terms:

But by choosing your way carefully you could work to your right around the grey and white stone church and reach the rue de l'Odéon and turn up to your right toward Sylvia Beach's bookshop and on your way you did not pass too many places where things to eat were sold. The rue de l'Odéon was bare of eating places until you reached the square where there were three restaurants. (70)

In order to follow Hemingway's steps, one has to take the Rue Palatine on the right of the Eglise St. Sulpice, turn left on the Rue Garancière, then right on the Rue St. Sulpice, then left on the Rue de Condé, and then, at the Carrefour de l'Odéon, right on the Rue de l'Odéon. By going that way, Hemingway could indeed have avoided most of the restaurants of the neighborhood, although he could hardly have avoided the restaurants at the Carrefour de l'Odéon.[37] Although it is no longer the case, in the 1920s the Rue de l'Odéon was bare of restaurants—but not entirely free of the sight or the smell of food, as there were a wine merchant at No. 5, a baker at No. 6, and a grocery store at No. 18, which might have tempted Hemingway's hunger. Finally, there were three restaurants at the Place de l'Odéon: the café Voltaire at Nos. 1 and 21 Rue de L'Odéon, the Brasserie Restaurant de l'Odéon at Nos. 7 and 1 Rue Corneille, and a bar at No. 5.[38] Today the only restaurant there is La Méditerranée. Another restaurant, Le Mazafram, is at 7 Rue Corneille, close to the Place de l'Odéon.

One might mention here that Flaubert, whom Hemingway greatly admired, had lived at 20 Rue de l'Odéon—four doors away from Sylvia Beach's store—and that Manet, whose paintings he used to admire frequently at the Musée du Luxembourg, had died in 1883 at 5 Rue des Saints-Pères—twelve doors away from Michaud.

The remainder of Hemingway's itinerary is generally accurate. It is actually a reasonably short walk from Beach's bookstore to Lipp's (72), which is situated at 151 Boulevard St. Germain, across the boulevard from the Deux Magots; and the Rues Bonaparte, Guynemer, and d'Assas would be the shortest way to the Closerie des Lilas from Lipp's (76). It is interesting to note that Hemingway's manuscript as well as his two typescripts read: "I went up Bonaparte to Guynemer, then to the rue d'Assas, *across* the rue Notre Dame des Champs to the Closerie des Lilas" (76) (italics added). The change from "across" to "up," which was made after Hemingway's death by his editors, alters somewhat Hemingway's walk. The use of "across" suggests that he had walked up the Rue d'Assas and then crossed the Rue Notre-Dame-des-Champs, as indeed he would have had to do to get to the Closerie. The change to "up" suggests that he would have crossed the Rue d'Assas to the Rue Vavin, then walked up the Rue Notre-Dame-des-Champs, or, possibly, that he might have walked up part of the Rue d'Assas to the Rue Joseph Bara or the Rue Le Verrier, turned right on either of them, and then left on the Rue Notre-Dame-des-Champs. Clearly, this is far more complicated. Thus, the change made by the editors seems not only gratuitous but also ill-advised, in that, without improving anything, it complicates rather than simplifies Hemingway's itinerary and opens more alternatives than his original description.

"Ford Madox Ford and the Devil's Disciple" unintentionally offers some surprising information about Paris—the result, as in some other instances, of Hemingway's occasionally careless proofreading. It has to do with the clientèle at the Closerie des Lilas. The original manuscript sentence reads:

> Most of the clients *knew each other only to nod and there* were elderly bearded men in well worn clothes who came with their wives or their mistresses and wore or did not wear thin red Legion of Honor ribbons in their lapels. (File 151) (italics added)

In the transcription of this sentence, the typist—probably Mary Hemingway—skipped the italicized section of the sentence (which corresponds to one line of Hemingway's handwriting), thus altering significantly its meaning. Hemingway did not notice the omission when proofreading, since it was not corrected when other errors were, and the maimed sentence was eventually published (81–82). The statement it makes is rather amusing, for no French café situated on a main artery and in as highly artistic a quarter as the top of the Boulevard du Montparnasse would ever have, whether in the 1920s or today, a clientèle composed mostly of "elderly bearded men." One need only glance at the professions of the inhabitants of, say, the Rue Notre-Dame-des-Champs to see that the *quartier* was inhabited by highly artistic types in the 1920s and 1930s—people who are traditionally associated with youth.[39] In any case, one could go as far as saying, without much risk of error, that no centrally situated Parisian café would ever have such a clientèle, even after World War I.

On the other hand, Hemingway is right when he writes that the Closerie des Lilas had been a café where poets used to meet regularly (81). Apollinaire, André Salmon, Paul Fort ("Le Prince des Poètes"), Baudelaire, Moréas, and also Gide, Jarry, Charles Louis Philip, Max Jacob, Picasso, Ingres, and other artists and writers frequented the Closerie at various times. But around 1912 a large number of the artistic patrons of the Closerie moved down the boulevard to the Dôme and the Rotonde. The Dôme and the Rotonde, which Hemingway scorns, had in fact as illustrious an artistic and literary past as the Closerie—the Rotonde in particular, which, under the ownership of Libion, was the haven of Modigliani, Apollinaire, Salmon, Max Jacob, Jean Cocteau, Picasso, Braque, Kissling, Derain, Vlaminck, and others. During World War I, the Rotonde was probably the café most closely watched by the police because of the former patronage of Trotsky. In fact, after the war, tired of police harassment, Libion sold the Rotonde to a "good business man" who expanded the café repeatedly and transformed the tiny, colorful, and smoky center of Parisian bohemia, where starving artists could get easy credit and pay, as Modigliani often did, with paintings no one wanted, into a prosperous café. It became more of a competitor to the Dôme which had long attracted rich Germans and Americans as an important part of its clientèle.[40]

Hemingway's comments about Blaise Cendrars and war casualties are interesting. Of course, in the 1920s, war casualties were a common sight in France. But one wonders what Hemingway would have liked Cendrars to do with his empty sleeve. Pinning up very neatly a well-ironed sleeve or a trouser leg was a normal thing to do for a man who had lost an arm or a leg. There was nothing flashy about it. It saved having alterations made by a tailor for people who had little money and, in fact, looked neater than anything a tailor might have done. This also was a very common sight in France for a long time. Hemingway's suggestion that the clientèle of the Closerie would mock Cendrars because of the ostentatiousness of the "pinned-up" (82) sleeve could hardly have applied to the French clientèle, in particular since it was well known that Cendrars had lost his arm up to the elbow while serving in the French Foreign Legion—the military corps that traditionally had the highest level of casualties, and which was respected far more than mocked.

Finally, the Bal Musette, which is partly the subject of the conversation between Hemingway and Ford in this chapter, was called the Bal du Printemps—"a charming little spot. It showed a row of electric lights across an angle in the Rue du Cardinal-Lemoine. . . . Inside the rough tables and wooden benches were painted scarlet and the walls around the dance floor were set with mirrors and painted pink, with garlands all done by hand." Although it seems to have come into existence in 1923, according to *Didot-Botin*, one should probably take Hemingway's word that it already existed in 1922, when he lived at Rue du Cardinal-Lemoine, for he wrote to Dos Passos on 16 February 1922 and described it.[41] It is thus possible, however unlikely it may seem (except if he went there before the Bal closed), that Hemingway's early-morning glass of wine was taken at the counter of the Bal Musette rather than at the counter of the wine shop that was at No. 74 before the Bal du Printemps.

"Birth of a New School" offers no information about Paris, aside from mentioning the Petite Chaumière (92); but "With Pascin at the Dôme" introduces a few new elements, in particular the bakery Hemingway used as a shortcut and the Nègre de Toulouse. Gajdusek identifies the bakery as the one situated at 151 Boulevard du Montparnasse with a backdoor at 110 Rue Notre-Dame-des-Champs.[42] There is still a bakery there today, and it is apparently the one Hemingway used. A slight detail is awry, however, in Gajdusek's identification—namely, that the bakery is still at 151*bis* Boulevard du Montparnasse, where it was in the 1920s.

The Nègre de Toulouse was situated at 157–59 Boulevard du Montparnasse, and Lavigne was indeed its proprietor, as Hemingway indicates (99). Apparently Lavigne became proprietor in 1924, roughly when Hemingway came back from Canada and settled in the neighborhood, and it is likely that he gave the restaurant its name. Before Lavigne, there was a restaurant at that spot listed under the name of Amagat in 1922 and 1923; and, as of 1929, the restaurant was no longer listed under Lavigne's name but under the name of Vieillescazes.[43] There is still currently a restaurant there—an Italian restaurant named La Padova—but it is smaller than Lavigne's used to be, as it occupies only No. 159.

Hemingway would indeed have had to walk *up* the boulevard from the bakery to the Nègre de Toulouse; but if he continued on his way and *"went on up the street* looking in the windows and happy with the spring evening and the people coming past" (99; italics added), he would have very shortly reached the Closerie des Lilas instead of the "three principal cafés" (99–100). The Dôme, the Rotonde, and the Sélect are and were situated some three blocks down the Boulevard du Montparnasse from the bakery, while both the Nègre de Toulouse and the Closerie were farther up the boulevard.

The remainder of the information provided in this chapter involves merely a mention of the three main cafés and their relative locations, which is accurate. The last piece of information given, the mention of the restaurant Les Vikings, is difficult to verify, since it is listed neither in the *Annuaire des Abonnés du Téléphone,* which lists restaurants according to their names, nor in *Didot-Botin,* which lists them according to either the name of their owner or their location. Since Hemingway provides neither the name of the street nor the owner's name, it is difficult to verify its existence. However, Clara E. Laughlin lists The Viking at 29 Rue Vavin as a Norwegian restaurant in *So You're Going to Paris.*[44] Thus, Hemingway may simply have recalled the name inaccurately, or Clara Laughlin perhaps anglicized it.

Neither "Ezra Pound and His Bel Esprit" nor "A Strange Enough Ending" offers much information about Paris. One might simply add that Ezra Pound lived at 70*bis* Rue Notre-Dame-des-Champs to the first of these two chapters (107). On the other hand, Hemingway's sole piece of information in the second one is debatable. He writes: "It was a lovely spring day and I walked down from the Place de l'Observatoire through the little Luxembourg. The horse-chestnut trees were in blossom and there were many playing on the graveled walks . . ." (118). If there was no "Place de l'Observatoire," there was a "Petit Luxembourg" which, however, was not a garden, as Hemingway intimates. The "Petit Luxembourg" was a section of the Palais du Luxembourg and included the former Hôtel du Luxembourg given to Richelieu by Marie de Médicis in 1627, as well as the cloister and the chapel of a convent founded by the queen. The Musée du Luxembourg occupied the Orangerie du Petit Luxembourg in the 1920s. However, it is now reduced to occupying a smallish room of the Petit Luxembourg. One should note, though, that in local and student parlance the Square de l'Observatoire is often referred to as the Petit Luxembourg, as it is a smaller garden than the Jardin du Luxembourg itself. It also precisely fits Hemingway's description.

"The Man Who Was Marked for Death" and "Evan Shipman at the Lilas" also have little to say about Paris. Hemingway merely mentions two types of oysters available in French restaurants—the "portugaises" and the "marennes"—in "The Man Who Was Marked for Death." In the next chapter, he writes:

> Later after leaving Ezra's studio and walking along the street to the sawmill, looking down the high-sided street to the opening at the end where the bare trees showed and behind them the far facade of the Bal Bullier across the width of the Boulevard St.-Michel . . . . (135)

Hemingway's description of the perspective is accurate, except for the detail that he would have been looking *up* the street rather than *down* the street, as the Rue Notre-Dame-des-Champs is in mild ascent between Pound's studio at 70*bis* and Hemingway's flat at 113. Further up the street one can indeed see the trees of the beginning of the Square de l'Observatoire and the Carrefour de l'Observatoire. The notorious Bal Bullier, which had been redecorated in an oriental style in 1850, was one of the last great establishments of popular entertainment, along with the Jardin Mabille and the Grande Chaumière. Among the famous people who danced at the Bullier, one should mention Béranger, Murger, Théodore de Banville, Vermesch, A. Vitu, Clara Fontaine, Rigolette, and Mogador. Repossessed during World War I by the army, the Bullier reopened in 1920 but disappeared before World War II.[45] The Bullier was situated at 31–39 Avenue de l'Observatoire, across from the Closerie des Lilas, and its name has been perpetuated by several cafés in Montparnasse, in particular the Bullier at 22 Avenue de l'Observatoire.

Further details provided in this chapter are accurate. The wife of the sawmill owner, whom Hemingway describes in unsympathetic terms, was Mrs. Chautard. The Chautards apparently ran the sawmill between 1923 and 1926.[46] Montrouge was indeed a suburb of Paris where people had small flower and vegetable gardens which they cultivated for both pleasurable and practical reasons.

"An Agent of Evil" introduces little new information about Paris; what it mentions in passing is partly accurate and partly inaccurate, but it is definitely colorful, although Hemingway does not make much of it:

> The Hole in the Wall was a very narrow bar with a red-painted facade, little more than a passageway, on the rue des Italiens. At one time it had a rear exit into the sewers of Paris from which you were supposed to be able to reach the catacombs. (143)

The Hole in the Wall (Le Trou dans le Mur) was not, and still is not, situated on the Rue des Italiens, but at 23 Boulevard des Capucines, across the boulevard from the Café de la Paix. During the 1920s it was listed as an American bar.[47] It was indeed very narrow, as it still is, its facade not much more than two meters wide. Whether it had at one time a direct entrance into the sewers of Paris is difficult to verify beyond question, but in all likelihood it did. If one examines the plans of the sewers of Paris, one sees that the sewers follow exactly the pattern of the streets of Paris under which they flow, each gallery bearing the name of the street, avenue, or dead end above it. There are, and in the 1920s already probably were close to, some 25,000 *regards d'égouts* and 17,000 *bouches d'égouts*, which allowed entrance into the 2000 kilometers of Parisian sewers. And there actually were a couple of *regards d'égouts* roughly at the level of the Trou dans le Mur on the side of the Boulevard des Capucines across from the large Hôtel de la Paix in 1903.[48] Whether one of these actually allowed entrance into the bar is hard to know, but it would be quite likely if one considers one aspect of the hidden history of the Paris sewers. The underground quarries situated in peripheral sections of Paris, and later the sewers, provided ideal channels for the smuggling of merchandise in and out of Paris. All merchandise, in particular alcohol, incurred a tax on entering Paris in the sixteenth, seventeenth, and eighteenth centuries; therefore, contraband thrived. By its very nature it had to be carried out discreetly, and going underground was natural for such activity. Cafés, bars, cabarets, and *guinguettes* were ideal covers to hide the points of access. Therefore, entrances to the underground galleries were usually found in the basements of such commercial establishments. In 1777, however, the creation of a service to inspect these underground galleries dealt a sharp blow to the smugglers.[49] Thus the presence in close proximity both of two entrances into the sewers and that of the Trou dans le Mur (a most suggestive name) leads to the logical assumption that one of these entrances led directly into the Trou dans le Mur. The sewers and the catacombs, however, are entirely different things, and it is unlikely that one could reach the catacombs from that exit of the sewers, for at least two reasons. The catacombs are located miles to the south of the Trou dans le Mur, on the other side of the Seine; and the catacombs are limestone quarries that were transformed into an ossuary in the late eighteenth and early nineteenth centuries, receiving the bones of over six million people that were previously in various cemeteries of Paris, as well as the bones of many of the dead of the Revolution of 1789 and later ones. A connection with the sewers is therefore hardly likely, nor does it seem to be documented.

"Scott Fitzgerald," of course, introduces the relationship between Hemingway and Fitzgerald, a relationship which, according to Hemingway, began at "the Dingo bar in the rue Delambre" (149). The Dingo bar was situated at 10 Rue Delambre. It is interesting to note that it is possible, indeed probable, that the Dingo bar received its name only in 1925 when it became the property of, or merely was run by, Mr. Wilson. The

Dingo bar does not appear in the *Annuaires du Téléphone* until 1925; but there was a café-restaurant at the same address before 1925, under the names of Saint Martin in 1922, Bidault in 1923, and Harot in 1925.[50] Although it is impossible to rely completely on these directories, they tend to be accurate enough, and one might legitimately surmise that the Dingo was not called the Dingo until 1925—roughly the time when Hemingway and Fitzgerald met, according to Carlos Baker.[51]

The remainder of this chapter provides a few more pieces of information about Paris and France—although it is information of a very general order—and it is the last chapter to do so. Neither "Hawks Do Not Share" nor "A Matter of Measurements" brings anything new to the book as far as the background is concerned. The last chapter, "There Is Never Any End to Paris," on the other hand, introduces Schruns, in Austria. The last details about Paris found in "Scott Fitzgerald" have to do with French trains, Lyon, and the car trip back to Paris.

It is indeed true that there were fast trains from the Gare de Lyon down to Lyon. These trains were called *rapides,* meaning fast trains, as opposed to *express,* which meant slow trains (155). It is also true that they stopped only once or twice before reaching Lyon—at Dijon, as Hemingway indicates, and also usually at Mâcon—and that one could get excellent lunches and dinners in the dining cars, with first-class service. Lyon, which Hemingway describes as "a big, heavy, solid-money town" (159), is a typical French bourgeois city; but the qualifier "heavy" is a trifle exaggerated. Hemingway's description of the trip from Lyon to Paris is basically accurate in the few details it gives about France—for example, that Mâcon, Chalon-sur-Saône, and the Côte d'Or are definitely on the main road between Lyon and Paris. One might also note that if Hemingway and Fitzgerald covered only the distance between Lyon and Chalon on the first day, they drove barely eighty miles.

Paradoxically, "There Is Never Any End to Paris" deals exclusively with Austria as far as the background is concerned. The description of the train ride to Schruns is absolutely accurate:

> We went to Schruns in the Vorarlberg in Austria. After going through Switzerland you came to the Austrian frontier at Feldkirch. The train went through Lichtenstein and stopped at Bludenz where there was a small branch line that ran along a pebbly trout river through a valley of farms and forest to Schruns, which was a sunny market town with saw-mills, stores, inns and a good year-round hotel called the Taube where we lived. (198)

The train ride is still the same today. However, the implication that there was only one good year-round hotel is inaccurate, as there were four hotels in the 1920s in Schruns, with the old Lowen Hotel, in particular, almost across the street from the Taube.[52] There is now a modern and luxurious Lowen Hotel close to where the old one used to stand. The number of hotels has multiplied since the 1920s, and now there is hardly a house in Schruns that does not partly function as a hotel, but the Taube remains one of the cheaper hotels in the village. What Hemingway writes about the Alpine Club Huts also appears to be accurate. The Lindauer-Hutte is in the Lunersee, the Wiesbadner-Hutte (not the Wiesbadener Hutte as published) is in the Silvretta at 2443 meters of altitude, and the Madlener-Haus at 1986 meters. Basically, all the factual details Hemingway gives about Schruns and Tschagguns, about the Austrians greeting each other with *Gruss Gott* (God's greetings), and about the ski slopes are accurate. One might also say that he captures the atmosphere of the village rather well—although, of course, much has changed since the 1920s. Hemingway seems to have had a comfortable life at the Taube, where he had two rooms, one for the family to sleep in and one for himself to work in. Hadley also had a piano, and Bumby's nursery was next door. He would be taken care of at the nursery during the day, and at night they had a young girl, Mathilda Braun, to look after him. Thus, Hadley and Ernest could enjoy almost complete freedom, while still being able to keep a close eye on Bumby. The two rooms and the full pension for the three of them cost about two dollars a day.

Much of what Hemingway writes about Paris, Lyon, and Schruns is thus essentially accurate, if pervaded by errors of detail, such as the names of streets, the physical location of some buildings or their functions. It seems clear that what Hemingway actually recalled from his early life in Paris, such as the milk goats or the atmosphere of the Latin Quarter, is accurately described. It is also clear that he had little interest in the historical aspects of Paris, for the historical details he provides are rather limited and often inaccurate. That he forgot in the late 1950s things that had struck him in the early 1920s is not entirely surprising. For instance, the charcoal braziers that were lit outside the main cafés in order to keep outdoor customers warm and Hadley's addiction to French pastries, which he commented upon repeatedly in his early letters from Paris, do not appear in *A Moveable Feast*.[53] What is more puzzling, however, is the inaccuracy of his spelling of street names coupled with the general accuracy of his description of these same streets, which suggests that he had a remarkably accurate visual memory and a certain disregard for spelling accuracy, or that he checked the location of these streets on his maps of Paris without paying close attention to spelling. In fact, one of his errors (the intersection of the Rue Descartes and the Place de la Contrescarpe) could easily have been made even after having checked his maps. While Hemingway's spelling of English was itself notoriously idiosyncratic, his lack of knowledge of French made things even worse for his spelling of French words. It does not seem, however, that Hemingway totally disregarded the need for accuracy, for, among his notes for the book, one may find the following notations:

F-Page 5 =
Put in name of Painter (impresioniste) who painted Bas Meudon
Page 14—Lyons or LYON—Believe it should be Lyons as you say
Rome instead of Roma and Milan instead of Milano.
L-Page 4—Check whether Tchagguns on North or South side of the
Valley—Believe South—
 Write story of Harold and Evan. (File 189b)

In fact, in 1961 he complained of his lack of documentation: "It's hard to work without your library and sourcebooks"; and he asked Brague to send him twenty-six books, including *Paris in the Twenties* and *Paris fin de siècle,* where he presumably intended to check some of his information.[54] Although the inaccuracy of Hemingway's spelling of foreign words, names, and expressions is not unique to *A Moveable Feast,* and therefore cannot be blamed entirely on his poor health or on the unavailability of source material, it can certainly be blamed, particularly in this book, on his editors, who owed it to him to check carefully. Hemingway had always asked Maxwell Perkins to check the spelling of foreign words for him and protect him from mistakes, so that he would not appear ignorant.[55] One might, of course, say that Hemingway owed it to himself and his readers to do his own checking, at least in his previous books, since he had always wanted to project, and indeed projected successfully, the image of the artist who would rather starve than compromise the integrity of his work—the very image that aroused the admiration of Gus Pfeiffer and of so many Hemingway readers and critics[56]—never using words ornamentally, nor without first considering whether they were replaceable or absolutely necessary.[57] But the case of *A Moveable Feast* is peculiar, not only because of Hemingway's physical and mental condition, but also because of the intense emotions that dealing with the past clearly aroused in him.

CHAPTER FOUR

Fact and Fiction

*M*OST, IF NOT ALL, of Hemingway's fiction contains numerous autobiographical elements, and his protagonists are often conscious projections of himself. Indeed, Philip Young was right when he remarked that it would be hard to think of even an autobiographical writer "who gave a more exact account of his own experience in the guise of prose fiction."[1] At the same time, Hemingway's openly autobiographical writing, *Green Hills of Africa* and *A Moveable Feast*, are barely more autobiographical than his fiction, and in many ways just as fictional, illustrating how fine and shaky the dividing line between fiction and autobiography may be. But *A Moveable Feast* is particularly complex because Hemingway was clearly conscious that it would be his literary testament. Thus, in writing it, he dealt with issues that had been important to him and settled old scores. Among the reasons that motivated this portrayal of self and others were clearly the need to justify himself, for he felt that he had been unfairly portrayed by some of his contemporaries, the desire to present his own version of personal relationships as well as the desire to get back at people against whom he held a grudge, the need to relive his youth and his first marriage in an idealized fashion and thus recapture the past at a time when his life was going to pieces, the need to impose a form of artistic order on his life and at the same time trace his own literary development, and, finally, the wish to leave the world a flattering self-portrait. Moreover, he was still involved emotionally with his subject matter and had clearly not yet come to terms with his role in the breakup of his first marriage, as repeatedly evidenced by the manuscripts. Thus, *A Moveable Feast* could hardly be an objective portrayal of its author and his contemporaries, and one might tend to agree with Katherine Porter's opinion that Hemingway's memoirs are "as false and incomplete and superficial as any memoirs of an ex-wife."[2]

The question of accuracy is therefore challenging, particularly since Hemingway both insisted that his memoirs would be based on documentary evidence and on an excellent memory in his letters to the likes of Malcolm Cowley, Ezra Pound, and Maxwell Perkins,[3] and, paradoxically, emphasized in the many drafts of the Preface that the book is, and should be read as fiction. On the one hand, it is clear that Hemingway was well aware that it is impossible to recapture the past accurately almost forty years after the fact ("All remembrance of things past is fiction," "No one can write true facts in reminiscences"), that he consciously made a selection of his material in order to create an artistic whole, just as he had, for instance, in *The Sun Also Rises* ("I have left much out and changed and eliminated"), and that he often distorted reality in order to make it fit into that artistic pattern ("It would be fine if it could all be true but lacking that I have attempted . . . only to make it interesting").[4] On the other hand, he went to some lengths in order to convince his readers that he was reporting accurately, evidence in hand, on what he had seen and felt some thirty years earlier.

There is little doubt that Hemingway loaded the dice against some of his contemporaries and that he somewhat exaggerated, not to say invented, his condition as a young, starving writer in Paris, one who would rather not eat than compromise his artistic integrity—a rather stereotyped and romantic image of the apprentice artist in a Paris garret. In fact, his emphasis on the inadequacies, perversions, and neuroses of others, intended to show him by contrast as youthful and innocent, tends to suggest malice rather than candor. At the same time, the choice of the episodes concerning Gertrude Stein, F. Scott Fitzgerald, Ford Madox Ford, Cheever Dunning, and others suggests an appeal to sensationalism. Whether these anecdotes were based on fact or not, their very subject matter indicates that Hemingway intended to expose the most intimate secrets of those he resented. Various critics have pointed out that *A Moveable Feast* contains not only distortions but also serious factual errors—which it does. But, given the background to the book and Hemingway's obvious resentments and self-idealization which clearly colored the choice of the anecdotes and the method of their narration, one is almost surprised to discover that many of the episodes are probably based on reality, in general terms if not in specific instances. In fact, the book appears as a fascinating composite of relative factual accuracy and clear dishonesty of intent, while it evidences that Hemingway was decidedly consistent in his view of others and in his portrayal of them. As George

Wickes once wrote, "*A Moveable Feast* . . . is subtly compounded of nine parts fact to one part fiction."[5] The proportion may be off—I would perhaps make it half fact, half fiction—but the concept is indeed valid.

The anecdotes related in the book are almost all of an intensely personal nature and therefore difficult to verify objectively, since most of them took place without any other witness than Hemingway himself. As he often indicated in his correspondence, he intended to write the things that no one else knew.[6] It is thus difficult to find corroboration for them outside Hemingway's own letters to others. The letters themselves are unfortunately not very reliable for two main reasons: Hemingway does not narrate in them all of the anecdotes narrated in *A Moveable Feast*, and "Not all of the stories relayed in his letters can be trusted as true."[7] Hemingway's imagination was vivid from his early youth, and he seldom felt bound by the requirements of truthfulness in his fiction or in his correspondence. Creative reporting was his trademark, and one cannot rely completely on his own words to authenticate the episodes of *A Moveable Feast*. But there is little else, and one must recognize that, if he invented, he invented along lines of greatest probability. Although one cannot discuss every single anecdote appearing in the book, one may distinguish among them four types: the incidents that were described by Hemingway in the 1920s almost exactly as they are described in the book; the events that he narrated later, especially in his correspondence of the 1950s; the events for which there seems to be no early narration; and the ones in which Hemingway is obviously or probably wrong.

I

Perhaps the most startling of the anecdotes narrated early in Hemingway's correspondence is the Cheever Dunning episode which Hemingway described to Ezra Pound in a letter dated 15 October 1924:

> Your old concierge showed up at seven O'clock Sunday morning with the news that Dunning was back since the night before. He had climbed up on the roof and insisted on sleeping there but the husband of the concierge pursuaded him it was a little late to stay on the roof so he came down.
>
> He declared you had stolen all his money and had pretended to gain his friendship in order to do this.
>
> The concierge wanted me to come and see if I could quiet him.
>
> I arrived with the little jar you left thinking that was what he

needed. Dunning shouted at me from the stairs—"So your in on this business too" and threatened me with a broom handle.

I said, "Here's something Pound left for you Dunning."

Dunning took the jar and said, "Oh yes, something Pound left for me."

He looked at the jar and then threw it at my head saying, "You son of a bitch I'll kill you."

I picked up the jar thinking of its thousand Franc value and Dunning threw a milk bottle.

I retreated down the stairs and have not seen Dunning since. He threw the broom after me.

Most of the elements of "An Agent of Evil" are present in this letter, and the closeness between the two narratives is amazing. Of course, the book version is more detailed and colorful, and Hemingway has to tell the reader who does not know Dunning things that Pound well knew, such as the facts that Dunning smoked opium, did not eat, and often drank milk—the staple diet of the opium addict. Sisley Huddleston, among others, verifies this:

> At no time could I ascertain that he ate—what we call eating. He would drink a glass of milk and perhaps nibble at a *croissant*. I would ask him to have dinner with me, and he would reply: "I eat very little just now, but I will willingly accept a glass of milk." A glass of milk it, accordingly, was; and I am sure that on many days it constituted his dinner.[8]

Indeed, with such a diet, Dunning must have looked like a skeleton! The fact that the lovers of poetry rallied to Dunning's aid also appears repeatedly in Hemingway's letters to Pound, in particular in the 15 and 22 October letters in which he writes that McAlmon has again placed Dunning in a *Maison de santé*, "rallied a collection of his friends recently returned to town," and made some arrangements with a banker to look after his money. Moreover, the dislike for Dunning, which seeps through "An Agent of Evil," was voiced by Hemingway in no uncertain terms in various letters,[9] and perhaps nowhere more colorfully than in his November 1925 (exact date illegible) letter to Pound in which he writes that he would put his last nickel on the fact that "Dunning, Cheever, is Shit." Dunning may have written "eight lines that somebody confused with you or Keats," but on the whole "Dunning is really puke producingly bad." Hemingway also claims that his attitude toward Dunning was not conditioned by his having had milk bottles thrown at him, and that he felt that

Dunning was "faecal" before that incident. That is indeed a strongly negative reaction to the man Huddleston felt was "the queerest and most likeable."[10]

There seems to be little doubt that the Cheever Dunning episode did occur as Hemingway describes it. Hemingway refers to it in his letters to Pound too often for it to have been merely a figment of his imagination. Moreover, it does seem to correspond to general facts recorded by others, and Pound's solicitude for others' needs was well known. In fact, another poet-and-opium episode is recorded by Robert E. Knoll, this time involving Robert McAlmon.[11]

The Ford Madox Ford and the Lost Generation episodes were borrowed from the manuscript of *The Sun Also Rises*. The idiosyncrasies of Ford that Hemingway focuses on—his snobbery, his lying, his not listening to others—have been confirmed by many people. However, many think that he did not lie deliberately:

> Another distinctive trait was Ford's inability to separate fact from fiction. Nearly everything he remembered—and his memory seemed to be prodigious—came out distorted. . . . What stayed in his mind was the significance—the humor, the piquancy, the moral or drama of what had taken place. But the actual event was lost beyond recapture.[12]

Stella Bowen agrees with Loeb's interpretation, and feels that "words to Ford were simply the material of his art, and [that] he never used them in any other way. This created confusion in his everyday life, for words are not like dabs of paint. They are less innocent, being the coin in use in daily life."[13] Hemingway never seems to have understood this, and he bitterly resented Ford's creative imagination. The Belloc-Crowley episode may or may not have taken place; but, if it did, it may well have been a joke at Hemingway's expense, the point of which Hemingway probably did not understand:

> Ford had known Belloc since his teens, and there is not the remotest possibility that he actually mistook Crowley for Belloc. This little display of British snobbery with its characteristic carelessness about the literal fact was surely intended as a parody of what Ford knew to be Hemingway's idea of him. It is unlikely Ford was unaware of Hemingway's need to think badly of anyone to whom he was indebted, as he was indebted to Ford for his kindness during the Transatlantic Review days, and Ford may well have wanted to see if

that need would blind Hemingway to what he otherwise could hardly have missed.[14]

Indeed, it seems surprising that Hemingway did not know who Aleister Crowley was, when he "used to parade around the Quarter with his head shaved, save for a waxed forelock. . . . A pudgy man of fifty or thereabout, [who] was addicted to kilts and plus-fours."[15] Crowley was a man whose specialties included black magic and devil-worship, alchemy and hypnotism, who boasted of his sado-sexual relationships with women, and who frequently played chess with his friends in a bar of the quarter. Indeed, he was one of the most colorful figures of the quarter with both Kiki and Jimmy the Barman, to whose autobiographies Hemingway wrote introductions. Jimmy was in fact a great friend of Crowley's.[16]

One is left here with a puzzling assemblage of facts and cannot help wondering that Hemingway should have been taken in by Ford's joke. If Ford wanted to see how fast on his mental legs the know-all Hemingway was, he must have been rewarded beyond expectation—a small personal revenge, perhaps, for having been played false by Hemingway concerning *The Making of Americans.* One also wonders that Hemingway used the episode in *A Moveable Feast,* where he always strives to present himself in a positive light. Or was he attempting to turn the tables on Ford, trying to make a fool of him by narrating the very episode in which he was perhaps himself made a fool of? Or did Hemingway simply never realize that it may have been a joke, and that he had been the butt of it— all of this, of course, assuming that the incident did take place! In any case, it is rather amusing to note that his final comment concerning the incident in the manuscript of *The Sun Also Rises* is that he "never felt the same" about Ford afterwards.

Gertrude Stein does not remember the "Lost Generation" remark as having come about in the way Hemingway describes it, whether in the less disparaging version of the manuscript of *The Sun Also Rises* or in the more condemnatory one of *A Moveable Feast.* In *Everybody's Autobiography,* she describes it as having taken place as follows:

> It was this hotel keeper who said what it is said I said that the war generation was a lost generation. And he said it in this way. He said that every man becomes civilized between the ages of eighteen and twenty-five. If he does not go through a civilizing experience at that time in his life he will not be a civilized man. And the men who went to the war at eighteen missed the period of civilizing, and they could

never be civilized. They are a lost generation. Naturally if they are at war they do not have the influences of women of parents and of preparation.[17]

Here it is difficult to ascertain which of the two writers is correct, but at least Stein's version has the advantage of being firsthand. James Mellow, however, feels that Hemingway's last version could well have the ring of truth, for "Gertrude did have the notion that, in France, creative artists and professionals were commonly granted special privileges. . . . She might have easily complained, therefore, if a garage mechanic had kept her waiting. Nor did she approve of the young expatriates she saw crowding in cafés in the twenties."[18] But Stein was not always truthful either in her autobiography and may well have been, like Hemingway, taken in by jokes.[19]

Some of the characteristics of the trip down to Lyon with F. Scott Fitzgerald are verified in various ways. For instance in a letter to Fitzgerald dated about 24 December 1925, Hemingway writes that Scott would be glad to read in the *New York Herald* that two men died of cold in Chalon-sur-Saône, where Scott nearly did the same; it was a good thing they got out in time. Then Hemingway asks, "By the way, where the hell is your car?"[20] Hemingway also refers to that trip in a letter to Ezra Pound dated 11 December 1925, in which he writes that he went down to Lyon with Scott to drive his car up: "Didn't miss one vintage from Montrachet to Chambertin. Elaborate trip." And Fitzgerald himself wrote to Stein in June 1925: "Hemingway and I went to Lyon shortly after to get my car and had a slick drive through Burgundy. He is a peach of a fellow and absolutely first rate."[21] Clearly, Hemingway's and Fitzgerald's views of the trip differed. Whether the conversations that Hemingway relates actually took place, and whether Fitzgerald behaved in such a hypochondriac fashion as Hemingway recounts, is anyone's guess, but what Hemingway reports seems consistent with conversations Fitzgerald had with others. For instance, the story of Zelda's infatuation with a French air-force pilot was well known and repeatedly told by Scott in a dramatic fashion. One conversation, however, did take place, in general terms at least, for Hemingway refers to it specifically in at least two letters. On 12 April 1931, he writes that, if Scott is still in Switzerland, he will come down there to see him in the fall. They might take one of those "topless motor trips" and Scott could give him a "cultured synopsis" of what "Arland" and the other boys have been doing, since he has not kept up with their activities.[22] Earlier, on 7 December 1926, Hemingway had related to Max Perkins how Fitzgerald had instructed him on Michael Arlen, writing that his contact with Arlen had been through Scott's talking about him and his work when they drove from Lyon to Paris. He remembered telling Scott who the people were who had taken Arlen up, and getting quite irritated about Arlen. Don Stewart had also talked about it, but Hemingway had taken it for granted that *The Green Hat* must be a cheap book when he heard that the heroine killed herself.[23]

As for the other conversations Hemingway reports having had with Scott during that trip, it is most likely that he made a hodgepodge of things Scott had reportedly told others, things Scott might have told him at various times and possibly during that very trip, and probably things he invented to make a point. As a matter of fact, it would be impossible for anyone to recall so specifically conversations one had more than thirty years previously, unless the topic were particularly memorable. It would be even more surprising if one recalled conversations one did not have, as Hemingway claims he did:

> I thought of Evan Shipman and I thought of the waiter at the Closerie des Lilas who had been forced to cut his mustache when they made the American bar at the Closerie, . . . I thought of telling Scott about this whole problem of the Lilas, . . . but I knew he did not care about waiters nor their problems nor their great kindnesses and affections. At that time Scott hated the French. . . . (168)

Hemingway had already dramatized in the manuscript of *The Sun Also Rises* the story of Jean who was forced to cut his mustache, and who, as a reprisal against the Closerie, and perhaps also out of friendship for Evan Shipman, poured glassfuls of whisky for Hemingway and Shipman instead of the normal measure:

> At that time a fellow named Dos Passos was in town and we were accustomed to go and drink in the cool of the evenings to a place called the Closerie des Lilas . . . where we knew a waiter who would give us two whiskey's for the price of one whiskey owing to a dislike he had for his boss. This waiter raises potatoes on a garden outside Paris beyond Montrouge. . . .[24]

This anecdote seems to have been dear to Hemingway's heart, for, when he was not sure whether to include the chapter on Shipman, he intended to have two paragraphs in the first Scott Fitzgerald chapter on Jean and the Closerie des Lilas. One way or the other, this anecdote was to appear in the book after having been deleted from *The Sun Also Rises*. Such determination on Hemingway's part suggests that the story may be true. However, since he decided to include the Shipman chapter, there was no need to mention the anecdote of the waiter again in the Fitzgerald chapter, and Hemingway seems to have done it for no other reason than not to miss an opportunity to attack Fitzgerald for not liking waiters and the French. Why Hemingway should have resented Scott's not liking the French is not clear, as he himself at times did not like them any more than Scott did, especially when they wanted to raise his rent. Moreover, he seldom resisted the impulse to attack French writers who were his contemporaries; but this may have had as much to do with the fact that they were both writers and his contemporaries as with the fact that they were French.[25]

Several of the things mentioned in "There Was Never Any End to Paris" are described in Hemingway's early correspondence, such as the fact that Bumby had a beautiful nurse, that Ernest played poker, that a German naval officer gave a lecture on the war, that a party of Germans were killed in an avalanche, and, of course, that "the rich" and the "pilot fish" joined him and Hadley, and that he read to them "the part of the novel that [he] had rewritten" (209).

The beauty of Mathilda Braun, Bumby's nurse, seems to have struck Hemingway, for he continually refers to her in his letters in terms of beauty, in particular when writing to Sylvia Beach on 15 January 1925, and to Gertrude Stein and Alice B. Toklas on 20 January 1925.[26] Hemingway also mentioned his poker games, especially in his letter to his mother, dated 14 December 1925, in which he writes that he plays in the weekly poker game, and in his letter to Fitzgerald of 24 December 1925, in which he complains that he played poker the night before and drank too much beer.[27] The lecture on the war did not take place in Schruns as suggested in *A Moveable Feast* but in Bludenz, a town nearby, and it did not have to do with the Battle of Jutland but with the Battle of Skaggerack. Hemingway gives details to Archibald MacLeish on 20 December 1925:

> Thursday we were in town, in Bludenz, and heard Kapitan-Lieutenant Mumm lecture on the Battle of Skaggerack in which he and a few other Germans made bums out of Jellicoe and Beatty and sunk the Warrior, the Indefatigable, Queen Mary, the Warspite etc. etc. . . . Moving pictures largely faked but splendid moving diagrams. Kapitan Lieutenant Mumm was something to see. One of those completely shaved heads. . . . Fish eyes. No lips. The Aus-

trian kids got very restless. . . . Kapt. Lieut. had to bawl them out
several times. He was very worked up about the battle but he
couldn't get any applause. . . .

He also refers to it in the 24 December letter to Fitzgerald, in which he
points out that Hadley hated Mumm.[28]

Hemingway relates the episode of the Germans killed in an avalanche
to Gertrude Stein on 13 February 1925:

> There were four men killed in avalanches. One German, a Saxon,
> weak and nervous, rotten skier, was buried for 35 minutes and as
> soon as he was buried looked at his wrist watch under the snow and
> resolved to shout every 3 minutes which he did till 15 minutes was
> up by the watch! Real efficiency. They heard him on the 5th shout
> after which he became unconscious until dug out. It's been such a
> warm winter that the snow avalanches in explosions—caused by the
> snow pressure on air pockets with warmth coming up. We've seen
> some funny ones. They had a big funeral for the dead ones and the
> priest would not let the bell be rung nor the one they buried in the
> local cemetery go into consecrated grounds. So the Saxon who was
> dug out made a dreadful oration at the grave.

This is not quite the way Hemingway describes it in *A Moveable Feast*
(203–4). The four men become nine in the book, and the self-controlled
behavior of one of the Germans is not recounted—perhaps because Hemingway seems intent on giving a negative picture of them. It is also interesting to note that the details of the death of the man who was refused
burial in consecrated grounds are not given in this letter, while they are
given in a letter to Pound dated 16 March 1925 in which Hemingway's
description of the accident is somewhat closer to that in the book. The
letter to Stein emphasizes the story of the survivors, thus illustrating how
Hemingway told Gertrude about the happier side of things rather than
about the gloomier one, as she did not like to hear "really bad nor tragic
things."[29] Hemingway's memory is thus partly at fault here, as it was in
the narrative of Mumm's lecture.

That Pauline, the Murphys, and John Dos Passos joined Hadley and
Hemingway in Schruns is verified in various ways, and in particular by
their signatures in the guest book of the Hotel Taube; Sara and Gerald
signed it on 18 March, and Dos Passos on 15 March 1926. Pauline came
down to spend Christmas with the Hemingways, arrived on 25 December, and stayed for New Year's.[30] However, the suggestion that Heming-

way read to them the manuscript of *The Sun Also Rises* is not borne out by evidence. One should note that Hemingway is very cautious and does not give the book's title, merely referring to it as "the novel that I had rewritten" (209); but earlier in the same chapter, he had been more precise: "I did the most difficult job of rewriting I have ever done there in the winter of 1925 and 1926, when I had to take the first draft of *The Sun Also Rises* . . . , and make it into a novel" (202). The implication is therefore clear. But it seems that it was not the manuscript of *The Sun Also Rises* that Hemingway read to the Murphys and Dos Passos but that of *The Torrents of Spring*. Moreover, he did not read it to them in Schruns but in Paris. Hemingway complained to Fitzgerald on 15 December 1925 that he had been suffering from a sore throat for a week after reading the whole of *The Torrents of Spring* to the Murphys "as an act of bravado after not being able to talk all day." Since the Hemingways arrived in Schruns on 12 December, the reading probably took place in Paris around the 7th, which is confirmed by Calvin Tompkins. Hemingway also read *The Torrents* to Dos Passos over lunch, and Dos Passos tried to argue him out of publishing it, but to no avail. "The rich" did not find the book truly great, either; Dos Passos, for one, did not like it and felt that it was not "quite good enough to stand on its own feet as a parody." Sara Murphy slept through the reading of most of it. In fact, Pauline seems to have been the only one who liked it. It is also important to note that Hadley did not recall Hemingway's reading of *The Sun Also Rises* to their friends in Schruns when she was interviewed by Carlos Baker.[31]

Other vacation trips described or mentioned by Hemingway in the book did take place, although not necessarily in the order in which they appear there. The trip to "below Les Avants" referred to in "A Good Café" (7) took place during the winter of 1922. The Hemingways had first stayed at the Gangwischs' pension from mid-May to mid-June 1922, and returned there from December 1922 to February 1923. Hemingway described aspects of his stays there in letters to his father and to Stein and Toklas, in particular, while Hadley wrote to her mother-in-law, Grace Hall Hemingway, from Lausanne on 11 December 1922, describing the trip they had just taken to Chamby and Les Avants, with "lovely jam and toast and nut cake at [their] own chalet" and "the most glorious rosy sunset in the midst of all those snow covered mountains wooping down toward the lake."[32] The trips to the Near East and Germany referred to in "Une Génération Perdue" are the trips to the Black Forest (August to September 1922)—a holiday trip rather than a business one, but which he put to good use by sending an article to the *Toronto Star* describing how a mob had murdered a German policeman—and the trip to Adrianople to cover the Greco-Turkish war (25 September to 21 October 1922). The political conference he also refers to is the Lausanne Peace Conference which he covered between 22 November and 16 December 1922.[33] Finally, Hemingway refers in "A False Spring" (53–55) to crossing the St. Bernard with Chink and Hadley, to Hadley's feet swelling at Aosta after the climb in the snow, to going to Biffi's in Milan, and to the Inn at Aigle. All this goes back to the spring 1922 stay in Chamby. The hike over the St. Bernard Hemingway described several times in letters, the two 1922 letters to his father and to Stein and Toklas, and also in letters of 1923 to William D. Horne and to James Gamble, among others. Most of the details seem accurate. Hemingway does not seem, in general, to have a very good opinion of the Biffi which, according to him, was the haunt of "Milanese profiteers" who preferred to eat there where they got miserable food rather than at Canpari's—by far the best restaurant in Europe, cheap and with excellent service. Hemingway mainly describes fishing the Rhône canal in his letter to his father of 24 May 1922.[34]

Several other episodes, such as the loss of his manuscripts, his meeting Edward O'Brien, his boxing with Pound, his seeing a lot of Gertrude Stein, also appear in the early correspondence, and cannot be doubted as far as concrete dates and facts are concerned. His borrowing books at Shakespeare and Company, his helping Stein publish *The Making of Americans*, his friendship with Sylvia Beach, his going to the races, Ford Madox Ford's parties at the Bal Musette, and Gertrude Stein's visiting the Hemingways in their flat are well-established facts which have been discussed repeatedly and which cannot really be doubted.[35] Other details, such as James Joyce's eating at Michaud's, O'Brien's taking "My Old Man" for the *Best Short Stories of 1923* and dedicating the book to Hemingway, Fitzgerald's resolutions to work and not drink, as well as his turning up drunk at the flat over the sawmill, are well-known facts which Hemingway related early.[36]

Clearly, then, many events recounted by Hemingway in the 1920s, whether in letters or in the manuscripts of *The Sun Also Rises*, are narrated in *A Moveable Feast*. Some of these events are recalled with accuracy, in particular the Dunning episode; others have been distorted to various degrees either willfully or by the insidious work of time. Most of them did doubtlessly take place, with the exception, perhaps, of the Ford anecdote. However, if Hemingway invented or exaggerated in his portrayals of Ford and Fitzgerald, which he probably did, his creative memory focused on recognizable idiosyncrasies of both men, thus making it, in the absence of other evidence, difficult to separate fact from fiction.

II

Other events are less easy to verify in that there is no early narration of them among Hemingway's papers and letters. A number of them, however, were related by Hemingway in his letters of the late 1940s and the 1950s, a long time after they allegedly took place. It is difficult to determine what credence one should give these stories Hemingway wrote to various friends—usually several of them at the same time, as if, having recalled or invented the story, he had to publicize it widely—for, by the 1950s, he had developed strong antagonistic feelings for the two people most involved in those anecdotes: Stein and Fitzgerald. In any case, whether they actually took place or not, Hemingway narrated them in *A Moveable Feast* very much as he had in his personal correspondence. Two of these anecdotes concern Stein's lesbianism and one her advising him against journalism.

Hemingway writes to Edmund Wilson on 8 November 1952 that, in the matter of Stein's homosexuality, he wishes that Wilson had maintained his position rather than qualified it. He offers Wilson all the material he might possibly need to back up his earlier position. He relates that Stein had talked to him once for three hours, telling him that she was a lesbian and explaining why the act was not disgusting or degrading. At that time she was against male homosexuality, but she later changed her mind. Hemingway concludes that three hours was a long time with Gertrude crowding him, and that he was eventually so sold on her theory that he went out and "fucked a lesbian" that night "with magnificent results"—they slept well afterwards.[37] Hemingway had already told the story in fewer details to W. G. Rogers on 29 July 1948, when he wrote that she used to talk to him about homosexuality, and how it was fine in and for women and no good in men, and that he always wanted to "fuck her," and that she knew it.[38] Hemingway also described the story of his breakup with Stein to various people, in particular Donald Gallup and Edmund Wilson. The two accounts are very much alike, the latter being more detailed. According to it, Stein had told Hemingway to come in at any time, and that he had the "run of the house." On that particular day, he rang the bell, and the servant let him in and took him into the big room, saying that Mademoiselle was busy but would want him to wait. She and Alice were packing to go away on a trip. The servant left, and while Hemingway was looking at the pictures, he heard Stein's voice, loud and anguished, plead: "Pussy! Pussy please don't. Oh please don't say you will do that. I'll do anything if you won't. Please Pussy. Please—" According to Hemingway, he left immediately and had shut the door before the next words reached him. He did not want to hear any more than he already had. The Gallup account talks about the *bonne* giving him a drink of kirsch and indicates that he heard Toklas saying things to Gertrude and Gertrude's pleading. He went out not listening, and trying to forget what he had heard.[39]

It is interesting to note that these accounts are all written to literary critics working on Stein. Could he already have been preparing the grounds for his own dramatization of his break with Stein a few years later? Surprisingly, he does not mention either Stein's homosexuality or the circumstances of his breakup with her in his letter to Charles A. Fenton of 23 September 1951, in which he tells Fenton that Stein read his early stories—the ones he had written before he went to Paris—which would tend to substantiate what he narrates of her visit to his flat soon after he and Hadley had met her (15–16). Of course, her reading of his stories could have taken place anywhere. He also tells Fenton that she "advised [him] to get out of journalism and write as . . . the one would use up the juice [he] needed for the other." He felt that she was right and that it was the best advice she ever gave him.[40] Hemingway also remembers that she told him that he "would never be able to write for the Saturday Evening Post or the Atlantic (those were her ambitions)," but that he might be a "good writer of some new kind"—all of which appears in "Miss Stein Instructs." Instead of telling Fenton, though, how he dropped Stein, he indicates, or rather suggests, that she was the one who dropped him: "Later she became angry at me because Alice was very jealous of our being friends and she was dominated by Alice." In fact, he indicated in several letters of the 1930s that it was indeed Stein who dropped him as a friend. He wrote to Pound that he stuck to "that old bitch until she threw [him] out of the house when she lost her judgement with the menopause," and to Dos Passos that he understands that Stein, "who dropped [him] when she went in exclusively for feathered friends," proves in her autobiography that he, Hemingway, is a "fairy" or a "fag," and continues: "Miss Stein should never have had the menopause. It haywired her judgement and made her into a missionary."[41]

Hemingway's letters of the 1930s reiterate that Stein was a fine woman until she reached menopause and opted for "fags and fags alone," and his most colorful description of Gertrude's change of life may be found in his letter to Janet Flanner of 8 April 1933:

> I never cared a damn about what she did in or out of bed and I liked her very damned much and she liked me. But when the menopause hit her she got awfully damned patriotic about sex. The first stage was that nobody was any good that wasn't that way. The second was that anybody that was that way was good. The third was that anybody that was any good must be that way. Patriotism is a hell of a vice. Mabel Dodge is a hell of a rival.[42]

It is of course rather ironic to think that it may have been Stein who dropped Hemingway because of her homosexuality, and not the opposite as dramatized in *A Moveable Feast*. It is also probably likely, for Stein claims that it is she who has broken up with her young friends: "Otherwise we have been having a nice peaceable time having really quarrelled for keeps with all our young friends and there are lots of stories that will amuse you."[43] She had effectively summarized her opinion of some of these young friends on 7 March 1927: "McAlmon is pretty bad. Fitzgerald and Cummings are the best of the crowd, the rest are fairly weak in the head." In fact, Stein's, Beach's, and Toklas's accounts of the breakup are definitely at odds with Hemingway's.[44]

It would indeed make much more sense if it had been Gertrude who broke up the friendship because of Alice's demands. This would account not only for Hemingway's resentment but also partly for his dramatization of his overhearing the quarrel during which Alice laid down the law. Portraying himself as the one who left would allow him to salvage his pride and still retain an element of truth, however twisted. The episode could, of course, have actually taken place: as James Mellow writes, "It is entirely possible that he had overheard a particularly bitter quarrel between Gertrude and Alice, one that established the Lesbian nature of the relationship beyond doubt for him, one in which the steely character of Alice's will was revealed, privately, as it had never been revealed in public."[45] However, even if the episode did take place, the shocked dismay that Hemingway supposedly experienced and the implication that it was at this point that he became aware of their homosexual relationship are most unconvincing. Lesbians like Nathalie Barney and Gertrude Stein lived openly in Paris, and only through incredible naïveté could Hemingway have avoided knowing how things were. Thus, his dramatization of the event in the book is at the very least hypocritical and suggests that he was trying both to put the blame for the breakup of their friendship on Stein and at the same time to portray himself as an innocent, just as he clearly attempts to put the blame for the breakup of his marriage on Pauline, the Murphys, and Dos Passos. The responsibility was probably Stein's, but not quite as Hemingway describes it.

Hemingway relates the anecdote concerning Fitzgerald's fears of sexual inadequacy to Mizener, telling him that Zelda had ruined Scott in two ways. She told him first that he had never given her sexual satisfaction, and second that it was because his sexual organ was too small. Scott confided this to Hemingway while they were having lunch at Michaud's, where Scott had wanted to eat because James Joyce used to patronize the place. Hemingway took Scott to the lavatory and told him that his organs were perfectly normal, but Scott was unwilling to believe him, saying that his organ did look small. Hemingway explained that it was because he was looking at it from above, and thus saw it foreshortened. But nothing would convince Scott.[46] In that same letter, Hemingway also mentions Zelda's saying "Don't you think Al Jolson is greater than Jesus?" and his replying "No," which was the only answer he could think of. It is particularly interesting to note that Zelda made that same remark to Gerald Murphy.[47] Whether Zelda repeated herself, or whether Hemingway attributed to himself (by implication, since he is the one who replied) something that happened to Murphy, or, finally, whether the comment was made sufficiently loudly at the table for everyone to hear is difficult to determine. Obviously, Zelda did make that comment, and since Murphy informed Nancy Milford of it on 26 April 1963, that is a year before *A Moveable Feast* was published, it seems unlikely that he borrowed it from Hemingway, if there was borrowing on either part.

Hemingway related the Michaud restaurant anecdote again to Harvey Breit, giving a great deal of information about Fitzgerald that one also finds dramatized in *A Moveable Feast*, such as Scott's passing out cold after a few drinks, his not having slept with any other woman than Zelda, his face changing into a death mask after four drinks, and his making Scotty "pe-pee" on the floor at the foot of the stairs, just outside the landlord's door. The urine had run under the door, and the landlord had come out of his apartment, and, thinking that the child had been caught short, told Scott that there was a toilet under the stairs. Scott replied rudely: "I know there is you son of a bitch. . . . And I'll take you and shove your head in it."[48] Like Mizener, Breit was working on Fitzgerald's life, in this case preparing a play. Clearly, these colorful anecdotes about Stein and Fitzgerald were related purposefully to people who would spread them through their works. In these letters and in his book, Hemingway never focuses on positive anecdotes, on Scott's "complicated tragedies, his generosities and his devotions," thus making the anecdotes he relates partly suspect, in particular since they cannot be verified objectively. Kenneth Lynn has, however, shown recently that Fitzgerald *had* slept with other women, and detailed some of his affairs. Lynn believes that the scenes at Michaud and at the Louvre are Hemingway fantasies.[49] Of course, this does not mean that Scott did not *tell* Hemingway that he had slept with no other woman than Zelda. In any case, this is an idea Hemingway seems to have clung to, for he keeps referring to it, in particular to Maxwell Perkins, to whom he writes that he imagines a love affair would help Scott if he had anything "left to love with" and the woman were not so "awful" that he had to "kid himself too much."[50] The "anything left to love with" can be understood both as an emotional and a physical comment. It is revealing, too, that Hemingway cannot imagine that Scott could have an affair with a beautiful woman, despite Zelda's good looks. In the earlier Fitzgerald narrative, Hemingway makes two comments which tie in well with this. First, he comments on Fitzgerald's looks withering by the day, like a cut flower's (". . . at thirty-five, if he had been in a vase in your house you would have had him thrown out long ago" [File 486]), and he links this decay to the withering of virginity: "Now virginity withers like an apple, although in the sun of religious devotion, it may dry as sound and as healthy as a dried apple, but partial experience withers like carnations." The implication is fascinating: Scott loses his good looks because he sleeps only with his wife! In that same narrative, Hemingway comments on Zelda's looks, saying that, by 1925, one could see that Zelda had been beautiful; but her face was too drawn, she was badly groomed and badly dressed. The only things that were beautiful about her were "the tawny smoothness of her skin, the lovely color of her hair, . . . and her legs which were wonderful; light and long as nigger legs." Again, the comments are two-edged.

It was also essentially in the 1950s that Hemingway began spreading the rumor that Zelda made Scott drink so that he could not work because she was jealous of his work, in particular in letters to Mizener and Breit, thus more than adequately avenging himself for Zelda's having called him a "phony."[51] He also told Breit on 17 January 1951 about Ford's having told him that "a writer should write every letter with a view to it being published for posterity." He had already written Mizener the same thing, with the added comment that it had made such a bad impression on him that he had burned every letter in the flat, including Ford's[52]—an obvious example of misinformation, given the volume of letters in the Hemingway collection.

Hemingway also describes his meeting with Ernest Walsh in Ezra Pound's studio to Charles Scribner on 20 November 1952, saying that Walsh had just arrived on the *Aquitania* and that he had two blondes with mink coats with him. They had all been staying at Claridge's and one of the blondes told Hemingway that Walsh was the highest paid poet in the world and that he had received $22,450 for poems published in Harriet Monroe's magazine, *Poetry*, which, according to Hemingway, was at the time paying only five to twelve dollars a page for verse.[53] The story of Walsh's staying at Claridge's, of the two blondes, and of his being bailed out of Claridge's by Pound (Hemingway writes that Walsh was thrown out in his letter to Scribner) is probably true, whether or not Hemingway met him with the two blondes as he describes, for Sylvia Beach tells the story of her first contact with Walsh as follows:

> One day a note was brought to me from Claridge's, from a young man named Ernest Walsh. . . . Walsh apologized for not coming himself. He was too ill to leave his bed. He told me his situation. His funds had given out and unless he could get help, he would have to move away from Claridge's.

Sylvia Beach sent a friend who reported that Walsh had arrived in the company of two delightful young persons whom he had met on the boat, and that his illness was due to a cold he had caught driving with them in the Bois de Boulogne.

> The girls had disappeared, probably to look for someone with plenty of money. Walsh spent all he had. My friend noticed the gold-stoppered whiskey bottle on the table, the magnificent dressing gown thrown over a chair, and the fine clothes in the open wardrobe.

She also indicates that Walsh had also written to Pound, and that Pound, "who made a business of rescuing poets, hurried around." Thus, Beach's account verifies some of the details given by Hemingway. However, there are some discrepancies between the three accounts—Beach's account and Hemingway's 1952 and book accounts—and one might wonder to what extent Hemingway had heard some of these details from her or had re-freshed his memory when reading her memoirs, since it appears that he was sent the manuscript of her book on 7 September 1956, shortly before he began to think about his own memoirs.[54]

Among other aspects of *A Moveable Feast* foreshadowed in the 1950s, one should note Hemingway's writing to Lillian Ross that he wanted to write one day of Marshal Michel Ney's covering the retreat of the French army from Moscow, which he does in *A Moveable Feast* (30–31). In ad-dition, his description of walking "dangerous" in that same letter—he learned early to walk very "dangerous" so that people would leave him alone: "think the phrase in our part of the country was not fuck with you. Don't fuck with me, Jack you say in a toneless voice"—clearly foreshad-ows what he would tell Gertrude Stein in "Miss Stein Instructs" (18–19).[55]

III

While the anecdotes which appear in *A Moveable Feast* and which are also related in Hemingway's correspondence of the 1920s appear accurate and credible, some anecdotes narrated in the 1950s concerning Stein and Fitzgerald are much less credible—not that they do not dramatize rec-ognizable characteristics of both writers, but they seem too pat, too con-venient. One might say that they fall in too well with Hemingway's cruel pattern of denigration of the character and profession of those to whom he was indebted not to have been invented. They become particularly suspect when one realizes that there are clear factual errors in the book, some of which cannot have been anything but deliberate.

Three of these misrepresentations involve Fitzgerald. The first one is minor, and may or may not be actually misleading. Hemingway claims that Scott was with Duncan Chaplin when he first met him at the Dingo, while Chaplin himself denies it, which makes it difficult to trust either one at face value.[56] What could perhaps make one lean more toward trust-ing Chaplin's word is that, in the other Fitzgerald narrative, Scott is with a nameless college friend when he and Hemingway first meet at the Dingo. In fact, this earlier narrative of that first meeting is quite different from that published in the book. Instead of being at the Dingo with some "completely worthless characters" (128), Hemingway is there having dinner with Hadley and a few friends. The incidents about Scott's Guards' tie, about his praising lavishly Hemingway's work and asking if

Ernest had slept with Hadley before they were married are not present in that earlier narrative. Instead, Fitzgerald indicates that he wants to meet Jean Cocteau as much as he wanted to meet Hemingway, which of course does not please Ernest, and they talk about literature, although Ernest cannot remember specifically what about; however, it was all serious: "the question and answer school of conversation." Hemingway finds that, although Scott embodies everything he dislikes in a writer, except his talent (which he envies), he still likes him as a person, with his fresh looks, his youthfulness, and ingenuousness. The incident about Fitzgerald's passing out, his face looking like a death mask, and his having to be shipped home in a taxi are common to both narratives, although the details differ. But Hadley and their friends are not there to witness it, since they left the Dingo when the conversation became too literary. In the earlier narrative, the second meeting of the two writers does not take place at the Closerie des Lilas but again at the Dingo, which Hemingway feels was the wrong place to meet in on a Sunday afternoon because of its gloomy emptiness. In that version, Hemingway remembers nothing of their conversation, nor whether anyone else was there aside from the two of them and their wives. From the Dingo they went to the Fitzgeralds' apartment and had dinner. Hemingway makes some negative comments about the way the Fitzgeralds ran their household: the apartment was expensive but dirty, the food elaborate and expensive, and the wines did not go well with the courses served. Scott shows them his books about the war and shows them the large ledger in which he entered the sums he was paid each year for his writing, which clearly foreshadows the first paragraph in "Hawks Do Not Share." The story ends with Bumby grabbing hold of Scott's glass of wine and swallowing it all down, which broke up the meeting, since they had to take Bumby home and put him to bed. Unlike Fitzgerald at the Dingo, Bumby, however, did not show the effect of the wine.

This is reminiscent of the deleted chapter on Bumby. Indeed, the similarity between some of the themes developed, such as Bumby's drinking alcohol and Fitzgerald's showing up drunk at the sawmill apartment, as well as the fact that the two narratives were written on the same kind of paper, suggests not only that they may well have been written at the same time, but also that they may be two sections of the same narrative, one section of which Hemingway contemplated rescuing for publication in the book.[57] This narrative also foreshadows themes that were developed in different chapters of *A Moveable Feast*, suggesting again that it was indeed an earlier manuscript, most probably the one drafted for the *Atlantic*. It could not have been a manuscript of the 1920s, however, since it makes implicit but clear reference to *Tender Is the Night*. This narrative is also more mellow than Hemingway's later descriptions of Scott in the book, also suggesting that it was an earlier narrative, written at a time when Hemingway had not yet hit his stride in the systematic denigration of other writers characteristic of *A Moveable Feast*. However, the obvious differences between the events related make clear that at least one of the narratives contains numerous elements of fiction, the obvious candidate being the "Scott Fitzgerald" chapter in *A Moveable Feast*.

Much more important is the fact that Hemingway claims that Scott had not helped him revise *The Sun Also Rises*:

> Scott did not see it until after the completed rewritten and cut manuscript had been sent to Scribners at the end of April. I remembered joking with him about it and him being worried and anxious to help as always once a thing was done. But I did not want his help while I was rewriting. (184–85)

This particular lie was revised at the various stages of the manuscript. The first stage was less deceptive, as it read that Scott had not seen it "until the completed manuscript had been sent to Scribners"—which is technically correct. Then Hemingway continues that he thinks that he first showed it to him in the first proofs, "in which [he] made several cuts." This is definitely less correct and sins by omission, by not indicating that it was at Fitzgerald's suggestion that he made the changes and cuts. These two sentences were heavily revised in the typescript, and it is interesting to note that each revision moves further away from factual accuracy toward even clearer levels of deception. First of all, there is the tense switch and the addition of "that summer," which changes the meaning of the sentence by suggesting that Scott had seen it only after the cuts had been made: Hemingway thinks that he first showed it to him "in the first proofs *that summer* in which [he] *had made* several cuts." Then there is a long sentence added after several (unfortunately unreadable) others had been heavily crossed out, stating that Hemingway does not remember when he first showed finished things to Fitzgerald that year nor when Fitzgerald first saw the proofs on the rewritten and cut version. They had discussed them, but Hemingway had made the decisions: "Not that it matters." He remembers the cuts were his suggestion: "Not that it matters." Of course, it did matter to Hemingway. Very much so. Otherwise, he would not have repeated so often that it did not or spent so much time lying about it or making fun of Scott's advice concerning the end of *A Farewell to Arms* in letters to friends.[58] Then Hemingway hesitated, crossing out several unfinished (but revealing) sentences, such as "He [Fitzgerald] saved the letters." "I know I met him first at June probably in Juan les Pins." "But his help was not." The last cut at Scott, suggesting that he was always willing to offer help "once a thing was done"—that is, when it was no longer needed—seems to have come as an afterthought, for "Once a thing was done" was in fact the beginning of an unfinished sentence coming two sentences after "anxious to help as always." Thus, what was a positive statement is turned neatly into a negative one by amalgamating the two disconnected sentences.

In fact, Hemingway had invited Fitzgerald's advice in a letter of 20 April 1926, writing that he was going to Antibes in August: "I'll have a copy of Sun etc. there and w'd welcome your advising me or anything about it." The list of suggested changes that Scott submitted to Hemingway is now a matter of record, and specifically his request to cut out at least 2500 words from the first section:

> From here Or rather from P. 30 I began to like the novel but Ernest I can't tell you the sense of disappointment that beginning with its elephantine facetiousness gave me. Please do what you can about it in proofs. It's 7500 words—you could reduce it to 5000. And my advice is not to do it by mere pareing but to take out the worst of the *scenes.*

Fitzgerald had clearly seen *The Sun* in typescript and not in proofs, as the date of his letter (early June 1926) and the page numbers indicated make clear, and Hemingway immediately took his advice and wrote to Maxwell Perkins on 5 June 1926 that he now wanted the book to begin with what was page 16 of the manuscript, since there was nothing in those first sixteen pages that was both necessary to state and not stated or explained elsewhere in the book. Hemingway acknowledged that Scott had seen the manuscript and had suggested some cuts, but he thought it better simply to delete the first sixteen pages. It is interesting to note that Hemingway presented the deletion of these pages as his own idea, with which Scott agreed, and not as having originated with Scott, as it clearly did.[59] By 21 August Hemingway seems to have had second thoughts about cutting out that first part of the book, but Perkins's unwillingness to publish the Belloc section with Belloc's name in it left Hemingway little choice, as he felt that it would be pointless to publish it with the Belloc part eliminated.[60]

It is hardly possible that Hemingway could have forgotten Fitzgerald's help in the matter of *The Sun Also Rises*, and Hemingway's claim in *A Moveable Feast* is an obvious instance of deliberate distortion. Not even the awareness that Fitzgerald must have kept the letters invalidating his claim could detract Hemingway from making it.

Moreover, it seems that Hemingway's final disparaging comment concerning Scott in "A Matter of Measurements" was a fabrication. Hemingway describes his conversation with Georges, the barman at the Ritz, where Fitzgerald was a regular customer (191–93). Georges supposedly does not have the faintest remembrance of Scott, and asks Hemingway to tell him things about Scott so that he might pass them on to people asking about him. Of course, Georges remembers everyone else who came to the bar in the 1920s! A French scholar, Françoise Féret, interviewed Georges, who was then head barman at the Ritz, in 1957, and reports that he had been a great friend of Fitzgerald's and remembered him very well.[61] Again Hemingway reverses the roles, for it was the successful Fitzgerald who helped Hemingway in 1926 and, in the 1950s, had no need for Hemingway's help, as his work had been successfully revived by literary criticism and his personality was in no danger of being forgotten. However, one is again confronted with conflicting evidence, for, if, as according to the Ritz, Georges did not start working there until 1947, he could not possibly remember Fitzgerald or anyone else coming to the Ritz in the 1920s. Thus, Hemingway could be right in indicating that Georges did not remember Scott, but it would not be for the reason he implies. Much, of course, depends on when Georges actually started working at the Ritz, whether as a barman or as a busboy.

The one instance of misrepresentation which was picked up quickly by critics is Hemingway's claim that "This quarterly [referring to the *Dial* in the preceding paragraph], of which Walsh was one of the editors, was alleged to be going to award a very substantial sum to the contributor whose work should be judged the best at the end of the first four issues" (125), and that the award had been promised to him, as well as to Joyce, by Walsh. In 1966 William Wasserstrom commented that the chapter on Ernest Walsh "transforms actual events into artifacts not of history but of delusion," that Walsh was not an editor of the *Dial* as Hemingway claims, and that Hemingway speaks nonsense in his comments about the *Dial* and the award it was supposed to make. Wasserstrom also suggests that

Hemingway manipulated evidence in order to damn the *Dial*, which had rejected his poetry for publication, and to revile Walsh, who might have promised more than he could deliver.[62]

The manuscript verifies Wasserstrom's theory, and the paragraph referred to reads as follows in the first draft: "This quarter, of which Walsh was co-editor, offered two thousand dollars to the contributor whose work should be judged the best at the end of the year." In the transcription of the manuscript, the typist typed "This quarterly" instead of "This quarter"—an error that Hemingway did not correct, although he corrected this very sentence to read as the published version, and added the whole next paragraph in the margin. It is likely that the typist's error gave Hemingway the idea of creating the delusion, and one suspects that it was done purposefully, as it allowed him to cast doubt on the integrity of the *Dial* as well as on that of *This Quarter*, thus conveniently killing two birds with one stone. In fact, the first draft of the whole chapter was generally more vicious than the last and evidenced that he intended to expose Walsh's "bad faith." Thus, a little added duplicity might have alleviated the regret of having to cut out much insulting material concerning Walsh.[63] Although one might conceivably argue that Hemingway simply did not notice the error, that he was perhaps tired or sick on the day he reread the typescript, it seems that, in that case, he would have made no correction at all and let the sentence stand as the typist had it, instead of reworking it entirely so that it would carry a message entirely different from the one originally intended. In the manuscripts there are several instances of errors of typing he did not notice and let stand.

However, it seems that Walsh had actually promised Hemingway an award, as evidenced by a letter from Hemingway to Walsh dated 20 July 1925:

> I wont say anything about the award to anybody including myself because I dont want to figure on anything that would be so damned wonderful and then may be lose out on it. Money is so important to us that I cant play around with the idea of it.

Indeed, according to Nicholas Joost, there were an "impressive pair of awards promised by the co-editors of *This Quarter*, all quite frankly premissed on two points: the generosity of rich donors and the eager reception of their gifts by *This Quarter* for dispersal to deserving writers. In their joint 'Editorial' in the first number, the co-editors announced that [they had] received checks toward the sum of 2000 dollars or 500 pounds to be given to the contributor publishing the best work in the first four numbers. . . ." The second number again sought funds for awarding to a contributor "with special reference to youth, of that talent and need which shows promise, as opposed to absolute success, of enriching the civilization of his age." [64]

Apparently, Hemingway never forgave Walsh for a promise that might have been made more out of impulsive generosity than anything else, for, according to Pound, "Walsh was impulsive; the impulse more often generous than not; and nearly always at least grandiose. Better than Coolidgism. Though more obviously open to attack." [65] Neither did he forgive him for having reviewed *The Torrents of Spring* in *New Masses* as the cheapest book he had ever read (and not *The Sun Also Rises*, as he recalls in the manuscript). This is perhaps the major reason for Hemingway's bitter resentment of Walsh, which Pound wisely could not take seriously, but which Hemingway refused to let go of and vented with a vengeance in *A Moveable Feast.* [66] The least that one can say of Hemingway's portrayal of Walsh is that it is disingenuous—a lack of honesty which appeared early in his correspondence concerning Walsh. For instance, on 11 April 1930 Hemingway wrote to Maxwell Perkins, asking him to send him his letters to Walsh which had come into the auction market, requesting him not to read them and saying that he had been "bitched" by Walsh "in true Irish fashion" when Walsh reviewed *The Torrents.* He also indicated that Walsh had created a prize of $2000 to be given to the writer who would contribute the best material to the magazine, that Walsh had promised the award to Joyce, Pound, and himself, and that, on the strength of this promise, he obtained "swell things" from the three of them. [67] Clearly, Hemingway had given "Big Two-Hearted River" and "The Undefeated" to Walsh not on the strength of the award promised but on the strength of the cash that Walsh paid on acceptance. As he wrote to Pound on 16 March 1925: "Walsh pays for stuff by return mail." He had paid him "1000 francs for [his] Big Two Hearted River fishing story. Thank Gawd for Walsh." Walsh also accepted and paid for "The Undefeated," which had been rejected by various magazines, in particular the *Dial.* [68] According to Hemingway, Walsh paid as much for the fishing story as Hemingway had earned in the whole of 1924. [69] One would believe that the near-assurance of immediate and substantial cash was sufficient reason for him to send his work to Walsh.

Whether the meeting with James Joyce took place as Hemingway relates at the end of "The Man Who Was Marked for Death" is anyone's guess, but, if it did, it probably did not take place before February 1932, for on 2 February Hemingway asked Pound if he supposed Walsh had also promised the award to Joyce ("James Jesus") in writing after having asked Pound whether Walsh promised him the $2500 prize in writing or only verbally. What is particularly intriguing is that Hemingway states in that chapter that he liked and admired Walsh's co-editor, because she only wanted to build a good magazine, paid her contributors well, and had not promised him any award, while he had written to Scribner in 1952 that it was in fact Ethel Moorehead who had promised him the prize:

> At three different intimate little dinners she told me, Jim Joyce, and Ezra Pound that we were going to get the prize for the first year. To me she said I was getting it the first year, Pound the next and Joyce the third. To the others she said Pound 1, Joyce 2, Me 3 and Joyce 1, Pound 2, Me, 3.[70]

This letter contradicts what Hemingway writes in *A Moveable Feast*, but then it also contradicts what Hemingway told Perkins in 1930. With such conflicting evidence, one can almost expect that the truth lies elsewhere and that neither version is quite true. In that same letter, Hemingway also claims that Walsh reviewed *The Sun Also Rises* as "The Cheapest Book I Ever Read," which is indeed inaccurate, since it was *The Torrents of Spring* Walsh reviewed in such a way. However, the manipulation of facts makes sense, for, while Walsh would appear a fool for reviewing *The Sun Also Rises* as a cheap book (although many of the models for the protagonists of this roman à clef would disagree), few people would quarrel with him for reviewing *The Torrents of Spring* as such.[71] Since Hemingway is clearly intent on damning Walsh for every possible reason (even his dying from tuberculosis, which he alternately implies is faked or used as an emotional weapon), one can easily believe that the whole lunch-with-Walsh episode is a Hemingway fantasy. This is not to say, of course, that Hemingway never had lunch with Walsh, but merely that the conversation and the atmosphere of the lunch were probably invented much later.

The greatest falsehood of all, however, surely is Hemingway's oft-repeated claim of poverty. The book is crammed with such claims, and so is his correspondence of the 1920s. His contemporary and later accounts of his life in Paris with Hadley is a continuous sob story concerning money. He had no qualms about claiming that he often had to skip lunch so that his wife and child might eat (69–75), or that he could not afford to buy books or have a cat (35, 16), and that he looked longingly at the beautiful cats in restaurants and concierge windows—forgetting that elsewhere in the book he makes clear that they had a big, loving cat "named F. Puss"—a pun on F. Scott?—(96, 197). Hemingway even tries to arouse the reader's sympathy by explaining that he must renounce gambling on horses because he cannot afford to lose money, being a young man "supporting a wife and child" (100). His letters to the likes of Walsh, McAlmon, Pound, Loeb, and Stein involve endless complaints about money, and he apparently made a practice of sponging off his friends, McAlmon in particular, and did not always pay his debts.[72] In 1927, he seems to have written Gus Pfeiffer a very touching account of his hardships in Paris, and of his determination not to compromise the integrity of his craft, no matter what the consequences.[73] In fact, it would be impossible to list all the references to his dreadful poverty and to the greatness of soul with which he met these financial difficulties. Indeed, Hemingway got a great deal of mileage out of this identification with the artists who did actually starve in Paris garrets or hovels. What makes this game playing unpalatable is the fact that his so-called poverty was a deliberate fabrication from the beginning, and that he capitalized on the real suffering of others to build his own myth. But Hemingway was a good salesman, and he well knew that a writer living in Paris in poverty would be much more attractive to readers and critics than a well-fed writer living in comparative luxury, mostly on the income of his wife. And it worked, as he knew it would. As McAlmon observed perceptively, "I think he's a very good businessman, a publicity seeker who looks ahead and calculates, and uses rather than wonders about people."[74]

In fact, the Hemingways were far from poor. As Michael Reynolds established recently, Hadley's income was by itself sufficient to keep them in comfort even in the United States, let alone in France where life was cheaper. Hadley's share in her mother's estate was to be $15,636 plus $5357 put in trust for any child she might have in the future, plus $5000 should she still be single one year after her mother's death in 1920. Moreover, she had inherited almost $10,000 from an uncle, and she had a trust fund from her grandfather's will which had been accruing interest for twenty-seven years and was worth about $30,000. Thus, without even counting her uncle's $10,000, she had at her disposal more than $50,000 in 1922. As Reynolds points out, such a sum, safely invested, would provide an income of $3000 a year, while the average working man in the United States was earning only $1342. They were thus rather well off, and in Paris they were even better off. In October 1925, the average daily salaries in Paris were 36,40 francs for a printer, 30,80 for a binder, and 32 for a cabinet maker. Averaged over twenty-one professions, the daily income was 41,45 francs in 1926, 42,75 francs in 1928, and 53,76 francs in 1930. In 1922, the average income was around 22 to 25 francs a day— roughly a maximum of 7775 francs a year, based on an average of 311 working days. If one takes into account the advantageous exchange rate for the U.S. dollar, which ranged from 2.84 to 35.84 francs between 1920 and 1930, averaging some 25 francs, the young couple had some 75,000 francs a year to live on, without even counting Hemingway's remuneration from his various jobs. In short, based on Hadley's income alone, they were about ten times as rich as the average worker in France, if only a little over twice as rich as the average worker in the United States. They were obviously well enough off to live in Paris in what would have been considered luxury by Parisian living standards of the time. Thus, the very cheap apartment, the dowdy clothes, not to mention the sponging, were sheer game playing to attract attention and arouse pity as well as admiration. Of course, the maid, paid only a pittance of sixteen cents an hour in 1922, the nurse for Bumby later on, the brand-new piano for Hadley (a Gaveau upright), the extensive traveling and hotel living make a lot more sense when one realizes they were very well off.[75]

Despite the fact that they were living mostly on Hadley's money, it was Ernest who was handling the bank accounts and giving Hadley money only as she needed it. There may well therefore be some truth to his comment that "[he] had been stupid when she needed a grey lamb jacket and had loved it once she had bought it" (51). Indeed, it seems that Hemingway was rather tightfisted about Hadley's spending her own money on herself, and he seems to have kept the strings of the purse tightly tied, as shown in particular by Hadley's letters to him when Bumby had whooping cough in Juan les Pins and Hemingway was off in Spain. Hadley's protests that she was living very sparingly and that the Murphys were covering the medical costs indicate that Hemingway was complaining of her living too well. For instance, she writes on 21 May 1926:

> As to money—Gerald insisted on paying my hotel & the doctor wouldn't let me pay him so I suppose Gerald did that also. I paid everything before I left—two months of bakery, milk bill, dress-maker, 400 to Marie (50 Frcs. of it advance) and a lot of small neces-

sities, cleaning too, so now with tips and all I am down to 440 Frcs.
I am charging the grocery but later I will need more. Leave it to
you. . . . Of course the whole thing is dreadful bad but I am so
lucky to have a few grand things like the rich friends, so kind and
the villa & the splendid climate.

After leaving the Villa America because of possible contagion to the Murphys' children, Hadley moved to the Hôtel Beausite at Cap d'Antibes,
and, almost immediately, to the Villa Paquita, lent to her, free of charge,
by the Fitzgeralds. Hemingway seems to have been reluctant to understand the generosity of the Fitzgeralds—never acknowledging it in
"Hawks Do Not Share," when he refers to the *inexpensive villa* (185)—
for Hadley wrote to him the next day:

> You didn't know I had taken a villa. . . . Mais quand même ce n'est
> pas moi qui est riche pour prendre un villa! It's Scott's and Zelda's
> *given* for our use until June 10th when we shall fumigate (probably
> at Murphy's expense as they are [they think secretly] paying the doc-
> tor's fees).

On the 24th, she again tried to make Hemingway understand that the
villa had been lent to her for free, and that she was not spending much
money, protesting that she could do nothing else but stay in France, and
could not possibly join him in Madrid, and that she was not having a
great time:

> We are *not* in the hands of Scott and Zelda but I am using their villa
> at *no* cost (they are *giving* it) and being largely supplied with food
> even by Gerald and Sara. . . . I don't even spend money on drink,
> however bad I feel—until yesterday when I had the curse and got so
> low I went down town and spent 8 Frcs on whiskey & felt repen-
> tant. . . . I'm living here the cheapest possible and not being bad.

It is indeed surprising that Hadley, whose income was in fact keeping
Ernest and Bumby, should have found herself in such a position of inferiority vis-à-vis her husband and should have had to justify herself in
such a way when she was probably denying herself the pleasures of life
far more than he was. This may of course reflect the condition of women
in the 1920s—for instance, it seemed to be Ernest and not Hadley who
could take money and sign checks out of her bank accounts. It may also
reflect Hadley's willingness to indulge Ernest's social pretense that he was
the family's provider, and thus soothe his male pride. Indeed, he spends
much time in *A Moveable Feast* dramatizing himself as a good and re-

sponsible provider for his wife and child, which abundantly suggests that
he needed to think of himself as such.

IV

Aside from the events that Hemingway narrated in the 1920s and in the
1950s more or less as they are related in the book and the statements that
are obviously untrue, one finds in *A Moveable Feast* a number of episodes
that Hemingway does not seem to have related in either his early manuscripts or his correspondence. The most important of these are perhaps
the "Birth of a New School," what Hemingway tells us of his involvement
in Bel Esprit, his seeing a girl in "A Good Café on the Place St.-Michel,"
his meetings with Pascin at the Dôme and with Evan Shipman at the
Lilas, and his meeting Wyndham Lewis in Ezra Pound's studio.

Hemingway mentions that he was interrupted while writing "Big Two-
Hearted River" in a letter to Robert McAlmon dated 15 November 1924,
just when he was "going good," and that he could never get back into it
and finish it.[76] But he neither describes the scene nor indicates who dis-
turbed him. In the manuscript of that chapter he had named the intruder
Harold, and the name was changed to Hal by the editors after Hemingway's death, leaving the reader to wonder whether Hemingway might be
talking of Harold Loeb, Harold Stearns, or Harold Acton. Carlos Baker
believes Hemingway is talking about Acton, but there are definite traits
in the character that remind one of either Loeb or Stearns. Moreover,
there are other possibilities, although none is named Harold, such as
George Horace Lorimer and Lewis Galantière in particular.[77] However,
one cannot help wondering whether Hemingway is not creating here a
composite character embodying characteristics he disliked intensely in
others: homosexuality, self-pity, talking about one's work, and, even
worse, complaining about one's work, being a literary critic, and not re-
specting the work of others.

Hemingway does not write much about his involvement with "Bel Esprit" in his correspondence either. He occasionally refers to Eliot in his
letters, usually in a disparaging fashion,[78] but never describes the extent
of his involvement in "Bel Esprit." That he was involved, though, is
doubtless and evidenced in particular by a letter from Pound to Hemingway dated 11. 1. 1922 (probably November 1, 1922):

> Re Bel Esprit. Bring O Neil round. I cant be bothered with moral
> scruples. . . . Also will you invite the Parker-Williams family to tea,

i.e., D. asks if you will bring them to tea on Friday or Saturday, and SAY which day.

These matters have been dragging too long. Must get some action.[79]

How much money Hemingway collected is also unclear, but it seems that it is not only his own money—which he "had earmarked for getting the Major out of the bank" (112)—that he gambled at the races, but also the money that he had collected from others—something Nathalie Barney neither forgot nor forgave.[80] This may be why he avoids the topic in his correspondence, and, in *A Moveable Feast*, pleads guilty to a much more favorable version of the facts than apparently actually took place (111–13).

The final irony comes at the end of the chapter, when Hemingway writes that he "would have been happier if the amount of the wager had gone to Bel Esprit," but that he "comforted [himself] that with those wagers which had prospered [he] could have contributed much more to Bel Esprit than was [his] original intention." He then deletes the sentence "It turned out all right though as we used the money to go to Spain." The double-entendre throughout this section is astounding (Hemingway merely suggests that it is his own money that he gambled but never actually states it clearly), and it is also amazing that Hemingway should have felt it was "all right" for him to use money others had given to get Eliot "out of the bank" so that he and Hadley could go to Spain.

The episodes involving Hemingway's seeing a pretty young woman in a café and his chatting with Pascin and Shipman in cafés may have happened any number of times and are merely dramatizations of common events. Seeing a girl waiting for someone in a café is something that will happen every day of the week in a café. Moreover, he describes the girl with "hair . . . black as a crow's wing and cut sharply and diagonally across her cheek"—a stereotypic hairstyle for French women. Here Hemingway is giving the reader a bit of *couleur locale* and trying to establish himself from the outset as an insider.

"With Pascin at the Dôme" dramatizes in passing the well-known fact that Harold Stearns was interested in horses and spent time in cafés but concentrates on Hemingway's meeting with Pascin and the two models and his refusing the sexual overtures of one of the models—the one who was built better than anyone else in Paris.[81] Whether the episode did take place is anyone's guess, and nearly impossible to verify. The devoted-husband attitude of Hemingway, though, fits in well with the general pattern of the book, but may not be entirely true to facts, as suggested by the "Madame Louisette" business card found among his early notebooks (kept as a souvenir, perhaps!), and by ulterior facts and the testimony of his sons, as well as by his adulterous relationship with Pauline during his marriage to Hadley.[82] This episode could also be wishful thinking on Hemingway's part. This chapter also favorably introduces Jules Pascin, a painter who committed suicide, and who had agreed to illustrate a book of Hemingway's "dirty poems."

"Evan Shipman at the Lilas" also dramatizes a meeting that might have taken place many times—the meeting of two friends—since Shipman was one of the few people Hemingway was genuinely fond of. Hemingway's fondness for Shipman was evidenced repeatedly, and it is indeed a fondness that endured to the end of Hemingway's life. For instance, on 1 July 1947 he wrote to Lanham that he had only three friends "of the head" left: Lanham, Shipman, and Charley Sweeney. On Thanksgiving Day 1927, Hemingway wrote a long laudatory letter to Max Perkins about Shipman and decided to dedicate *Men Without Women* to him. Dedicating a book to Shipman was on Hemingway's mind for a long time, and he had contemplated dedicating to him *A Farewell to Arms*, as evidenced by a letter to Mrs. Pfeiffer dated 1 October 1929, in which he comments that Shipman is a young poet "who is having a hard time getting any recognition for his stuff," which is extremely good. Hemingway's high opinion of Shipman's poetry, which he feels is superior to Archibald MacLeish's, and of his other work is stated repeatedly in his correspondence. While he could not always resist a little dig at Shipman, as evidenced by his letter of 20 November 1924 to Robert McAlmon, in which he describes a fight that Shipman had with Nathan Asch, commenting that after a half hour of slugging neither of them had a mark— "Neither packs much of a punch, I guess"—he felt sorry for Shipman's misfortunes. Hemingway refers to these misfortunes in the manuscript of the Preface as Shipman's having been induced or helped in squandering his inheritance by Harold Stearns—the very inheritance he had waited a long time for and had so many plans for.[83] It seems that Hemingway had intended to express his love for, and pride in Shipman by writing a story about him for many years; but he never seems to have done so, unless one considers "Evan Shipman at the Lilas" or the unpublished chapter about him as such.[84]

Finally, it seems that Hemingway never related his encounter with Wyndham Lewis in Pound's studio in either his early or his later correspondence. However, Lewis's own account apparently verifies Hemingway's, at least so far as mere facts are concerned:

> A splendidly built young man, stript to the waist, and with a torso of dazzling white, was standing not far from me. He was tall, handsome, and serene, and was repelling with his boxing gloves—I thought without undue exertion—a hectic assault of Ezra's. After a final swing at the dazzling solar plexus (parried effortlessly by the trousered statue) Pound fell back upon his settee. The young man was Hemingway.[85]

If Lewis was as admiring toward Hemingway as this account suggests, it is quite likely that Hemingway did not feel negatively toward him until 24 March 1934, when Sylvia Beach showed him Lewis's article "The Dumb Ox," in which he criticized witheringly Hemingway's anti-intellectualism.[86] Hemingway was so angry that he punched a vase of tulips on Sylvia's table. Lewis's was indeed a crime of *lèse majesté* which could not be punished too severely, even thirty years later.

Discussing every episode, anecdote, or allusion in *A Moveable Feast* would take a book in itself. However, the selected anecdotes discussed here should give an idea of the complex mixture of fact and fiction that pervades the whole book. Indeed, *A Moveable Feast* is autobiographical, not in the sense of faithfulness to events as they actually happened, but in the sense that Hemingway was faithful to his personal vision of things. What we get in *A Moveable Feast* is the past seen through the colored lenses of Hemingway's old age, regrets, bitterness, and resentments, instead of the past seen through the reasonably colorless lens of an honest attempt at objectivity and factual accuracy. Hemingway, in fact, describes many aspects of his own self-projection in *A Moveable Feast* in the first narration of his meeting with Fitzgerald, when he talks about Fitzgerald's leaving an account of his own life in his fiction:

> These accounts were, of course, fictional in the sense of being untrue and the ending was never the real ending but the reality in them was the reality of what had happened to him in his life. It was as though that reality, in the amount that he had seen, had been followed and outlined with one of those instruments we had as children, composed of many wooden arms jointed together and holding a pencil at each extremity that, when you followed the outline of some simple object, traced a romanticized version of that object for you, while still following, as a base, the original fact.

The various pencils outlining and, occasionally, distorting the facts are Hemingway's mixed feelings about the past, those who played a part in it, and his own role as apprentice writer and devoted husband. It is terribly difficult to differentiate and decide whether specific errors are due to mere failure of memory—a normal thing after some thirty years—or to a deliberate and conscious distortion of the truth. In fact, both probably merged: for Hemingway, as for every human being, the unconscious mind often chooses to forget or distort what is usually most unpleasant or difficult to deal with—blanking out the memories one would prefer not to recall. Thus, the scholar can only examine carefully the physical evidence, tie it in with known facts, and hope to draw the proper conclusions.

CHAPTER FIVE

Autobiography "by Remate"

*A*FTER A CLOSE EXAMINATION of *A Moveable Feast*, of the rationale given by Hemingway for writing it, of the almost even proportion of fact and fiction contained in the narrative, and of the rather amazing steadfastness Hemingway evidenced in his lying and fabrications,
even at a time when he had achieved fame and no longer needed to attract
attention by false pretenses, one is left with the obvious question: WHY?
Why did he probably invent the discovery of the Ritz Hotel papers? Why
did he purposefully straddle the genres of autobiography and fiction, creating a background of fact, accuracy, and personal responsibility through
the discovery and purported use of early manuscripts and documents,
while claiming in the manuscripts of the Preface that the book is fiction,
as it indeed largely is? Why did he continue to lie when he should no
longer have had anything to prove, and when any logical or coherent reflection would have shown him that his reputation had everything to lose
by it, since it was only a matter of time before a responsible scholar would
bring out the lies and prove beyond question, for instance, that he had
never been poor?

The answer to these questions would involve an in-depth discussion of
Hemingway's psyche, which is not the purpose of this book. That he was
aware to some extent of his lies and misrepresentations, and that he was
deeply troubled by them, is obvious in his manuscripts; but what really
troubled him was not so much the fact that he had been unjust to a number of people as the fact that it might backfire on him and that people
might sue him. What he never seems to have realized, at least so far as
manuscript evidence suggests, is that he was doing himself a disservice
by using every means at his disposal to show himself as virtually perfect
and almost everyone else as extremely flawed.

There is much truth to William Wasserstrom's description of the book as a "triumphal banquet in self-celebration, a feast of victims."[1] Indeed, the major aim of the book is self-celebration. Hemingway tells the reader throughout: I was young, I was good, I was talented, I was self-disciplined and self-sacrificing, I was honest and true to myself, my wife, and my genius. This he achieves by direct self-description, but also indirectly—by "remate"[2]—by contrast and by implication. Throughout the book Hemingway attempts to elevate himself by aggressive, direct destruction of others who were also talented and had achieved fame, including Stein, Ford, and Fitzgerald. Hemingway portrays favorably only nonentities and, paradoxically, turns into a nonentity anyone he has something nice to say about, which is particularly evident in the case of Pound and Shipman, and above all in Hadley's case. But the result of the whole exercise which was to present to the world a flattering self-portrait of the writer as a young man and, by implication, of the writer as an old man—even though, by this point, it was obvious that he had not been faithful to his wives—is not the one Hemingway had intended, for, instead, he appears as a man who is petty, resentful, ungrateful, hypocritical, and incredibly self-centered.

The three means through which Hemingway achieves his "flattering" self-portrait are consistent throughout the book, in great as well as small instances; while the direct self-description is, of course, the most obvious, much significant information is given indirectly, although transparently. Hemingway describes himself as a thoughtful husband who defers to his wife's wishes (7–8, 37, 51, 56), as a loving and happily married man (14, 38, 57–58, 176) faithful to his lovely wife (102–4), as a young writer whose work is good but who is nevertheless humble about his craft and knows that he has much to learn from older writers (73, 135, 155), as a poor but self-sacrificing man who does not have money to buy books (35), who does his best to give his wife the comforts of life to the extent of allowing her to buy a lamb jacket she needed for the winter (50–51), who could not afford a cat (16)—but who strangely enough had one (96, 197)—and who often had to go hungry so that his wife and child might eat (69–72, 75, 100–101). Hemingway also describes himself as a man who, despite his poverty, will not accept handouts such as a trip paid for by others (157), and who therefore pays more than his share when he is traveling with Fitzgerald (161); a man who cannot afford to waste money, but who generously buys the fire-eater dinner (159); and as a man who, while he has no qualms about accepting a very expensive lunch from

Walsh (125–27), whom he despises, will not accept an expensive drink from a friend such as Pascin (102). He also describes himself as a good friend who does his best to like the friends of his friends, who tries to make his friends look good (108–10) regardless of the odds, and who will help them in their generous endeavours (110–13, 143–46). Hemingway is even generous and high-minded enough to acknowledge some of his faults, such as the fact that he is less generous and kind than Ezra Pound (108), that many of his complaints are phony ("You God damn complainer. You phony saint and martyr, I said to myself" [72]), and that he had in those days a "bad, quick temper" (157). However, these examples of self-criticism are not meant to be taken seriously by the reader, for who could blame anyone for being less kind and Christian than a saint, or for having a bad temper in the face of such provocation as Fitzgerald offered? And who could accept self-criticism of phoniness coming from someone who is apparently not eating so that his family might eat? While the statement that Hemingway is a "phony saint and martyr" is perfectly accurate, it is disingenuous and made in such a way as not to be believed.

W. A. Bunnell sensed the importance of the negative and contemptuous descriptions of others as a means of self-elevation: "The purpose of the frontal attack and direct insult is to show us everything the new hero [that is, Hemingway] is not, and, by implication, all the good things he is. It is made palatable primarily by the elements of humor and expository excellence, but nonetheless it is fictional deception and factual distortion."[3] Indeed, Hemingway's major means of self-description is by contrast with others who are always by implication less perfect than he is. Gertrude Stein, for instance, is described as a writer who wanted recognition but was too lazy to make her writing intelligible, whose great ambition was to be published in the *Atlantic Monthly*, who knew how to win critics over so that they would praise her work (it "had been well praised by critics who had met her and known her" [17]—implying that critics who would have based their judgment on her work alone would never have praised it), and whose opinion of other writers was based on whether they had written favorably about her own work (27). Her judgment of other writers is in fact dramatized by Hemingway as incoherent and unsubstantiated: she sees Aldous Huxley as a dead man and D. H. Lawrence as preposterous, pathetic, and sick; she praises lavishly Marie Belloc Lowndes and begins to praise Sherwood Anderson's work only when he has "cracked up as a writer" (26–28). She is also portrayed as prudish about words and life, not allowing Hemingway to use slang and words that are not *accrochables* or to talk about "the real and the bad"; but she is a lesbian and completely irrational in her opinion of other lesbians and homosexuals (18–20). "A Strange Enough Ending" is a masterpiece of hypocritical character assassination and, to use Bunnell's words, "reeks of the worst kind of melodrama," but it does not really work for the perceptive reader, because Hemingway's reaction of disgust is just not in character with a worldly-wise man who knows all about "perversions." By contrast, we are of course supposed to infer that Hemingway is none of these things, that he is hard-working and disciplined, that his writing is good and deserves better than the *Atlantic Monthly*, that he does not need to court critics so that they will praise his work, that his opinion of other writers is sound and not based on their attitudes toward himself, that he is coherent in his judgments and can face up to reality, that he is honest, logical, not perverted, and that his marriage is natural and pure. While Gertrude Stein is disposed of as undisciplined and perverted, Hemingway is made to represent courage and moral rectitude.

Ford Madox Ford, Ernest Walsh, and F. Scott Fitzgerald also undergo a masterful destruction, the aim of which is to elevate Hemingway by direct contrast. While Hemingway indicates in his own defense that Ford's "ignoble presence" (86) made it impossible for anyone who was not a saint to be fair to him, and while he suggests that there may have been extenuating circumstances for Ford's being the way he was (never mentioning, of course, that the reason Ford was wheezing was that he had been gassed during the war), he happily dramatizes him as a liar and a fool who gave off a foul body odor, a snob who did not know what he was talking about and never listened to others. Walsh is dispatched as a fake in art as well as in life, a man who supposedly had to be bailed out by the generosity of others, but who stayed at Claridge's and was paid $1200 for a poem when, most unfairly, Hemingway got only $12 a page. Hemingway even suggests that Walsh pretended to be sick—"He knew I knew he had the con . . . and he did not bother to have to cough" (126)— and used his "marked for death look" to manipulate people. To express his contempt for Walsh, Hemingway accepts an expensive lunch from him, which he orders himself, suggesting that, just as Ford cannot order a drink properly, Walsh does not know how to order a good lunch (125–27). Again Hemingway attempts to arouse the reader's disgust in an underhanded way, never acknowledging that Walsh was actually dying of tuberculosis. By contrast, we are expected to see Hemingway as a man who is no fool, does not lie, knows how to behave, and is "the real thing" in life as well as in art.

F. Scott Fitzgerald undergoes the most extensive and vicious attacks. Throughout, Hemingway is patronizing toward Scott and describes him as physically effeminate (149), unable to hold his liquor but refusing to acknowledge it (152, 161, 174), as a hypochondriac who knows nothing about sickness and can be fooled by the most obvious stratagem (163–71), as an artist whoring his art for money (155–56, 179, 181–82) who has unsound ideas about the novelist's craft (151), and who cannot spell (172–73)—a lovely instance of the pot calling the kettle black. He also dramatizes Scott as a man who has feelings of impotence and is extremely unlearned about sex (190–93), so much so that Hemingway has to explain the facts of life to him—" 'It is not basically a question of the size in repose,' I said. 'It is the size that it becomes. It is also a question of angle.' I explained to him about using a pillow and a few other things that might be useful for him to know" (191)—and to take him around to a museum for visual aid. Fitzgerald is portrayed contemptuously and patronizingly, and at the same time Hemingway is depicted as the exact opposite, as masculine, virile, knowledgeable about life and sex, and as a writer of great integrity who does his best to help a writer of lesser integrity. Of course, Scott is properly admiring of Hemingway's work, and he praises it lavishly, thus eliciting Hemingway's embarrassment.

Occasionally, Hemingway's self-portrayal or self-reassurance is achieved merely by implication, usually in minor instances, such as his statement that he kept away from the Café des Amateurs "because of the smell of dirty bodies and the sour smell of drunkenness" (3), or his assertion that he knew the price of a bunch of small twigs he would have to buy to make a fire (4). We are supposed to infer that he is no drunk, and that he has to be very careful about money, even for necessities, given his dreadful poverty. Similarly, when he reassures himself that he can still write—"Do not worry. You have always written before and you will write now. All you have to do is write one true sentence. Write the truest sentence that you know"(12)—we are supposed to understand that in the late 1950s, at the time he is writing *A Moveable Feast*, he is just as able to write as he was in the 1920s, and that what he writes is just as true. Indeed, he was able to write in 1957–58 when he wrote the book, if not later when he was attempting to revise it. However, he no longer trusted his own creative ability, and it is clearly his own doubts he was trying to appease. When he writes a few lines later that he decided then that he would write one story about each thing that he knew, we are of course expected to understand that each chapter of the book is about one thing that he *knew* about, thus emphasizing once more, but more subtly, the premise that everything he writes is true. The last section of "There Is Never Any End to Paris" is of course packed with such innuendos, all of which tend to suggest that Hemingway was not guilty of what happened to his marriage; he was merely a helpless innocent in the hands of calculating and irresponsible people. There are decided overtones of *The Great Gatsby* in that section, for it is indeed the rich who break things up and leave others to clean up the mess. For instance, when Hemingway writes, "During our last year in the mountains new people came deep into our lives and nothing was ever the same again," we are supposed to understand that it was the new people's responsibility for invading the lives of the Hemingways, and, therefore, that it was their fault that nothing was ever the same again. The short statement "The pilot fish leaves of course" (207) suggests that the pilot fish leaves when his harm is done and, therefore, that it is his fault that harm came to the Hemingways, that he evades responsibility, and that he even perhaps intended to do harm. When Hemingway tells us that the rich would never have come a year before, when it was not yet sure that he would write a good novel (208–9), he is telling us that the rich do not waste their time on others until they are sure that there is something worth destroying. In fact, this whole section is a fine piece of dramatic personal dishonesty and a remarkable demonstration of how to avoid responsibility for one's own actions by shifting the blame onto others.

Indeed, it seems that Hemingway could never wholly bring himself to granting anyone qualities or a stature that could match his own. The only people he portrays positively are usually literary nonentities, such as waiters and restaurant owners or managers, with the notable exception of Sylvia Beach. Mr. Lavigne, for instance, knows better than to interrupt him when he is working at the Closerie des Lilas (99), unlike the would-be writer in "Birth of a New School." At the same time, he manages to damn with faint characterization people whom he portrays sympathetically. While Hemingway appears to praise Ezra Pound lavishly, telling us he is nothing short of a saint in his generosity and faithfulness to his friends (witness his *Bel Esprit* undertaking), that he is a gentle man and a great poet, he still portrays him as hopeless at boxing, so much so that he embarrasses Hemingway in front of others, as physically awkward (he broke or cracked the chair he sat on at Gertrude Stein's [28]), and as having disastrous judgment in the matters of friends and of art, the latter being conditioned by the former since he always liked the work of his friends (107–8). Similarly, while Hemingway praises Evan Shipman and Pascin, the former comes across as a nice boy, slovenly dressed, rather dirty, with bad teeth, who misplaces his clothes and his poems, and who somehow appears to be properly grateful for Hemingway's friendship. Pascin, the "lovely painter" (104), is portrayed as drunk, promiscuous, and perfectly happy to share his models and sex partners with others, even making his own studio available. These three friends of Hemingway's seem to be undone by their virtues, and are finally dramatized as friendly mediocrities.

Hemingway is unfair even to Hadley in his portrayal of her, as he well knew. Although he claims continuously that she was a wonderful woman and wife, her most important quality in the book seems to be that she is blissfully in love with her husband, admiring the smallest of his decisions as if they were wonders of life. Throughout, her conversation is limited to such perceptive statements as: "I think it would be wonderful, Tatie," "Oh, I want to right away. Didn't you know?" (7), "I'm sure it will be," "Weren't you good to think of going, too" (8), "Of course, Tatie" (31), " 'My,' she said. 'We're lucky you found the place' " (38). Occasionally, she is dramatized as being slightly motherly—"But, Tatie, you must go by this afternoon and pay," "No. Don't forget we have to pay the library" (37), "But didn't you have any fun or learn anything, Tatie?" (175)—and always as behaving in accordance with her husband's wishes, even if she is occasionally hesitant, as in the case of going racing (50–51). Hadley is generally portrayed as subdued and full of sympathy and pity for others, whether they are racing horses or F. Scott Fitzgerald (52, 176). Whenever there is a more serious conversation involving Hadley, she is dramatized as being somehow in a position of inferiority, as being conscious of it, and as being properly grateful when she is treated as an equal. For instance, she is happy that Chink Dorman-Smith and Hemingway include her in their conversations (54), but she does not take it for granted that she has the right and the brains to talk with them on an equal footing. Moreover, as everyone else in the book, Hadley is under attack for irresponsibility. After all, she did lose her husband's manuscripts—a terrible instance of carelessness—and she often leaves her husband to take care of Bumby, in particular in the mornings while she is sleeping late. Since she is portrayed as having absolutely nothing else to do but look after her husband

and child, the indictment of her performance as wife and mother is implicit. It is most likely that Hemingway never really forgave her for having lost his early manuscripts, and that he may more or less consciously have felt that Hadley's accidental loss had been subconsciously willed. This is indeed suggested in *The Garden of Eden*, where Catherine, who is keeping David and footing all the bills, as Hadley largely did, willfully and spitefully destroys David's manuscripts because she is frustrated at his having an affair with Marita and at his not writing about herself. There is little doubt that Hemingway's resentment of Hadley's loss of his juvenilia finally comes out in *The Garden of Eden*, a resentment that he must have suppressed for many years but which may still have colored his portrayal of Hadley in *A Moveable Feast,* despite his oft-repeated protestations of love and admiration.

That Hadley was a bright and talented woman is never brought out in the book. Hemingway never mentions that she was a talented pianist who had sacrificed her work to her husband's, that he relied on her for the mundane aspects of life in France, since her French was much better than his (for instance, she ended up writing letters to their landlord, because Hemingway was unable to write anything intelligible in French[4]), that she was a personable, secure individual who could in fact handle heartbreaking situations far better and with more dignity than her husband, that she was a woman who could face up to reality and accept the world and herself without wallowing in self-pity and self-justification. In fact, a reading of her correspondence and of the anecdotes that surrounded the breakup of her marriage to Hemingway arouses far more admiration for her than for her illustrious husband.[5] But none of this ever comes through in *A Moveable Feast,* which offers a very unfair, simplified, and infantile view of her as mother and child-wife.

It seems that Hemingway desperately needed to believe that he was the only artist and the only man, and that the eventual aim of his autobiography was self-deception, which would largely explain why he had to straddle the genres. He does not want to be held liable for the accuracy of what he narrates and therefore claims it is fiction; but he wants readers to believe it as fact and, in order to make that possible, he creates through devious means a context that will influence their judgment. If the readers take the narrated events as fact, they will also accept as fact the glorification of the author/hero which results from such a reading.[6] That Hemingway did not see that the device was transparent and did not credit his readers with enough intelligence to see through it suggests either that he had lost much of his clear-sightedness by the time he wrote the book, or perhaps that the neuroses he was suffering from had become overpowering. *A Moveable Feast* is a book written by a man who was psychologically sick, but it is perfectly in line with his life and work, and it is the logical product of his personality.

Hemingway's mental condition during the last years of his life, which eventually led to several suicide attempts before he finally succeeded, has by now been well documented. His inability to accept old age, accompanied as it was by a normal weakening of his powers as a man and a writer, and his transference of responsibility onto the outside world, evidenced by his delusions of persecution, suggest that he had never come to terms with himself. Gerry Brenner suggests that it is his relationship with his own father that Hemingway had never come to terms with, and that his attacks in *A Moveable Feast* on any man who might be remotely considered a father figure, be it Ezra Pound, Ford Madox Ford, or Al in "Birth of a New School," evidence his need to justify himself before his father and demonstrate that, unlike everyone else, he had not been irresponsible.[7] That Hemingway had deeply unresolved feelings toward his father is certain. These feelings were more complex than usually granted, for a glance at the family letters shows that Clarence Hemingway could not possibly have been the man his son wanted so desperately to see in him. There was much of the professional victim and self-sacrificer in Clarence, who loved to dwell on how he deprived himself so that his family might have all the comforts of life.[8] Hemingway was clearly his father's son in more ways than he would have cared to admit. Similarly, Hemingway's attacks in *A Moveable Feast* on Gertrude Stein, who must have reminded him in many ways of his own mother, mirror the way he shifted the blame for whatever negative things happened to his father onto his mother. Neither Clarence nor Ernest was to blame for what he did. It was always the fault of somebody else, and preferably, whenever one was available, the fault of a strong woman. Even Fitzgerald, despite all his faults, is portrayed as a pawn in the hands of a strong—if crazy—woman.

That Hemingway had elaborated a glorious and exacting self-image or persona that led him to live a spectacular life, never giving him respite from the need to prove himself, and that this self-image severely limited his relationship with others, prompting him to see them merely as the witnesses of his accomplishments and to feel an interest only in those who possessed the qualities he admired, finds its ultimate autobiographical expression in *A Moveable Feast*. It is indeed logical that he should have felt the need to turn to the past at a time when he was no longer feeling secure in his creative ability, and to flog the ghosts of those he had competed against all his life when they were no longer around to be measured against, either physically or as producing artists. It is also psychologically understandable that, feeling that he had behaved irresponsibly and needing to convince himself and others that he had not, he should have focused on the real or fancied irresponsibilities of others. *A Moveable Feast* makes too strong a case for Hemingway, either directly or indirectly, not to reveal a deep, underlying uneasiness. Unable to come to terms with his own irresponsibilities and failures, he projects them onto others.

Indeed, *A Moveable Feast* dramatizes Hemingway's competitiveness, for he measures himself against others in every possible situation, and largely in situations that do not call for it.[9] Do his readers really care to know that he can order a meal better than Walsh or a drink better than Ford? that he is less awkward physically than Pound? that he likes waiters or knows the usefulness of a pillow in lovemaking better than Scott? Such things, even if they were true, are trivial and uninteresting except to someone who desperately needs self-reassurance and grabs at any straw to gain it and persuade himself and others that he is indeed superior. There is, of course, a great deal of hostility in his choosing mostly episodes that show his contemporaries in the worst light. The greater the competition they offered, the more negatively and at a greater length they are portrayed. Ford and Walsh rate only one chapter, while both Stein and Fitzgerald rate three each. However, in page count, Fitzgerald's chapters are twice as long as Stein's. The lack of subtlety of Hemingway's attack is surprising, but it corresponds to a deep-seated reality. Scott was his greatest competitor in the literary field; therefore, he needed to be destroyed more thoroughly than anyone else, and since he could not be attacked credibly on the artistic level, he had to be destroyed as a man and as an undisciplined writer. Hemingway's hostility can be perceived, too, in his patronizing attitude toward those he describes more positively. As Sherwood Anderson understood as early as 1937, Hemingway could not "bear the thought of any other men as artists" and wanted "to occupy the entire field."[10] Almost every page of *A Moveable Feast* validates this opinion, and, of course, Sherwood Anderson does not escape its pages unscathed, despite the fact that for a couple of sentences Hemingway voices a positive opinion of his work in order to damn Stein's more effectively.

That Hemingway inordinately needed others to be witnesses to his greatness is evidenced by the care he took to always keep himself in the public eye and by his inability to accept criticism. He needed public adulation, and he had not been unaware of the reading public's lack of interest in his last books, except for *The Old Man and the Sea*, and of the critics' unfavorable comments. Despite its stylistic excellence, *A Moveable Feast*, written at a time when he was losing his self-confidence as a man and a writer, is in many ways a last and pathetic attempt at verifying his self-image. But, because it appears vital to him that he prove that he is indeed the best and the only man and artist, there is little honesty in his self-scrutiny and in his approach to others. Moreover, what honesty there was was largely edited out after his death. That Hemingway wanted to leave a flattering self-portrait is obvious; that he fails in doing so is also obvious. The very reasons which make it imperative that the self-portrait be unqualified self-glorification make it unavoidable that the self-glorification backfire and result in a revealing but unflattering self-portrayal. It is impossible for Hemingway to convince himself and his readers of something he knows to be untrue.

If the Hemingway hero changes in *A Moveable Feast*, it is only superficially, for the author/hero is still the traditional Hemingway hero; but he is now a man who can no longer acknowledge his own failings openly and find a way to transcend them. An entire universe has not perished or "at least become terribly inverted," as W. A. Bunnel believes; it has merely become more obvious or incoherent. Winning is what the Hemingway hero has always wanted; but for a time he was content with winning victories within his range and transforming failures into moral victories. Hemingway's heroes were always fictional visions of himself, but they usually had the virtue of being other than himself, so that, whatever their victories or defeats, the fictional distance served as a buffer, as a screen behind which the author could hide. In *A Moveable Feast* the screen has been removed, with all the attendant advantages and disadvantages. Now the glory can be laid directly at Hemingway's door, but also the false glory, the lying, and the pettiness. Wanting directly the credit for the glory but not the discredit for the failures in accuracy and honesty, Hemingway had to straddle the genres of fiction and autobiography, probably subconsciously hoping to get the best of both worlds.

Eventually, one must wonder if the manipulation of genres and of facts turned out to be such a liability to the book. Human nature does like gossip, in particular ill-intentioned gossip that talks about the great of this world. Beautifully written, with passages about Paris that are as charming as any in *The Sun Also Rises, A Moveable Feast* will satisfy any reader in search of juicy literary anecdotes. Moreover, it is a book full of nostalgia and regrets for lost love and happiness that would affect the romantics. It is a book about Paris in the 1920s, the Jazz Age as lived on the Left Bank, a book about a young budding talent suffering in a Paris garret for the sake of art. Few topics have more general appeal to the reasonably literate. So what does it matter when a book has all it takes to make a best-seller that facts should have been distorted? It is only the critics' problem. However, for anyone interested in the man behind the book it is important to know what happened to the facts, to the man, and to his text after his death.

CHAPTER SIX

Borrowings from Early Manuscripts and Discarded Material

ESPITE CLAIMS that Hemingway used drafts and manuscripts of the early 1920s to write *A Moveable Feast*, it seems that he made, in fact, relatively small use of early manuscripts.[1] There are two main instances of borrowing from *The Sun Also Rises* (the passage about Ford Madox Ford cutting Hilaire Belloc, and the passage about the Lost Generation), one from "Big Two-Hearted River," and a few miscellaneous borrowings from early manuscript fragments. On the other hand, Hemingway drafted several chapters which he eventually decided against including in the book—chapters which were also left alone by his editors.

Hemingway borrowed the passage about Ford's cutting Belloc from the first notebook of *The Sun Also Rises* (File 194), but it was extensively rewritten and integrated with other material. This passage disappeared when Hemingway decided to follow Fitzgerald's advice and lopped off the first fifteen typewritten pages of the manuscript.[2] The two scenes are in fact rather different, but they have in common a similar description of Ford, a similar description of Crowley, and the fact that Ford cuts Crowley. The scene in the notebook is much shorter: it begins with a description of the waiter at the Closerie des Lilas who would give Hemingway and Dos Passos two "Whiskey's for the price of one whiskey owing to a dislike he had for his boss." This waiter raised potatoes in a garden outside Paris, beyond Montrouge. These details tend to authenticate what Hemingway tells us about Jean in "Evan Shipman at the Lilas." In the notebook scene, Hemingway is sitting at the Closerie with Dos Passos who is in town when Ford—that is, Braddocks—joins them. Ford is described as "breathing heavily and wearing a black hat," while in *A Moveable Feast* he is described as "breathing heavily through a heavy, stained mustache and holding himself upright as an ambulatory, well clothed,

III

up-ended hogshead" (83). His description is obviously more cruel in the book, and, indeed, this is a constant difference between the two narratives. In both scenes Ford asks if he can join him/them: "May I join you?" in the notebook, and "May I sit with you?" in the book. In the notebook, Hemingway introduces Dos Passos as a famous author who wrote "a book called the Holy Grail" about the war and who got "half a million for the movie rights." After commenting "don't pull my legs," Ford indicates that he knows all about Dos Passos and settles heavily into his chair, "breathing with difficulty." In the book Dos Passos is not present.

The long description of the Closerie des Lilas and its *clientèle* (81–82), the parody of Ford's not remembering what drink he ordered and changing his mind twice, his not listening to what he is told, and his advising Hemingway to go to the Bal Musette are not present in the notebook version, nor are Hemingway's insinuations concerning Ford's bad breath, or Ford's comment about spending years of his life "that those beasts should be slaughtered humanely" (83). Crowley is introduced in slightly more detail in the notebook version, where he is described as a "rather tall grey lantern-jawed man walking with a tall woman wearing an Italian infantry officer's blue cape." In the book, Crowley is merely described as a "rather gaunt man wearing a cape" and walking with a tall woman (85). It is interesting to note how the details were probably switched around in Hemingway's mind; it is also possible that he switched them around purposefully, were he using the notebook as a model. In the notebook, Crowley is described as looking for someone, and, in particular, as scanning their table; while, in *A Moveable Feast*, Hemingway believes that Crowley has not seen them. The description of the cutting is rather different in the two versions, and much more extensively described in the book. In fact, the whole exchange about cads and cutting them is absent from the notebook version. In the notebook, Hemingway merely comments that he would never forget Ford's large, red face, with his walrus mustache, as he gloated over the episode. Hemingway was happy to see the literary life, and to have a piece of valuable gossip. The endings of the episodes are also different. In the notebook, it is the next day that Hemingway is able to avail himself of his new knowledge at the Café du Dôme, while sitting with several other people: " 'There is Hilaire Belloc,' I said to the people at our table. 'He has not a friend in the world.' " He then concludes that he never felt the same about Ford afterwards, and that, were Ford not a friend of Cohn's, he would prefer not to put him in the story. The ending of the episode in the book is, of course, different (88).

Despite the similarities between the two narratives, even very specific ones in the use of words, one cannot be quite sure that Hemingway used the notebook of *The Sun Also Rises* as a model for "Ford Madox Ford and the Devil's Disciple." There is always the chance that the episode could have been a product of his memory. However, if one cannot say specifically that he worked with the notebook at hand, he certainly remembered clearly enough how he had described the episode in the notebook. His using that particular episode in *A Moveable Feast* could also well be a way of recycling material he had been advised against publishing thirty years earlier.

Similarly, the episode about the Lost Generation was borrowed from the brown notebook containing the foreword to "The Lost Generation— A Novel," in which Hemingway explains why he decided finally not to call his first novel "The Lost Generation." The original passage, however, was very much reworked for inclusion in *A Moveable Feast,* and the overtone of war is entirely new. The notebook passage reads:

> One day last summer Gertrude Stein stopped in a garage in a small town in the Department of Ain to have a valve fixed in her Ford car. The young mechanic who fixed it was very good and quick and skillful. . . .
>
> "Where do you get boys to work like that?" Miss Stein asked the owner of the garage. "I thought you could not get boys to work any more."
>
> "Oh, yes," the garage owner said. "You can get very good boys now. I've taken all of these and trained them myself. It is the ones between 22 and 30 that are no good. C'est un generation perdu. No one wants them. They are no good. They were spoiled. The young ones, the new ones are all right today."
>
> "But what becomes of the others?"
>
> "Nothing. They know they are no good. C'est un generation perdu." A little hard on them, he added. (File 202C)

Hemingway continues by explaining that he did not hear the story until after he had written *The Sun Also Rises,* and why he had decided to use neither "Fiesta" nor "The Lost Generation" as a title for the book.

The difference between this passage and the version Hemingway published in "Une Génération Perdue" is obvious. In the notebook version the work done by the young mechanic is excellent, while in the book it is unsatisfactory. In the notebook it is the garage owner who talks about the lost generation, while in the book it is Stein who accuses Hemingway's generation of being lost. There are no overtones of drunkenness or war in the notebook, while in the book version Stein makes an issue of Hemingway's generation drinking itself to death and having no respect for anything as a result of the war. Clearly the book version is far more deprecatory toward Stein than the version of the 1920s.

Some of the comments Hemingway makes in *A Moveable Feast* about his learning to write in Paris and the influence of Cézanne on his craft are strongly reminiscent of the deleted passage of "Big Two-Hearted River," which has now been published as "On Writing" in *The Nick Adams Stories*.[3] Although there seems to be no direct textual borrowing, the ideas are similar and the attitude of the writer analyzing his own craft and giving clues to his characterization is already present in "On Writing." On 15 August 1924, Hemingway wrote to Stein and Toklas that he had finished the long short story he had been working on before going to Spain, where he had tried "to do the country like Cezanne and having a hell of a time and sometimes getting it a little bit." But by 15 November he realized "that all that mental conversation in the long fishing story is the shit" and cut out the last nine pages. The story was interrupted just when he was going well, and he could never get back into it and finish it.[4] The discarded passage makes some interesting points: it indicates in particular his belief that the "only writing that was any good was what you made up. What you imagined . . ." and that the Nick of his stories was never himself—that he, Hemingway, had never seen an Indian woman having a baby. He also feels that Cézanne was the greatest painter of all times, that he started with all the tricks, then broke the whole thing down, and then built the real thing. Nick wanted to write about the country so that it would be "like Cezanne had done it in painting." He had to do it from inside himself, and he could do it if he had "lived right with his eyes," but it was something he could not talk about. "You could do it if you could fight it out. . . . He was going to work on it until he got it." People were easy to do, but they were not the thing he was after.

Other minor borrowings are from File 484. Short passages from these manuscript fragments have been used and mostly reworked in the book. For instance, the first paragraph of File 484 appears to have served as an early draft for the first paragraph of "People of the Seine." In both cases there is a description of walking down from the top of the Rue du Cardinal-Lemoine to the Seine. The words used for describing the river bank and the Halle aux Vins are almost exactly the same: "a bleak, windy stretch of river bank" in the book, and "a dull, windy stretch of river bank" in the manuscript; "a sort of bonded warehouse where wine was stored against the payment of taxes and was as cheerless from the outside as a military depot or a prison camp" (41) in the book, and "a sort of bonded warehouse high fenced in wire [which] was as cheerless from the outside as a military depot or a prison camp" in the manuscript. Some of the ideas developed in another paragraph—for example, that novels would tend to lead up to one moment of intense truth, and that he wanted to write only that piece of truth and omit the rhetoric and the padding—are reminiscent of ideas developed in "Hunger Was a Good Discipline" (75). Similarly, the last paragraph strongly foreshadows "A Good Café on the Place St.-Michel" (7), with its talk of the weather having turned bad in Paris, and Hemingway's desire to go to the mountains with Hadley when he gets paid for the work he has done for the paper in Toronto. However, it is difficult to date the fragments of File 484, and there is always a distant possibility that they might have been merely an early draft for sections of *A Moveable Feast*.

Another likely borrowing is the headnote for the Fitzgerald section which Philip Young describes as "considerably older than the rest of the manuscript."[5] It does indeed look much older, and it certainly is written on a different type of paper, as it has been torn out of a small notebook. However, I have not been able to find among the early notebooks the one from which this small sheet of paper could have been torn. None of them has a similar format.

Hemingway may also have resurrected the idea for his break with Gertrude Stein from an early manuscript entitled "My Own Life: After Reading the Second Volume of Frank Harris' 'My Life.' "[6] If such should be the case, it would provide an added reason for considering the story of his breakup with Stein as fictional. In this sketch, which also includes how he broke up with John Wilkes Brook, with his wife and children, and with F. Scott Fitzgerald, it seems that it is almost always the others who break up with him: Stein closes her door to him or has the maid tell him that she is out, and his wife and children leave him notes telling him not to look for them.

Five of the chapters written for, but not included in, *A Moveable Feast* are of a mood with the published ones, but the sixth is different in that it deals mostly with a much later time, when Evan Shipman came to visit the Hemingways in Cuba shortly before dying. The four chapters on

Ford Madox Ford, F. Scott Fitzgerald, Larry Gains, and "On Writing in the First Person" were not numbered by Hemingway, and we seem to have no indication as to where he intended to use them in the book, if he intended to use them at all. On the other hand, the chapter on Bumby bears the indication in Hemingway's hand that it was to be used after chapter 17; on the Shipman chapter we have indications in Mary Hemingway's hand that it was a "possible finishing chapter," which is validated by the dates ranging from 1 to 3 April appearing on the various pages, and by the fact that Hemingway reuses at the beginning of this chapter many of the sentences and paragraphs that he had redrafted endlessly for his introduction and concluding chapter.

The Ford chapter is mostly a series of considerations on what Hemingway disliked about Ford and on what Pound had told him when he first introduced him to Ford. Hemingway recognizes that many people loved Ford, particularly women, but that some men also liked him after they knew him, and that many men, like H. G. Wells, who had seen him badly treated, tried to be fair to him. But Hemingway himself, who had never seen him at a good time in his life, despite the fact that many people considered his *Transatlantic Review* period a good one, did not like him because, among other things, Ford lied about money and about things that were important in daily living. The better his luck was, the more he lied and the more unbearable he became. If his luck ran badly, "he would sometimes give you close to a straight answer." Hemingway tells us that he tried not to judge Ford and just get along with him, but that writing about him with accuracy "was crueler than any judging" (File 180).

Hemingway narrates his first encounter with Ford in Pound's studio, when he and Hadley had returned from Canada with a six-month-old child and had found the sawmill apartment on the same street Pound lived on. Pound warned him that he must not mind Ford's lying because he lied only when he was tired. Ford apparently once told Pound that he had crossed the whole southwest of the United States in the company of a puma. Then Pound told Hemingway the story of Ford's inability to get a divorce from his first wife, how Ford had gone to Germany with relatives, and how he had stayed there until he had convinced himself that he had become a German citizen and had obtained a "valid German divorce." Pound also told him how Ford had been persecuted upon his return to England because his wife had not agreed to the divorce, and how his friends had behaved shabbily toward him. Hemingway waxes sarcastic in his response, wondering whether Ford was tired when he convinced himself that he had a valid divorce, and feels that a man who was persecuted for such a simple error deserved sympathy of a kind.

Hemingway then explains how Ford had started the *Transatlantic Review* and how he had edited a review in London before the war. According to Pound, Ford had done a "splendid job of editing" the *English Review* before his marital troubles. Now Ford was starting a new life with Stella Bowen, his new wife, who was a serious painter, and they had a daughter, "a large child for her age, who was very fair and had good manners." Finally, Hemingway describes the "completely unreasonable physical antipathy" he experienced toward Ford, an antipathy which included, but was not limited to, his bad breath. His "acrid" bodily odor also was unbearable to Hemingway, who could not stay in the same room with Ford, so that he always tried to see him in the open air. When Hemingway was proofreading or evaluating manuscripts for Ford, he would always take his work out of the shop and sit on the walls of the *quais* under the shade of the trees. He preferred to work outside in any case, but as soon as Ford came into the shop, he had to go out. On a page of the manuscript, Hemingway compares Ford to a "great gasping fish breathing out a fouler breath than the spout of any whale."

This is a very contemptuous description of Ford—one which, however, adds little that is new concerning Hemingway's feelings toward his former friend. Whatever reference Hemingway made to Ford in his letters was always pejorative in one way or another. For instance, he once wrote to Pound that Ford was in town "with his new teeth and his infant daughter." Another time, he wrote that he did not believe in "springing full panoplied from womb of Jove a la F.M.F.," and, elsewhere, that Ford was going like wildfire in America, and that he was already regretting having hailed Hemingway as the "world's greatest writer" because he now wanted the place for himself. And there is, of course, the contemptuous reference he made to Ford's writing a "collossal trilogy of The Soldier (British) as represented by the Master himself. This refers to Ford not to Christ." Hemingway felt that if Ford dared risk showing his soldier at the front, it would be an "orgy of stylistic faking."[7] Seldom did Hemingway have a kind word to say about Ford.

The unpublished Fitzgerald chapter is a narrative of returning from a Princeton football game with Scott and Zelda, Pauline, and Mike Strater on 17 October 1928. After the Yale-Princeton game, which Princeton won 12 to 2, the five friends rode back to Philadelphia in the crowded after-football train. Fitzgerald's Buick and his chauffeur, Philippe, were waiting there to take them back to his house, Ellerslie mansion, in Wilmington.[8]

According to Hemingway, Fitzgerald, who took football seriously, had stayed sober through most of the game, but on the train he started talking to people he did not know, annoying some girls. Strater and Hemingway tried to soothe rising feelings and keep Fitzgerald out of trouble, which angered him. Finding a Princeton supporter reading a medical book, Scott started referring to the medical student in a voice loud enough for all to hear as "clap doctor," eventually telling the young man that there was nothing to be ashamed of about being a clap doctor. While Strater was apologizing for Fitzgerald, and the young man was trying to study, Scott's final comment was "Physician heal thyself" (File 182). Zelda, all this time, was sitting quietly with Pauline, paying no attention whatsoever to her husband's behavior. When they arrived in Philadelphia, they found Fitzgerald's car and his driver, a Frenchman who had been a taxi driver in Paris and one night had kept Scott from being robbed. In gratitude, Fitzgerald brought him back to America as a chauffeur. As they drove toward Wilmington, the Buick started overheating, and Philippe explained to Hemingway that neither Scott nor Zelda would allow him to put oil in the engine. According to Scott, only "worthless French cars need additional oil." Although Hemingway urged him to stop at a garage to put oil, water, and gas in the car, the chauffeur was afraid that it would make a dreadful scene. Finally, Philippe asked Hemingway to come with him the next day while the little girl was at church and go to a garage where they could change the oil and buy some extra cans of oil. Fitzgerald finally caught on to the conversation and complained that Philippe had some fixation about putting oil in the car all the time as if it were that ridiculous Renault which he and Ernest had driven up from Lyon. He felt that Philippe was a "good fellow and absolutely loyal," but that he knew nothing about American motors.

Hemingway's final comment is that it was a nightmare ride which ended with Scott and Zelda arguing about the proper turnoff leading to the house. Zelda claimed that the turnoff was much farther, and Scott that they had passed it. Philippe, obeying first Zelda, then Scott, waited until both were napping to make the right turnoff.

This narrative is very disparaging toward Scott, if less so toward Zelda. While Hemingway deleted two contemptuous references to Scott—referring to him as a "shanty Irish drunken crut," and indicating that he was abusive to the medical student mostly because he knew that under Hemingway and Strater's protection nothing would happen to him—the narrative systematically points out Scott's failings: his lack of worldly knowledge, his drunkenness and abusiveness, and his needing people to bail him out of trouble, whether in Paris or in the United States. Again, this sketch adds little that is new about Hemingway's opinion of Fitzgerald—an opinion that he voiced repeatedly in his work and in his correspondence.

It is remotely possible that Hemingway drafted this story about Fitzgerald on board ship, for he wrote on 1 November 1959 a note delivered to Andrew Turnbull on board the *Liberté*: "Am trying to write a little about him [Fitzgerald] when I knew him."⁹ Hemingway was carrying with him, at that time, the manuscript of the book which he intended to deliver to Scribner's on arrival in New York, and he may be referring either to the manuscript he had with him or to the actual writing of a new chapter.

Hemingway always patronized Scott, and there are few instances of his talking positively about him. Whatever comment he ever made about Scott was always tinged with pity or contempt, but he still felt he had never done Fitzgerald any harm. He wrote to Pound on 17 August 1956 that the only harm he ever did Fitzgerald was "to try to keep him from getting beat up by people he used to insult, try to straighten him out when he would get mixed and not use his over-flogged talent as he should." One can only wonder at Hemingway's intense dislike of Fitzgerald—a dislike which Scott's drunkenness and his good advice in the matter of *The Sun Also Rises* can hardly seem to justify, but a dislike which suggests a projection of Hemingway's own fears of personal and professional failure. Indeed, it seems that Hemingway resented particularly what he called Scott's "cheap Irish love of defeat, betrayal of himself." He felt that Scott was "damned perverse about wanting to fail" and saw the cause of it in his "damned, bloody romanticism" and in his not having grown up.¹⁰ Hemingway certainly did not sin by excess of romanticism or by a love of failure, at least outwardly, but he knew something of self-betrayal and self-destruction, by alcohol or otherwise.

The next two sketches are much more positive, perhaps because they deal with two people who could not possibly offer Hemingway any competition: Larry Gains (or "Gaines," in Hemingway's usual spelling), an unknown boxer, and Evan Shipman. Gains is described as a tall, long-muscled Negro heavyweight, with a pleasant, unmarked face, good manners, and strange, long hands (File 185). Upon returning to their apartment on the Rue du Cardinal-Lemoine after a trip, Hemingway and Hadley found among their mail a letter from Lou March, the sports editor of the *Toronto Star,* asking Hemingway to look after Gains and a note from Gains himself giving his address. In the morning sporting paper was also an article about Gains, describing him as the Canadian heavyweight champion who was making his début in France the following Saturday at the Stade Anastasie, Rue Pelleport. Hemingway comments that the real heavyweight champion of Canada was a seasoned professional named Jack Renault and that Larry Gains could not possibly remain upright in the same ring with him for long.

Hemingway meets Gains at the Café Napolitain on the Boulevard des Italiens and notices in particular his extremely long hands for a boxer, which could not possibly fit into any ordinary boxing gloves. On his way to France, Gains fought in England with a middleweight named Frank Moody, and he explained to Hemingway that he was beaten because the gloves were too short for his hands, which were so cramped as to be useless. After he had seen Larry work, Hemingway could think of a number of reasons why Moody, who was quite a good fighter, should have beaten him. Together, Hemingway and Gains go to the Stade Anastasie, which was situated in one of the toughest neighborhoods of Paris (Hemingway provides details on how to get there), close enough to "draw" from the Père Lachaise cemetery, should any of the dead be fight fans. The Stade Anastasie "was a sort of dance hall restaurant" with a few rooms over the restaurant where some of the fighters lived. Located in a wooded vacant lot with a wall around it, it had a ring set up under the trees and boxing apparatus in the dance hall where they could set up a ring in bad weather. On Saturday nights, during good weather, there were fights in the outdoor ring. Spectators could eat first at tables set up in the dance hall, served by the fighters. One could buy numbered seats at the entrance, or one could just buy an entry into the grounds and stand to watch the fights, but the prices were low and the food excellent.

Hemingway describes at length how Gains trained and how poor his performance was despite his long reach, his good left jab and nice, straight right hand, and his fantastic footwork: "He had wonderful legs and he moved faster and further and more uselessly than any heavyweight I have ever seen." Against a welterweight from Marseilles, Gains was helpless. "Suddenly Larry's arms were too long, there was no place for him to dance to and the boy was inside of him any time he wanted to be with both hands to the body and Larry knew nothing except to grab."

Hemingway quarrels with Gains's trainer because he wants him to teach Larry how to protect himself, and the trainer does not want to spoil his great footwork. Against a carcass carrier who does nothing but what the trainer tells him to do, Gains does better but shows new weaknesses. We have a lengthy description of that fight with the carcass carrier: Gains cannot hit to the belly or protect himself against a right hand, and "any heavyweight on earth has a right hand." There is a new quarrel between Hemingway and the trainer who does not want to spoil Larry's style.

For his first fight in Paris, Gains is lucky enough to have an opponent who does not know much more than the carcass man. When the boy, who had a hungry look and was just out of the army, started to "go," "Larry forgot all he knew and started swinging and never stopped until the boy slipped off the ropes and head first down onto the canvas." The audience loves it, but Gains apologizes later to Hemingway, who concludes the sketch with a comment on how strange a fight club the Stade Anastasie has turned out to be.

It seems that Hemingway actually had taken a real interest in Larry Gains, for he wrote a long letter to a lawyer, Maître Fabiani at 5 Place Edward VII, Paris, on 29 August 1923, introducing Gains to him and explaining how Gains was introduced to Louis Anastasie six weeks after his arrival in Paris and was signed up by Anastasie to a three-year exclusive contract. Hemingway feels Gains was taken advantage of, as he speaks no French and the contract includes no protection for him but forbids him to fight any matches for himself or for any other manager. Hemingway wants Fabiani to help Gains file an objection to the contract with the French Boxing Federation, and to check into the overall validity of the contract. Hemingway vouches for Gains's character and indicates that he was amateur champion heavyweight boxer of Canada before coming to France. The fact that Gains was still fighting at the Stade Anastasie on 27 February 1924 suggests that Fabiani was unable to help him.

According to Mary Hemingway, the Evan Shipman episode narrated in the next unpublished chapter took place in Cuba in either 1956 or 1957. This sketch, which either Hemingway or Mary, or possibly both, considered as a possible finishing chapter, is a hodgepodge of ideas, paragraphs, and sentences drafted many times by Hemingway,[11] and it includes a narrative of Shipman's last visit to Cuba, when he was suffering from cancer of the pancreas.

The first four paragraphs indicate once more that the book would give an account of the people and the places Hadley and Hemingway had known when they believed that they were invulnerable. Speaking in terms of skiing, he mentions that people no longer have to climb on seal skins since they have new bindings and that, in the end, it may be easier to break one's legs than one's heart, although people are stronger at the broken places, whatever breaks. (People ski much better now and are better taught: "They come down faster and they drop like birds" [File 124a].) People know many secrets now, just as Hemingway and his friends knew in their time, even if the problems are different. If people start early enough, know the secrets, and have enough talent, nothing may break. The way things are organized everywhere, no one should get killed. Despite all the new conveniences, no one can expect not to break a leg. Breaking a heart, though, is different, and one cannot break it if one does not have it. Hemingway concludes these four paragraphs in a somewhat confused fashion by saying that there may still be nothing there, "Nada," and that philosophers explain it very well.

The fifth paragraph, which precedes the story of Shipman's visit, discusses writing. The ideas expressed in this paragraph are random, with little logical progression. Hemingway mentions that there are secrets in writing, that nothing is ever lost, and that what is left out strengthens what is left in (not a new idea for him, by any stretch of the imagination). He also mentions that a writer does not possess anything until he has written about it, and that sometimes one has to throw things away or they may be stolen again.[12] He also makes some remarks about critics, whom he calls "explainers," and of whom there are many more than good writers. A writer must not complain too much of these explainers who tell him how to write and why, even if he does not agree with them. Some of them wish a writer luck and others do not, but good writing "does not destroy easily." It is made by alchemy, and much is written about it by people who do not know the alchemy. Hemingway also makes a rather cryptic remark about the difficulty of reconciling the "nothingness" a writer knows "and the part where [he lives] in other people." He is presumably talking about a writer's characters and what a writer puts of himself inside each character. What he may well be questioning is the validity of writing at all. Indeed, why create life in fiction if all life is futile per se—NADA? His final remark is that a writer must be careful of making jokes—a worry he often expresses in manuscripts and letters—clearly feeling that his jokes have been misunderstood and have backfired too often.[13]

The story of Shipman's last visit is a sad one, not only because of the atrocious pain he must have endured, but also because the sketch evidences Hemingway's view of Shipman as planet to his sun. Indeed, the only thing that Hemingway seems to be able to do is to portray Shipman as a tight-lipped stoic, enduring pain without complaint (much like Hemingway's traditional heroes) and worshipping at Hemingway's altar.

Shipman, who was covering the races at Gulf Stream Park for the *Morning Telegraph,* flew over to visit Hemingway. Hemingway felt that he had come to say good-bye but did not want to acknowledge it. Suffering from a cancer of the pancreas which was draining and which he was dressing himself, Shipman had brought neither morphine nor a prescription for it because he assumed that it could be bought easily in Cuba, which was no longer the case. Waiting for a doctor's visit in Hemingway's company, he was enduring much pain, apologizing for being a nuisance, and trying to chat as if he were not in agony. They talked about the funny parts and the great people of the old days. They recalled Desnos and the wonderful book he had given Hemingway, and the time when Shipman had turned up in Madrid after having been discharged from a hospital in Murcia, and how he slept under the covers across the foot of Hemingway's bed—Shipman had been wounded, was on convalescent leave, and was wearing canvas sandals in the snow. John Tsanakas was with them, slept on the floor, and cooked for them. They also talked about Shipman's fighting in the "other war," and about his feeling that it was like being back in school, and very much like being with horses. He felt that combat was interesting as a problem.

When the pain gets to be very bad, Shipman starts asking Hemingway to write about the early days. He feels that it has been good talking about Dunning and "*le fou dans le cabanon* on that wonderful voyage on the old *Paris,*" about Mr. Vosper and the waiters André and Jean, about Joan Miró and André Masson, and about when Hemingway had him on an allowance from the bank. He feels that Hemingway writes for all of them, and that he must go on doing it. He wants Hemingway to put it all in, the best parts, the bad parts, and Spain; to put in "the fun and the other that only [they] know who have been at some strange places in some strange times." Although Hemingway might not want to think back on it all, he must write about it. Shipman being in great pain, they talk a little about each other's health, Shipman being concerned about Hemingway's. They wonder why the doctor is not coming, and Hemingway is sorry that he probably got rid of the morphine he used to have on the boat. Finally, Shipman decides to go and lie down in the Little House, making sure, first, that Hemingway will go on with his writing; and meanwhile Hemingway calls for another doctor. Alone, Hemingway thinks about writing, feeling that this is what he was born to do, and would do again, and that, in the long run, what critics had to say about his work did not matter.

The last paragraph of the sketch is one that Hemingway had drafted repeatedly for his introduction or conclusion. It talks about there being "remises," or storage places, in the mind where one can leave things as one does in a trunk or a duffel bag, such as personal effects, or the unpublished poems of Evan Shipman, or arms and marked maps that one should turn over to the authorities. He states again that the book contains material "from the remises of [his] memory and [his] heart," although "the one has been tampered with"—probably referring to the electroshocks he was treated with at the Mayo Clinic—"and the other does not exist"—probably referring to the fact that his heart has been broken. The theme of the broken heart is one to which Hemingway returns more than once, not only in the manuscripts of *A Moveable Feast* but also in a narrative entitled "A Story to Skip or A Badly Organized Story of No Importance" (File 721).

The chapter about Bumby dramatizes Hemingway's knowledge of French cafés, Bumby's oft-repeated presence with him while he was working in cafés, and Fitzgerald in a sober moment. The mood of the narrative and the tone of the conversation are peculiar in that Bumby is portrayed as a child but speaks in his father's voice. While children will tend to imitate their parents, the case here borders on parody, which is clearly not what Hemingway intended. There is some conscious humor in the narrative, though, when Hemingway reports that Bumby would confide in him some of the things he had learned from Tonton (Mr. Rohrback, their maid's husband, who had been a "MARECHAL De Logis or SERGEANT MAJOR in the PROFESSIONAL FRENCH MILITARY establishment"). Apparently, Tonton played a great part in Bumby's formative years, since Bumby spent the summer months with him and "Marie-Cocotte" at Mur de Bretagne when his parents were in Spain. After Hemingway had finished his work at the Closerie des Lilas or at the café on the Place St.-Michel, Bumby would sometimes come out with expressions learned from Tonton, such as *"Tu sais, Papa, que les femmes pleure comme les enfants pisse?"*[14] or "Papa four *poules* passed while you were working that were not bad." These attempts at behaving like a grown-up are amusing, in particular when matched with other childish traits, such as calling Sylvia Beach "Silver Beach." However, the rest of the time Bumby is made to speak and behave sententiously, in his father's fashion. For instance, he comments that he observes the Parisian *poules*—"One observes them"—and that Tonton is a great soldier who has taught him much. When his father tells him he is going out to lunch with some people, Bumby asks if they are interesting people; when he is told that Scott is sick because he drinks too much and cannot work, he inquires whether Scott does not respect his *métier* and, later, whether Scott has been demolished mentally by the war. When the three of them meet in a café and both Hemingway and Fitzgerald order mineral water, Bumby orders a beer to make an example, because "Tonton says that a man should first learn to control himself." There is also bitter irony at the end of the sketch when Bumby concludes that he is very happy and that he and his parents have no problems of their own.

Hemingway discourses for a paragraph on French cafés and on the fact that people had private cafés where they never invited anyone, and where they would work, or read, or receive their mail. People would also have another café where they would meet their mistresses, and yet another, a neutral one, where they might invite friends to meet their mistresses. And finally, there were cheap, convenient places where everyone would go and eat on neutral grounds. Hemingway felt, though, that the organization of Montparnasse's cafés, with the Dôme, the Rotonde, the Select, and later the Coupole and the Dingo bar, was quite different.

Although Fitzgerald is dramatized in this sketch as being temporarily sober, the Fitzgerald-Hemingway relationship is a traditional one: Ernest is superior to Scott and instructs him about Tonton, the French military establishment, the Napoleonic campaigns, the war of 1870 and the war of 1914–18. Hemingway had friends who had participated in the wars of 1870 and 1914–18, and he could tell Scott things that would shock him. He told Scott about the mutinies in the French army after the "Nivelle offensive at the Chemin des Dames," and how such men as Tonton were an anachronism, "but an absolutely valid thing."

Hemingway, though, makes the point that Fitzgerald turns up drunk frequently, that his wife is jealous of his work, and that he faces almost insurmountable problems as a writer. Bumby is more optimistic, and feels that, since Scott was so nice and sober that day and did not molest his father, he might well surmount his problems.

"On Writing in the First Person" [15] is a very short essay—the equivalent of about two typewritten pages—in which Hemingway discusses very briefly three ideas: the art of writing in the first person, the pointlessness of biographical literary criticism, and the fact that he wrote not only from his personal experience but also from the experiences of people he knew. Hemingway thus points out that it is perfectly natural for people who read a story told in the first person to believe that the events related actually happened to the author—indeed that is the test of a well-told story, a story that has been made "real"—because the author had to make those events happen to the person telling the story. If the author is successful in making the story happen to the characters, the reader will also believe that it happened to him. The story will enter the reader's subconscious mind and become part of his experience and of his memory. Such a story is not an easy one to write.

But it is easy, or at least always possible, for what Hemingway calls "the members of the private detective school of literary criticism" to prove that what happens to the first-person narrator could not possibly have happened to the author, that the author could not have done everything the narrator does, or even any of it. This rather deprecatory comment about literary criticism is hardly surprising; in fact, it is rather muted in comparison with his usually vitriolic comments on literary critics, whom he occasionally called the eunuchs of literature. Although Hemingway displays here the antagonism and willful obtuseness that characterized his dealings with literary critics, his conclusion is not without merit: "What importance this has or what it proves except that the writer is not devoid of imagination or the power of invention I have never understood." This is clearly a valid point for fiction. But what about autobiography? What about *A Moveable Feast*, where the author and the narrator are both Hemingway, talking about Hemingway and the very real people he knew? Can imagination and the power of invention have a role in autobiography which is supposed to rely on facts and truth, at least to the extent of the writer's personal vision and honesty? There is little doubt that Hemingway was angered by critics and readers alike, as he felt that they really do not know what they want. He explained his position on 28 July 1957 to "Jake," again indicating that if a book is written in the first person and the writer has invented well enough, everyone will believe that it happened, which is as it should be, although the narrator is not the author; the narrator is somebody the author made up. "But people read a book invented in the first person and then if they find it is made up and invented away from life they start blaming the writer and call him a phony. If he invents so they believe it completely they say oh he is just a good reporter." While there is some validity to the point,

Hemingway forgets two major things, one which applies particularly to him and one which applies to all writers. In his particular case, he always obfuscated the issues of fiction versus fact or reporting, claiming that some of his books, such as *Green Hills of Africa* and *A Moveable Feast*, were absolutely true books about what had really happened when, in fact, they were just as fictional as anything else he had written. On the other hand, books marketed as fiction, such as *The Sun Also Rises*, were so closely and consciously based on actual facts that occurrences and characters were readily recognizable, and that some of the people who recognized themselves in the characters of *The Sun Also Rises* and had participated in the events called it thinly fictionalized reporting. In such a case, it is indeed not only normal but expected that critics should attempt to separate fact from fiction—the bait is ostentatiously there—and the author can hardly complain of a situation he has himself created. Indeed, establishing the relationship between fact and fiction in the contexts of fiction and autobiography will reveal a psychological pattern that will help one understand the writer better. What Hemingway refuses to accept the consequences of is that a writer, or an artist, can create only out of himself, out of his own experience (be it firsthand or secondhand), out of his own psychological makeup. Therefore, whatever he produces reveals him. This is exactly what Flaubert suggested when he said, "I am Madame Bovary." Obviously, he was not literally Emma, but she embodied what he might have been had he been born in her circumstances; she was a self-projection, embodying his fears, his romanticism, and his views on the dangers of the education of women in his time.

Flaubert based himself on fact, too—what he had witnessed or heard about, his experiences and those of his friends—just as Hemingway did, but he was willing to accept the relationship existing between the creator and his creation, which Hemingway was not willing to do. Hemingway's refusal to accept the obvious and the logical consequences of his *métier* is deeply revealing on the psychological level. One may also find there the reason he never offered a perceptive and coherent reflection on the art of writing—the whole theory of the iceberg having in no way originated with him. This complete refusal to accept the relationship between the mind that creates and that which is created, at least when he was himself concerned, accounts for his intense dislike of literary critics who presumed to establish that relationship. Critics, of course, do not escape the common plight, and they too write out of themselves, using the writer and his work as their *donnée*. Why, then, hate them so much, when they are doing in a different discipline exactly what the writer himself is doing?

When Hemingway was working in Paris in the early days, he would invent not only from his own personal experience but also from the experiences of the people he had known who were not writers. He felt lucky that his best friends were not writers and that he had known many people who were articulate. In Italy, during World War I, he learned of many things that happened to people who had been in the war in all its stages. Thus, he knew many hundred times as much as he had actually experienced, and his own experiences gave him a "touchstone by which [he] could tell whether stories were true or false and being wounded was a password." After the war, Hemingway tells us that he spent a lot of time in the 19th Ward and in the Italian quarters in Chicago with an Italian friend he had made while he was in the hospital in Milan. He also feels that his experience was expanded by the people he knew in the British army and in their ambulance service. Much that he later invented from was what he had actually learned from them. Then Hemingway begins to tell us, without naming him, about Eric Dorman-Smith—an Irish officer in the British army—who was his best friend for many years.

"On Writing in the First Person" ends with a couple of disconnected paragraphs: one that seems to be an early draft for the beginning of "A Matter of Measurements," introducing a lunch that Hemingway and Fitzgerald had at Michaud's before Scott "knew that Zelda was crazy." The second talks about learning to know one's quarter in Paris, where one could find everything one needed to live except books and money.

Hemingway was occasionally tempted to write about his craft, as he did in this unpublished section, in the deleted section of "Big Two-Hearted River," and in the long draft about writing in File 845, where he acknowledges at the end that writers will often lie. But his ideas about fiction and the craft of writing do not amount to anything like a coherent philosophy—at least, nothing half as coherent or perceptive as what was offered by such writers as Edgar Allan Poe, Stephen Crane, Frank Norris, Emile Zola, Flaubert, Jack London, and a hundred others.

There are a few rough drafts that could possibly have been related to the writing of *A Moveable Feast,* but the relationship is too remote for them to be considered as actual drafts for the book. Among these are a description of a man living alone in Paris with his three-year-old son (File 446a), an interesting sketch about Hadley's pregnancy before they left for Toronto (File 409a), and a sketch of a man living in Paris and getting a divorce (File 529a).

The sketch in File 409a is quite clearly an early manuscript, dealing mainly with Hemingway's inability to write: he cannot write because Hadley is pregnant and feels sick. Hemingway resents the days that are wasted on little things, such as making breakfast and housecleaning, which barely leave an hour to work before lunch. In the afternoons, people come to visit. The night before he could not sleep because Hadley was hungry and woke him up. They are leaving for Toronto in three weeks, and he wishes she would get well. The connection with *A Moveable Feast* resides mainly in the idea that people take time away from work and are the limiters of happiness.

According to Carlos Baker, the sketch of the man living alone with his three-year-old son in Paris, in a sixth-floor apartment with a balcony looking out into the street and across the roofs of other houses, because his wife is away, dramatizes Hemingway's taking care of Bumby while Hadley was in Chartres in 1926 and Hemingway was staying in Gerald Murphy's studio.[16] The son speaks French a little and loves papa very much but does not miss him, or anyone else, when he is away. There is no mention in the sketch of why the wife is not there. On the verso of the second page is a short sketch on Italy, suggesting that this may well be an early manuscript. This sketch is not very interesting, except that, by implication, it suggests that Hemingway felt abandoned: "his wife was not there." This ties in with "My Own Life" and suggests that Hemingway may have resented Hadley's not accepting his affair with Pauline and learning to live with it. In both these sketches it is Hadley who is gone, rather than he who left her. In fact, the forty-six-page story of a man living in Paris and getting a divorce makes it quite clear that Hemingway would have liked Hadley to beg him to stay.

There are in fact three versions of this story, one of which is quite different from the other two. The version in File 648b features the same characters as File 529a—James Allen and Dorothy Rogers—and the stories are similar. The version in File 648a, however, differs significantly from the other two, and the name of the male protagonist is Philip Haines. What seems particularly important about the version in File 529a is that starting with page eleven it is written on the same type of rather peculiar paper as the draft of his meeting Fitzgerald (File 486).[17] This suggests that the two sketches were probably written during the same period, although it is not in itself sufficient proof. The James Allen story is in many ways autobiographical and, as one would expect, involves some wishful thinking.

James Allen lives in a studio at the end of a courtyard closed by an iron gate and opening into a street that runs parallel to the Avenue du Maine. If Hemingway is talking about Murphy's studio, it is a little confusing, since the Rue Froidevaux runs perpendicular rather than parallel to the Avenue du Maine. This type of error would tend to link this story to the time Hemingway was writing *A Moveable Feast,* since there are several similar errors in the book. Allen has become a painter because he feels that the scenes which attended his breakup with his wife, Caroline, ruined him as a writer and made him lose confidence in his work. He is so poor that he has to cut pieces of cardboard to put inside his shoes, which need resoling. He thinks back on the five years of happiness with his wife, and how his writing was "very delicate and unreal," and how, four months earlier, he had fallen in love with Dorothy Rogers, who was now in America waiting for his divorce to come through. He also recalls how Caroline had found out about the affair and had accused him of it. There is a random encounter at the Closerie des Lilas with Caroline, who wants him to give up Dorothy and come back to her. She makes a scene, accusing him of marrying women for their money, and begs him to come back to her. They sleep together, have another scene during which he treats her in the most insulting fashion, thanking her for the "favor." She slaps him and starts crying. The next day, Allen experiences some remorse for his behavior and does his best to justify himself. His self-justification is a masterpiece of hypocrisy and self-righteousness: he is more remorseful for having betrayed Dorothy with Caroline than he ever was for betraying Caroline with Dorothy, and he broke up his marriage because he felt that Dorothy and he had something together that justified anything they did. He eventually concludes that this last betrayal is all right because "there could be no betrayal by his body unless there was one in the spirit." One need only read Hadley's letters to be convinced that she was not one to humiliate herself the way Caroline does and accept anything in order to keep her husband. That Hemingway would have wished her to be less strong and decisive when he was himself wallowing in self-pity is also easy to believe, for it was indeed Hadley who had made her mind up that she wanted a divorce and that there was nothing to talk about except details. As she wrote to him on 19 November 1926:

Haven't I yet made it quite plain that I *want* to start proceedings for a divorce from you—right away? Thus the three months separation between you and Pauline is nil as far as I am concerned—whether you communicate with her about any or all of your and my arrangements makes no difference to me. If you for any reasons that I don't know feel any hesitation I will start things myself—tho I think you are much more likely to find a *good* lawyer quickly.

We are indeed very far from the groveling Caroline, and Hemingway's ego must have suffered a blow to see that Hadley was not willing to fight for him on his own terms.

These three sketches are therefore only remotely related to the writing of *A Moveable Feast,* except for the James Allen one which seems indirectly related to it because of the mood of self-righteousness vis-à-vis one's own guilt which also pervades "There Is Never Any End to Paris," because it seems to offer an alternative, and, to Hemingway's ego, more satisfactory dramatization of his breakup with Hadley than that which is likely to have taken place, and because it was probably written shortly before Hemingway began the actual writing of *A Moveable Feast.*

It was probably a wise decision not to publish the six chapters Hemingway had drafted, as they bring little that is new. The two on Ford and Fitzgerald keep flogging horses that are already dead, the one on Shipman appears almost as a parody of the Hemingway hero, the one on Bumby is of little interest and appears as an unintentional self-parody; few people probably care to know about Larry Gains, and the chapter on writing is not elaborate or perceptive enough to add anything to literary theory. That Hemingway had wanted to write about many other people and events is repeatedly made clear in the drafts of his preface, but these seem to be the only other chapters he had drafted, despite his claims that much more had been written but that it was part of another book. It is interesting, though, to see how cleverly he recycled material that he had deleted from earlier books and stories for a variety of reasons. These borrowings from earlier manuscripts, whether they actually were textual borrowings or simply recalled from previous work, are in fact much fewer than one was led to believe.

CHAPTER SEVEN

Manuscript Revisions

A STUDY OF THE various stages of the composition of a book is usually remarkably rewarding in that it documents the creative process better and more objectively than any other type of study. In the case of *A Moveable Feast,* a detailed study of Hemingway's changes, deletions, additions, and corrections evidences his state of mind when he wrote the book, his hesitations, his emotional involvement with his subject matter, his nostalgia, and his awareness that his portrayal of others was not always accurate or fair, and that he chose to fictionalize reality in order to make it fit into an ordered pattern. It also documents his writing technique, the relative ease with which he wrote dialogue as opposed to the difficulties he experienced with descriptions and the structure of long sentences, as well as his subsequent breaking down of them into the short sentences that made him famous.

Hemingway wrote most of the chapters of *A Moveable Feast* in several stages. First, he wrote a longhand draft in pencil, the neatness of which depended on the difficulty he experienced in writing it. Generally, conversations are seldom changed or rewritten, but descriptions are often revised extensively, even at this early stage. Additions are integrated between the lines, sometimes in the margins, and occasionally all around the page, forming a circle around the original draft. This manuscript was then typed with a carbon copy. Some chapters were typed by "Betty" or by "Val," as evidenced by the directives occasionally found on the messier pages, but most were typed by Mary Hemingway, triple-spaced with paragraph indentations of some twenty to twenty-five spaces.[1] Very occasionally, Hemingway composed directly on the typewriter. In such cases, his typescripts are easily distinguishable because of the wide spaces he left between words and punctuation marks. After his manuscript had been typed, Hemingway corrected the typescripts, but did so in a very erratic fashion. He usually made changes and major corrections on only one of the copies, either the original or the carbon copy, the other one being left uncorrected or merely with some typographical corrections. Hemingway seems to have followed no pattern in these corrections, correcting at random either the original or the carbon copy, although most of the corrections were made on the carbon copy. The corrected typescript was then retyped professionally, perhaps by Betty, again with a carbon copy. These second-stage typescripts, originals and carbons, bear few corrections in Hemingway's hand, suggesting that he may not have reread all of them. Again, what corrections or changes there are appear on either the original or the carbon copy with no logical pattern, but mostly on the carbon copy.

Changes occurred at every stage of the typing. The variations existing between the manuscript and the first typescript consist primarily of corrections, insertions, or deletions of punctuation (occasionally ill-advised), corrections or insertions of spelling errors, the occasional breaking up of a lengthy sentence, the underlining of book titles, foreign words, and the names of some foreign places and products, corrections in the spelling of names, and minor (at times, less than minor) stylistic changes, mostly made by Mary. For instance, Hemingway's typical spelling of words such as "its-self" is corrected to "itself"; words such as "accrochable" and "inaccrochable" are underlined; and the spelling of names such as "Turgeniev" and "Doestoeiovsky" are corrected to "Turgenev" and "Dostoyevsky." Errors in the typing are usually obviously due to the difficulty in reading the messier passages, although, at times, they are also due to inattention. For instance, on various occasions, the typist read diagonally and skipped a line, thus changing significantly the meaning of a sentence, and at times making the sentence a statement puzzling in meaning if not necessarily in structure.

When the typescript corrected by Hemingway was retyped, new corrections and changes were introduced, similar in kind to the ones just described between the manuscript and the first typescript. Again, sentence fragments were occasionally dropped. For instance, in chapter 20, "There Is Never Any End to Paris," the italicized portion of the following sentence was dropped at the stage of the second typescript: "Another year a former German naval officer with a shaven head and scars came to give a lecture *with lantern slides on the great and unappreciated German victory of the battle of Jutland*" (203).

The manuscripts of *A Moveable Feast* are organized in two major groups. Files 121 to 185 are the drafts of *A Moveable Feast* arranged by chapters. For instance, Files 128, 129, and 130 are the manuscript and the typescripts for "A Good Café on the Place St.-Michel," with 130 being a carbon copy of 129. Originally, all the chapter drafts and typescripts were found in four groups, usually more or less reflecting an order of progressive development. Not all the chapters were found in all four groups, and their arrangement within the group was somewhat random. The groups were broken up and the manuscripts and typescripts reorganized so that the manuscripts and typescripts for each chapter would be together, but the individual drafts were numbered one, two, three, and four, so that the original organization of the manuscript might be preserved.

The second main group, Files 188 and 189, is composed of an entirely new typescript of the book, with the exception of "Birth of a New School," which Hemingway clearly did not intend to use in the book. Similarly, there is no Preface in this typescript, and the chapters remain untitled, as in the preceding manuscripts and typescripts, except for "Ford Madox Ford and the Devil's Disciple." Moreover, the chapters in this second group are still in Hemingway's original order, not in the order in which they were eventually published.[2] Generally, File 188 includes the originals of this typescript, while 189 includes the carbon copies. However, it is not always easy to differentiate the originals from the carbon copies. Files 188–89 also include two sets of chapters 5 and 6, one of which is identified in Mary Hemingway's handwriting as "Rewritten and Revised Chaps 5 & 6."

Most of the chapters are quite clean, having undergone no extensive rewriting; however, six chapters—"A False Spring," "The End of an Avocation," "A Strange Enough Ending," "The Man Who Was Marked for Death," "People of the Seine," and "Scott Fitzgerald"—bear many revisions at every stage of the manuscript. It is clear that Hemingway found it difficult to write them, but still much less difficult than writing the Preface and "There Is Never Any End to Paris," both of which were so extensively rewritten that it is almost impossible to find one's way through the maze of changes. Overall, one might say that Hemingway experienced few problems in writing the chapters where his memory served him well and which dealt with specific memories and experiences rather than general ones. But, more importantly, the very messy chapters are those which deal with issues with which Hemingway was still emotionally involved: the Preface, in which he tries to explain the rationale for the book and to defend both the point of view he adopts and the presence of inaccuracies; the last chapter which dramatizes his breakup with Hadley; and the negative dramatizations of his breakup with Gertrude Stein and of his relationships with Ernest Walsh and F. Scott Fitzgerald. "The End of an Avocation," in a way, also dramatizes a negative experience in the lives of Hemingway and Hadley because betting on horses came between them, and perhaps also because he still experienced a certain amount of guilt at having continued going to the races with Pauline immediately after having done so with Hadley. On the other hand, two chapters which are also negative portrayals of friends—"Ford Madox Ford and the Devil's Disciple" and "An Agent of Evil"—are extremely clean, perhaps because Hemingway had at hand the first notebook of *The Sun Also Rises* and either the original or a copy of his letter to Pound of 15 October 1924. "Hawks Do Not Share" and "A Matter of Measurements," paradoxically, are also quite clean, perhaps because Hemingway had no qualms about hating Zelda openly, and possibly because the incident with Scott at Michaud's had actually happened and he remembered it clearly—at least he had narrated it recently in similar terms in his correspondence.[3]

The most effective way of documenting the composition of the book may well be to examine the chapters in their published order and, not mentioning minor corrections or changes in punctuation or spelling and minor stylistic revisions, to discuss at each stage the changes that cast some light on the text, either stylistically, thematically, or psychologically. Direct quotations from the manuscripts and typescripts are shown in boldface.

THE PREFACE

There is no coherent manuscript or typescript of the Preface which can be attributed to Hemingway. There are some thirty pages of rough drafts[4] which Hemingway was uncertain how to use. These drafts include mostly disconnected sentences and paragraphs which might be organized into the following subjects: 1) whether the book is fiction and whether people, Hadley in particular, will understand; 2) Hadley as the heroine of the book; 3) Pauline and others; 4) Paris; and 5) skiing. There are also a few irrelevant sentences and paragraphs which seem only very remotely related to the topics of these drafts. Finally, Hemingway did not always know whether he wanted to use some of these topics in the Preface or in a concluding chapter.

It is clear that the book's being fiction was uppermost in Hemingway's mind, for he returns to this idea some eighteen times in those drafts, continuously rewording the statement and backing it up with various justifications. It is interesting to note that the editors printed almost verbatim, but with a very significant change, one of Hemingway's sentences: ***This book is fiction but there is always *a* chance that such a *work* of fiction may throw some light on what has been written as fact*** (I.W.D.F.P.T.).[5] One can only wonder that, despite the fact that he had stated unequivocally at least eighteen times that **the book is fiction**, his editors changed his statement to the more fuzzy **If the reader prefers, this book may be regarded as fiction**. Hemingway also repeats numerous times that he has left out much, altered, and distorted, and that he hopes that Hadley understands why he had to do it and forgives him. He is fully aware, however, that others might not be so forgiving and that they might even sue him. Hemingway states clearly that no one can write true facts in reminiscences, that all remembrance of things past is indeed fiction, and that he has tried above all to make the book interesting. The following paragraph, for instance, was not used in the published Preface:

> This book is fiction. I have left out much and changed and eliminated and I hope Hadley understands. A book of fiction may eliminate and distort but it tries to give a fictional picture of a time and the people in it. No one can write true facts in reminiscences. Evan would back you up but he is dead. Scott would disagree. Miss Moorhead would sue if you published anything against Walsh and she has many letters and much basis to sue on. The story about Walsh will have to come out.

Hemingway was worried that even if he changed the names and called it all fiction people would still sue him, even after he was dead. Of course, Hadley would not sue him because she is the heroine of the book. He returns several times to that idea, and to the thought that she would understand why he had to do what he did. There is a rather touching mention in File 122 of hearing someone's voice on the phone and knowing that **they still are and that they deserve it**, which can only refer to his call to Hadley of March 1961 when he wanted her to remind him of the names of the man and woman who had exploited young writers in Paris in 1925.

Hemingway was not sure whether he wanted to have a concluding chapter or not: on the one hand, he writes in File 122, **There is no last chapter**, and in File 124 he has a few pages headed **Last Chapter**, with insertions, false starts, and some questioning (**"Last Chapter/Still not right"**), as well as some dates: Feb. 7, March 9, March 14, March 20. Whether in the Preface or in a concluding chapter, he wanted to mention the things he had not written about and why. He felt that he had cut the book ruthlessly and had omitted many of the people and voyages. He returns about four times to the fact that he wrote about Pauline, and that this would have been a good way to end the book, but that he decided against it because it was a beginning and not an end. He saved what he wrote about her, though, for the beginning of another book to be entitled **"The Pilot Fish and the Rich, and Other Stories."**[6] There was much more to write about Fitzgerald too, **his complicated tragedies, his generosities and his devotions**, and about the Paris they both knew and loved. André Masson and Joan Miró are not in the book either as they should be (**and will be**—suggesting that Hemingway had hopes of adding some chapters), nor are the stories of André Gide's teaching him how to punish a cat and of Evan Shipman and Harold Stearns's running through Shipman's fortune when he came of age. Occasionally, Hemingway seems to be losing his memory for he also mentions among the stories that are not in the book that of Pound and Eliot and Bel Esprit and the story of the time when Pound left him a jar of opium for Cheever Dunning, both of which are, of course, in *A Moveable Feast*. One should recall that by 6 February 1961, as suggested by his letter to Harry Brague, he seemed no longer to want to use the Bel Esprit section of the Pound chapter or the chapter on Dunning in the book. Very conscious of his omissions, Hemingway states at least three times that he has tried to write by the old rule that a book should be judged by **the man who writes it, by the excellence of the material that he eliminates**. This particular statement usually comes as a conclusion to his discussions as to why he did not write more about Fitzgerald.

In the drafts of File 124, Hemingway makes two major attempts at a paragraph about there never being any ending to Paris. His editors used one of these two paragraphs, with some editing, at the end of the book. He also seems concerned by the impossibility of putting all of the Paris he and Fitzgerald knew into a single book. Hemingway mentions that it was the time when Hadley and he thought that they were invulnerable (though they were not), and that nobody climbs on skis any longer, that most people break their legs, and that it may be easier to break one's legs than to break one's heart, although people say that everything breaks and that, sometimes, many are stronger at the broken places. This topic seems to have been close to his heart for he has many similar drafts and statements in other files, in particular in 126-1 and in a draft of an unrelated short story tentatively entitled "A Story to Skip" or "A Badly Organized Story of No Importance," beginning, **And every July they took him out and broke his heart** (File 721).

Among the apparently unrelated statements, there is a two-page discussion on no one's agreeing with anyone, on his having seen in his time four honest people disagreeing about what had happened at a certain time on a certain day. Hemingway also makes some confused and confusing statements about tearing up orders, and about false statements written long afterwards being used as evidence and being presented to replace the written orders—all of which probably relates to his military hearing during World War II when he lied about bearing arms as a journalist. This whole discussion seems to be tied up in his mind with the idea that it is necessary to write about the past as fiction. The link is tenuous, but these statements seem related to his fears of being sued and of being proven a liar; however justified, his fears seem to tie in well with the persecution complex which plagued his last years.

"A GOOD CAFE ON THE PLACE ST.-MICHEL"

File 128 is quite clean. There is no extensive rewriting of any kind, merely occasional words added, deleted, or crossed out. Sentence fragments are often integrated within the text, either between the lines or in the margins; all the revisions evidence a descriptive and stylistic concern, but, unlike some of the revisions of later chapters, no emotional involvement. Among the stylistic revisions, one should note the following:

P. 3, ll. 4–6: the sentence is revised as follows: **The leaves *would* [C] lay sodden in the rain *and* [C] The wind *would beat on the drive* [C] drove the rain against the big green autobuse*s* [C] at the terminal and the café des Amateurs *would be* [C] was crowded. . . .** Clearly the deletions lighten the sentence, which was published with only one very minor change of punctuation

P. 3, l. 8: Hemingway replaces **bad-smelling** by **evily run**, with a question mark concerning spelling in the left-hand margin

P. 4, ll. 2–5: the sentence is revised as follows: **The tank wagons were painted brown and beige and in the moonlight** *when they worked the rue Cardinale Lemoine their wheeled horse-drawn cylinders* [A] **looked like Braque paintings**

P. 4, ll. 14–15: here Hemingway hesitates between the use of **you** and **I** in the sentence fragment **where I had a room on the top floor where I worked.** He first used **you** in both instances, then crossed them out and replaced them by **I,** then crossed these out and returned to the use of **you.** It is his editors who, after his death, changed back to the use of **I**

P. 4, ll. 29–30: the sentence fragment is revised as follows: **Place du Panthéon and cut in for shelter** *behind the sorbonne* [C] *and* **to the** *finally* [C] **right and finally came out**

P. 5, ll. 22–24: the sentence is revised as follows: **She was very pretty with a** *fresh new painted* **face** *like* [C] *fresh as a newly minted coin if they minted coins in smooth* [A] *flesh* [C] *flesh with rain-freshened skin* [A], **and her hair was black . . . .**

The typescripts were both corrected by Hemingway, although File 129, the original, bears fewer changes than 130, the carbon copy. The changes that occurred in the typing are minimal, and of the usual kind— the most interesting being the switching of the sentence **That was where we could go** from the beginning of the second paragraph on page 7 to the end of the first paragraph. The second paragraph thus begins in File 129 with **Travelling third-class on the train was not expensive.** File 129 bears few corrections, except for the correction of a few typographical errors. The first sentence, **The bad weather would come in one day when the fall was over,** is crossed out and replaced by a large "I." File 130 bears further corrections and additions. The corrections found in 129 are repeated here, and there are further corrections of typographical and spelling errors. The top of the page is annotated with "**Provisional EH**" and "**A**" on the left-hand side, "**Chapter One**" in the middle, and "**Ok?**" "**EH**" on the right-hand side. The following corrections should be noted:

P. 4, ll. 2–3: **beige** is changed to **saffron color**

P. 4, l. 16: Hemingway qualifies **eight flights** by adding **either six or**

P. 7, l. 5: the sentence is corrected as follows: *Below Les Avants there was* [A] *We Knew* [C] **a chalet** *where we had lived* [C] **where the pension was wonderful . . .**

P. 7, ll. 9–11: **Travelling third class on the train it was not expensive. The pension cost very little more than we spent in Paris.** is crossed out after an attempt at revision. An unreadable sentence is written above it, and then crossed out. **Was** is replaced by **would,** and **be** is added after **not,** thus suggesting that Hemingway considered writing **would not be expensive;** but these changes are crossed out too.

Files 188–89 incorporate all the corrections, additions, and deletions made to Files 129 and 130. They also correct a few errors still present in Files 129–30, such as **café,** instead of **cafè, cesspool** instead of **cesspool.** They also change **Taty** to **Tatie,** but leave misspellings such as **rue Cardinale Lemoine.** The i of **poivrottes,** which has been continuously misspelt as **povrottes,** is inserted in pencil. File 189 bears no handwritten corrections and is a carbon copy of 188.

"MISS STEIN INSTRUCTS"

File 131 is also a clean manuscript. The descriptions are more heavily revised than the conversations which bear almost no corrections. Hemingway has a tendency to refer to Gertrude Stein as Gertrude and then correct himself and use Miss Stein instead. Sentences such as **I was learning something from the paintings of Cézanne. . . . Besides it was a secret** (p. 13, ll. 17–23) are added between the lines, up the right-hand margin, across the top of the page, and then down the left-hand margin. Hemingway again hesitates between the use of **you** and **I** in the sentence **If I walked down . . . I could walk through the gardens . . .** (p. 13, ll. 10–11). The sentence fragment **the mores of the** *fifteenth street police station* **[C] different parts of that city** (p. 18, l. 22) is revised as indicated.

File 132 is headed in pencil with a "**II.**" The carbon copy, File 133, is headed in pencil "**B**" "**Chapter Two**" and there are a few pencil revisions and additions in Hemingway's hand. For instance: (p. 12, last line) **very** is crossed out before **good and severe discipline;** (p. 13, l. 15) **and the Jeu de Paume** is inserted after **the Louvre;** (p. 15, l. 3) **house** is crossed out and replaced by **flat;** (l. 7) **them all** is crossed out and replaced by **most of,** which is in turn crossed out and replaced by **some of them;** (p. 19, l. 14) **you** in **brought you a bottle of Marsala** is crossed out; (l. 16) **I asked** is added; (ll. 19–21) the sentence beginning **I gave his name** is inserted; (p. 21, ll. 4–5) **around it instead of through it** is inserted; (l. 6)

so is crossed out and replaced by **very** before **brightly**; (ll. 7–8) **almost in would cure almost anything** is crossed out and then reinstated.

There are four major revisions in File 133: 1) The two sentences **When I was through . . . in the room at night** (p. 12, ll. 4–8) formed a separate paragraph. In File 133 a pencilled arrow links these two sentences to the preceding paragraph. 2) The whole paragraph which is on p. 15, ll. 20–29 does not exist in File 131 and, of course, in Files 132–33. Instead, Hemingway has three sentences to the effect that he understood what Gertrude Stein was saying, but did not agree with her point of view. He did not want to argue with his elders and would much rather hear them talk; many of the things Stein said were very intelligent. That afternoon she told them how to buy pictures. Hemingway then tries to insert something like the text of the new paragraph, but gives up; instead he adds a handwritten page headed **"insert to page 7"** with what is basically the text of that paragraph. 3) The sentence **She had discovered . . . that were valid and valuable** (p. 17, ll. 21–24) was first added at the end of the first paragraph on page 17, and then crossed out in red pencil. This same sentence, with the ending **and she talked well about them** added, is then inserted in pencil at the end of the next paragraph after **judgement.** 4) After **Work would cure almost anything,** Hemingway adds in pencil at the end of File 133, after crossing out the period, **I believed then and I believe now . . . in the mountains** (p. 21, ll. 7–14).

Files 188–89 incorporate all the changes made in File 133 but drop the passage about Hemingway's not agreeing with Stein and his not wanting to argue with his elders. Apparently, Hemingway had not intended to drop this passage since he had not crossed it out in File 133; but he either did not object to its deletion or, more likely, did not notice its disappearance since he did not reintegrate it in either File 188 or 189. **Trying** instead of **tyring,** and **Boutet de Monville** instead of **Bautel de Monville** are corrected on File 189.

"UNE GENERATION PERDUE"

File 134 is a very clean manuscript. The deletions are the most noteworthy changes, in particular:

P. 25, l. 19: the first sentence of the third paragraph is followed by *Gertrude and I talked often about reading books.* [C]

P. 27, l. 13: the sentence continued with *and the good books of Raymond Chandler.* [C]

P. 27, l. 16: "**La Maison du Canal**" is followed by *they were given to me by Janet Flanner,* [C]

P. 28, l. 16: after **supporters,** the following sentence is crossed out but reappears in substantially the same form a few lines later in both Files 134 and 135: *She herself began* **to praise** *him* **lavishly after he had cracked up as a writer.** (I.W.D.F.P.T.)

Hemingway also intended to look up or have researched, as evidenced by a note on the manuscript, the book title he could not remember (p. 27, l. 6).

File 135 includes both the original (A) and the carbon copy (B) of the first typescript. A is headed in pencil with a large "**VII**" and B is headed "**D Chapter Seven,**" and there is a circled "**E**" in the upper left-hand corner. There are no corrections to speak of on A. B bears a few corrections of typographical errors as well as a query as to the spelling of **sérieux,** and Hemingway made a few changes such as:

P. 25, l. 12: **never the real, never the bad** is added
P. 26, ll. 9–10: **or, by now, find along the quais** is added
P. 26, last line: **Maybe that not so well** is added
P. 29, first line: **when we had come back from Canada and** is inserted between **It was** and **while we were living**
P. 30, l. 10: **and mental laziness** is added
P. 31, first line: a sentence is added after **easy labels,** and then later crossed out: **I** *had no idea* [C] **did not know then that anyone could hate anyone because they had learned to write dialogue with the quotation from the garage keeper from that novel**
P. 31, l. 8: **I'm a wife** is added.

Files 188–89 incorporate the corrections made to File 135 but include a few errors in the typing, such as **serieu,** a misspelling of **sérieux.** In Files 134–35, **When I got home and into the courtyard** (p. 31, l. 1) begins a new paragraph, but the typist, probably confused by the crossed-out sentence, did not paragraph properly. The error, however, was never corrected. Finally, **Taty** is again changed to **Tatie.**

"SHAKESPEARE AND COMPANY"

File 136 is a remarkably clean manuscript, except for the first page which bears various additions and deletions. Noteworthy changes are:

P. 35, l. 1: the first sentence is continued by the following crossed-out fragment: **except French books in cheap editions with paper covers**

P. 35, ll. 14–15: the section **she was kind . . . and to gossip** is added

P. 37, ll. 6–13: there is an annotation in Hemingway's hand next to this paragraph: "**fix this paragraph E. H.**"[7]

File 137 is headed in pencil "**III**" and File 138, the carbon copy, is headed in pencil "**C Chapter Three**" with another "**C**" in the top left corner. The usual changes were made in the typing; for instance, the spellings of **Turgeniev** and **Doestoeiovski** are changed to **Turgenev** and **Dostoyevsky**. The **to** before **gossip** (p. 35, l. 15) has been dropped. There is one annotation on File 137, "**Fix**," in the margin next to the paragraph beginning, **At home in our two-room flat . . .** (p. 37, ll. 6–13). Hemingway made a few corrections in File 138, in particular:

P. 35, ll. 9–10: **sharply sculptured face** is changed to **very sharply cut face**

P. 37, l. 7: **inside** is added before **toilet facilities**; and, as in File 137, "**Fix**" is written beside that paragraph in the left-hand margin, indicating that he still wants to rework the entire paragraph

P. 38, l. 9: **Foie de veau** is underlined in pencil.

Files 188–89 incorporate the corrections made in Files 137–38. One handwritten correction in File 139 shows that Hemingway reread the new typescript: in "**Do you eat at home?**" **at** was dropped by the typist and reinserted by Hemingway. **Taty** is again changed to **Tatie**. Some typographical errors remain uncorrected by Hemingway.

"PEOPLE OF THE SEINE"

File 136 is a messier manuscript which bears more inserts, deletions, and corrections than the manuscripts of the preceding chapters. In particular:

P. 41, ll. 6–7: **and the high-wired fence of the** is crossed out after **river bank**

P. 41, l. 17: **second hand** is crossed out before **American books**

P. 43, ll. 5–6: **and did not want to think** is inserted and then crossed out before **or when I was trying to**

P. 44, l. 2: **and watch the fishermen** is crossed out at the end of the
sentence

P. 44, l. 3: **I knew many of the fishermen** is revised to **I knew several of
the men**

P. 44, l. 9: **People** is replaced by **Travel writers**

P. 44, l. 25: the paragraph continued with two sentences describing how
admirable and human Paris was with all the big trees, the chest-
nuts, the elms, and the plane trees. Having so many trees in the
city and along the river banks made the spring. These two sentences are crossed out, and a new paragraph begun

P. 44, l. 28: **the small fast bateau mouche** is crossed out and replaced
by **pulling a tow of barges.** The remainder of that sentence and
the beginning of the next are revised as follows: **the great plane
trees** *by* [C] **on the** *banks* [C] **stone banks of the river, the elms
and sometimes the poplars** *and the* [C] **I could never be lonely
along the river. With so many trees in the city** *the spring was
violent when it came* [C] **you could see the spring comeing each
day until a night of warm wind would bring it** *with violence almost* [C] **suddenly one morning**

P. 45, l. 6: **Then the spring would be sadder than the fall** is crossed out
after **your life**

P. 45, ll. 12–13: **something died that could never be replaced** is crossed
out after **it was as though.**

File 140 is headed in pencil with a large "**IV**" and evidences nothing
but typographical corrections. File 141 is headed "**Chapter Four F**" in
pencil and there are a few corrections, such as **were** inserted before **not
at all oily** (p. 43, l. 24), **gougon** corrected to **goujon** (p. 43, l. 21), and
Sisley inserted in the blank space Hemingway had left when he could not
remember the painter's name (p. 44, l. 1). No unusual changes were
made in the typing, except, perhaps, that **these** is changed to **they** before
were delicious fried whole (p. 43, l. 21). Hemingway's inaccurate spelling of French names and words, such as **clientel, Boulevard St. Ger-
maine, rue du Cardinale Lemoine, Quai des Grandes Augustins,** or
Place de la Verte Galante were not corrected in the typing.

Files 188–89 incorporate the corrections in Files 140–41 but drop the
very in front of **expertly** (p. 43, ll. 18–19). Neither 188 nor 189 bears any
correction in Hemingway's hand.

"A FALSE SPRING"

File 142 is a very messy manuscript, with numerous revisions, deletions, and additions, as well as seven pages of discarded drafts, some of which are up to two pages long. The first of these discarded passages is a one-page dialogue between Hemingway and Hadley about their first spring in the Rhône Valley: the heavy wisteria vine in the garden of the inn at Aigle, the clear trout streams (the Rhône Canal and the Stockalper), drinking wine on the porch, and arguing about **making things and not describing them.** It appears to be an early draft of the passage on page 54. Another discarded page talks about spring coming in Paris and there being no problem except to make oneself work. He was always driven by **a devil** that made him write, and he solved the problem by working early on the dining room table before Hadley would wake up. Hadley too had **her own devil** which made her play the piano, but she did that elsewhere, and she had friends with whom she went out to lunch. Sometimes she and Hemingway would meet up somewhere and go to eat at a new place. Another two pages bear a draft of the first paragraph of "A False Spring" and continue by discussing the fact that **men friends in Paris were liable to have terrible wives,** and that if the wives came with them **it was another day, or another meal, or another evening wasted** out of one's life. He then goes on to talk about Hadley's friends from home whom he tried to like, and his own **equally horrible** friends, to whom she was kind and polite. They also had a couple of good friends, but, generally, people were **destroyers.** On a fifth page Hemingway discusses his very good friends Bill Bird, Guy Hickock, Mike Ward, and Charlie Sweeney, whom he would see when he crossed the Seine, each of whom was good enough to be a once-in-a-lifetime friend. But Hemingway dismisses them by saying that this is a book about literary friendships, which are **false and temporary** things, since writers are often the worst people, and not a book about true friends.

The sixth discarded page, bearing a "2" in the top left-hand corner, deals with racing. It describes the course for hurdle racing and steeplechases, and how Hadley and Hemingway rented a pair of glasses for ten francs, with a deposit of fifty francs, and how they found a spot on the grassy bank from where they could watch what was going on. They had brought their lunch and sat on Hemingway's raincoat spread out on the grass. They ate sandwiches of French bread with ham and pâté and studied the first race in the paper. They had money they could afford to lose.

The last page to be discarded bears a "**6**" in the top left-hand corner and is a short draft of a conversation taking place at the Café des Deux Magots, which Hemingway first locates on the **St. Germain de Pres side** and then at the **corner of the Boulevard St. Michel and the Luxembourg**. Hemingway and Hadley talk about racing and about Dorman-Smith.

All these discarded passages dramatize the fact that Hemingway experienced some difficulties in focusing the chapter, perhaps because it did not deal with any specific event. There are also many corrections to the manuscript. The crossed-out passages are not very illuminating, except, perhaps, for one that mentions taking the racing train from the Gare du Nord through the ugliest quarters of Paris (p. 50, l. 11), and one that explains more clearly how they spent their winnings—one quarter for fun, one quarter for fixed expenses, and half for betting capital (p. 53, ll. 7–8).

The typescripts in Files 143–44 are also more complex than most others. File 144 includes three typescripts: File 144-1 is titled "**Chapter Five**," and the first page bears a number of annotations in pencil: "**Question if put in after** *D* **E.H.**," "**Must decide E.H.**," "**Re-did Jan. 27th E.H.**," "**D Bis**," and "**Reworked 28th, 29th, 30th**." There is also a note to Betty asking her to head the chapter "**Five**," to type it double-spaced with two carbons, and not to capitalize **spring**. In addition to the correction of some typographical errors and some minor stylistic changes, a few changes are made, such as:

P. 49, l. 1: **even the false spring** is added
P. 49, l. 24: **flat** is replaced by **building**
P. 50, ll. 12–13: the first part of the sentence **Some money . . . newspaper work for and** is inserted
P. 55, ll. 17–20: this short paragraph is added
P. 58, l. 5: **the *lovely soft regular* breathing of some one . . . moonlight** (I.W.D.F.P.T.) replaces **the beating of your heart**.

File 143 is a carbon copy of 144-1 bearing some typographical corrections in pencil and blue ink. File 144-3 is an uncorrected carbon copy of 144-2, a typescript that incorporates the corrections made on 144-1 and bears further corrections and additions, among which one should mention:

P. 50, l. 3: **at the** added before **corner**
P. 50, l. 11: **after I had finished work** is added

Pp. 50–51, last line–first line: **which we often made** is added

P. 51, l. 9: **Especially if you buy pictures instead of clothes** is added

P. 51, l. 10: **think of ourselves as poor** replaces **think about being poor**

P. 51, l. 13: **later on** is added after **strange to me**

P. 53, ll. 10–11: **Another day . . . some track again** is added

Pp. 54–55: the long passage beginning **Do you remember the inn at Aigle** and ending on page 55, line 6 is added, replacing another long passage rather similar to the first discarded passage of File 142, but which included a discussion of the chestnut trees in bloom looking like waxen candelabras.[8]

P. 55, l. 15: **in the winter** is added

P. 55, l. 16: **when it is gone** is added

P. 55, l. 21: **next** is added

P. 55, l. 23: **time** replaces **spring**

P. 57, l. 1: **But that's gone now** is added

P. 57, l. 15: **again** is added

P. 57, last line: **first** is added before **morning**

P. 58, l. 1: **the false** replaces **it**

P. 58, l. 5: **lovely soft regular** is crossed out before **breathing**

Files 188–89 are a transcription of 144-2. Hemingway obviously proofread File 189 since there are some spelling corrections in his handwriting.

"THE END OF AN AVOCATION"

File 145 is also a very messy manuscript, bearing many corrections and deletions. The last three pages—a rough version of what became the last two pages of the published chapter, beginning **But for a long time**—are crossed out. There are also four discarded fragments: 1) A long passage about bicycle racing at the Vélodrome d'Hiver; this crossed-out passage has been integrated, however, almost word for word in File 147-2. 2) Various random sentences. 3) A passage about Hemingway going to the races on his own, and about racing never coming between Hadley and himself, **only people could do that**; this is a draft for page 61, lines 9–14. 4) The same fragment as the sixth discarded one in File 142.

File 147 comprises three typescripts (File 146 is an unmarked carbon copy of 147-3): 147-1 (the carbon copy of 147-2) is headed in pencil with a large "**VI**" and bears typographical corrections only; 147-2 is heavily revised in pencil, with instructions to Betty: **"Question if use after D Bis i.e.; D 2"**; **"Must Decide E.H.,"** "No D 3," "Reworked Jan 27, 61, 28, 29, 30"; 147-3 is the corrected typescript of 147-2.

The first paragraph, which had been already reworked three times in File 145, is again heavily revised in 147-2, crossed out, and rewritten on another page with instructions: **"To Betty Please head Mss Chapter 6,"** **"1st paragraph 1st sentence."** The original paragraph in File 145 is not very different from the version Hemingway finally settled upon. A little more romantic, it mentions **the moon full on a field of narcissus.** In 147-2 Hemingway adds some comments about Dorman-Smith being a professional soldier whom he had met in Italy, and who had been his and their best friend for a long time, and then crosses them out. Other revisions include:

P. 61, l. 14: **she was profitable** is changed to **she could be profitable**
P. 61, ll. 22, 23: **then** is replaced by **in their season; hard work** is replaced by **full-time work**
P. 62, l. 14: **jockeys and trainers and owners** is added
P. 62, l. 21: **and at the flat racing tracks too** is added
Pp. 62–63, last line–first line: **corner of the rue des Italiens** is added
P. 63, l. 17: **One with great horses** is added.

Files 145, 146, 147-1, and 147-2 end with what is an early version of page 64, lines 6–11. The last page of 147-2 is heavily revised, but the last three sentences and the revisions are crossed out (with instructions: **"Betty—Please continue from here on next page"**), and five pages of manuscript are added, which are essentially a revised version of the last three pages deleted from File 145, starting with **That was a new and fine thing**.

File 147-3, the typescript of 147-2, incorporates all the corrections, deletions, and additions made to 147-2 and bears some additional corrections in pencil, among which one should mention:

P. 61, l. 3: **very much** is added after **loved it,** and then crossed out
P. 61, l. 5: **walking down the road with the moon full on a field of narcissus** is crossed out after **chalet** and replaced by **with the lights of the town below on the shores of the lake, nor waking to the mountain spring,** which is itself crossed out
P. 61, l. 10: **it** is replaced by **for a long time** before **stayed**
P. 61, ll. 15–16: **and I had no time for that** is added

P. 61, l. 16: **was writing stories** is replaced by **wrote**

P. 61, l. 22: **when I could** is added

P. 62, l. 1: **each** is replaced by **a** before **jumping race**

P. 62, l. 2: **it was a fast climb up to** is added

P. 62, l. 11: **that you could be there** is added

P. 62, l. 16: **in principle** is added

P. 62, l. 17: **also** is replaced by **sometimes**

P. 62 l. 19: **all the time** is replaced by **very closely** in **You had to follow it very closely to really know anything**

P. 64, l. 6: **nothing** is replaced by **little**

P. 64, l. 7: **much** is crossed out before **later**

P. 64, l. 29: **exacting** is replaced by **exciting**

P. 65, ll. 2–3: **wall of air resistance hit him** is changed to **wall of air that he had been sheltered against hit him**.

File 188-1, headed "**Chapter 6**," is put together with the typescript headed "**Chapter 5**" and annotated in Mary Hemingway's hand, "**Rewritten & Revised Chaps 5 & 6**." This typescript is in fact the original of 147-3. Files 188-2 and 189, the original, both headed "**Chapter Six**," are a new typescript that incorporates the corrections made on File 147-3.

"HUNGER WAS A GOOD DISCIPLINE"

File 148 is a clean manuscript. The deleted sentences are, as usual, the most interesting. Specifically: 1) the first attempts at sentences at the beginning are crossed out. They comment on the fact that it was easy to decide to no longer do newspaper work, but that it was hard to eat regularly and that his wife was nursing a baby; 2) before **compromising on something else**, he had three sentences about messing up the stories so that they would sell (p. 72, ll. 17–18); 3) after **ahead of them** is a crossed-out sentence saying he ought to write **a long simple wonderful story** that everyone could understand, leaving out everything, and using everything he had ever learned (p. 75, l. 22).

File 149 is headed with a large "**VIII**" and bears only a few typographical corrections. File 150, the original, is heavily revised. The typist made many errors in transcribing the names of people and streets, and in the last sentence she transcribed **difficult** as **different**.[9] There are several instructions written in pencil and blue ink at the top of the page: "**not bad. E.H.,**" "**E. Bis?,**" "**if include E.H.,**" "**as of Jan 24 include E.H.,**" "**Rewritten Jan. 27. Include E.H.,**" "**If include is F,**" "**Re-read and wrote insert 29th. Re-read 30th. Believe should go in E.H.,**" "**Chapter Eight.**" Hemingway was clearly not entirely satisfied with the chapter and had qualms about it. Among Hemingway's corrections, one should mention:

P. 69: the first sentence, originally written in the present, is switched to the preterit

P. 69, l. 4: **at a time when you had given up journalism and were writing . . . lunching out with someone** is inserted between **When you were skipping meals** and **the best place to do it**

P. 69, l. 10: **always** is added

P. 69, l. 13: **much better** and **truly** are added

P. 69, last line: **scholars** is replaced by **bishops**

P. 70, ll. 8–9: **pass not too many places** is changed to **you did not pass too many places**

P. 70, ll. 26–27: **You like him** and **Or any one you really like** are added

P. 71, l. 19: **To him and the Frankfurther Zeitung** is added

P. 71, l. 24: **semester** is replaced by **quarter**, and **Three hundred Francs** by **Six hundred Francs**

P. 71, l. 28: **There is no money . . . journalism** is added

P. 72, ll. 15–16: **You quit journalism of your own accord** and **She has plenty of time** are added

P. 73, ll. 25–27: **so I could work . . . manila folders** is added (instructions to Betty in red pencil)

P. 73, l. 28: **it** is replaced by **the one story**

Pp. 73–74, last line–first 3 lines: **The other story . . . somewhere** is added; this may be the insert Hemingway wrote on 29 January. After having tried to insert it, he finally copied it on another page titled **"Betty Insert 1."**

P. 74, l. 5: **it** is replaced by **the racing story**

P. 74, ll. 16–27: **She had cried . . . casualties** is added, also on a separate page with instructions to Betty in red pencil

P. 74, l. 27: **him** is replaced by **O'Brien**

P. 75, l. 2: **that** is added

P. 75, l. 3: **about** is added

P. 76, ll. 1–2: **in the bag stolen at the Gare de Lyon** is added

P. 76, ll. 3–4: **probably** is added

P. 76, ll. 27–30: **The story was . . . war in it** is added

Files 188–89 are headed "**Chapter Eight**" and neither bears any corrections, except for the correction of one typographical error in File 189; **skipping meals** has been dropped before **at a time when you had given up journalism** (p. 69, l. 4).

"FORD MADOX FORD AND THE DEVIL'S DISCIPLE"

File 151 is a very clean manuscript. There are a few deletions of interest, such as a sentence fragment saying that the writers were all friends of theirs crossed out after **outside** (p. 81, l. 5); a sentence fragment saying that there was no wind from Ford to Hemingway is crossed out and replaced by **and the fallen leaves . . . past his** (p. 83, last line); **of all the good things** is crossed out after **remember** (p. 85, last line).

File 152 is titled and headed with a large "**IX**" in pencil. File 153 is a negative photocopy of File 152 with annotations in Hemingway's hand: "**Chapter Nine**" and "**Should be BLAISE CENDRARS,**" as well as a couple of corrections of **Cendrars** in the text. Some errors were made in the typing, in particular: the adjective **square** was added by the typist (p. 81, l. 6); on the other hand, the typist skipped a line—**knew each other only to nod and there** is skipped after **clients** (p. 81, l. 24). Hemingway made very few changes to the typescript, except for: **three** is changed to **two** before **years** (p. 84, l. 12); **been able to** is added after **never,** and **not** is added after **Ouida** (p. 86, l. 9).

Files 188–89 incorporate the corrections made in File 153 and are headed "**Chapter Nine**." There are no corrections on either to suggest that Hemingway read them.

"BIRTH OF A NEW SCHOOL"

File 154 is a relatively neat manuscript. Two crossed-out titles are at the top of the first page ("**A Non Friend in Full Cry**" and "**The Work Destroyers**"), leaving one remaining title, "**Birth of a New School.**" The most important aspect of this chapter is that Hemingway wrote two possible endings for it. The first section ends with '**That's perfectly right,' he said. 'I promised.'** (p. 94, l. 15). The first ending continues the conversation between Hemingway and the critic for only five lines and evolves toward a meditation on the work destroyer: Hemingway does not think the critic will come back since the Closerie is off his beat. Hemingway feels that it would have been worse if he had been civil to him, and that sooner or later he would have had to hit him. He did not want to hit him in his home café, and he must be careful not to break his jaw; it would be difficult to prevent his head from hitting the pavement. The best thing to do is to avoid him. Hemingway then meditates on the convenience of working in a café such as the Closerie and feels that it is worth taking the risk of being bothered. The last paragraph of the first ending is an early version of the last paragraph of the published chapter. The second ending is the one that was chosen by Hemingway's editors for publication.

There are a few crossed-out sentences in File 154, in particular: (p. 91, last line) **and after the anger wore out there was no damage done** is crossed out after **better**; (p. 92, l. 16) **The anger started. You had your own café which was just down the street** is crossed out after **Lilas**; (p. 94, l. 16) line crossed out in File 154, after which four more lines of conversation are crossed out—the other man repeats that he cannot write; Hemingway is sorry, and the other is skeptical; finally Hemingway lies in an attempt to be kind because he has worked.

File 155 is a typescript of File 154 which includes both endings. File 155 is headed in blue pencil with a large "**XIX**," which is then crossed out, and with a large "**IX**" also in blue pencil. It is titled in type as well, and there is only one handwritten correction to the dialogue. The typist forgot to transcribe some sentences in the first ending, in particular. She also added at least one word: (p. 92, l. 22) **like** in **It sounds like a charming place.** File 156 is a typescript of pages 5 and 6 of File 155—pages which are essentially a typescript of the first ending without the last paragraph and the five lines of transition at the beginning. This is mainly the section which was not published.

"WITH PASCIN AT THE DOME"

For two and a quarter pages, File 157 begins as a disorderly typescript on Finca Vigia stationery. There are many crossed-out typewritten passages that are unreadable. Among other additions and deletions, one should note:

P. 99, ll. 2–3: **out through the court yard with the stacked lumber, closed the door, crossed** is added, and **across** is crossed out before **the street**

P. 99, ll. 13–14: **It made me hungry to read the name** is added

P. 99, l. 23: **He was a great respecter of literature and this made him happy** is crossed out after **I said**

P. 100, ll. 12–13: **that were clearly marked on the saucers that were served with them** is added

P. 100, l. 17: **you** is changed to **I** before **could afford**

P. 101, l. 20: after **foresworn**, the sentence reads: **at Enghien to work *on this day* [A] as a serious writer; now full . . .**

P. 101, l. 29: **decoration** is crossed out and replaced by **part of the decor**, with a query in Hemingway's hand: "**Maybe only decoration is better. Think it over. E.H.**"

P. 102, l. 15: **You're too sensible** is replaced by **If you really liked . . . Lipps**

P. 103, l. 4: three sentences are crossed out: Hemingway asks if he can buy them a drink before sailing into the sunset. The reply is **no**, and he says good-bye and walks up the Rue Delambre

P. 103, l. 15: **Japanese** is changed to **Javanese**.

File 158-1, the original, is headed in pencil with a large "**X**" and bears a few typographical corrections, as well as some check marks. File 158-2, the carbon copy, is headed in pencil "**Chapter Ten**" and annotated: "**G**," "**H**," and "**J**" in blue ink. File 158-2 bears some supplementary corrections: (p. 101, l. 29) **part of the decor** is crossed out, leaving **decoration**, which had been put between parentheses; (p. 102, l. 12) above **Une demi-blonde**, Hemingway wrote a note to remind himself to check the spelling with "**old Picard**"; (p. 104, l.23) Hemingway corrected **Le Vikings** to **Les Vikings** adding, "**check spelling should be 'Les Vikings?' EH.**" One should also note that the word **completely** was omitted in the transcription before **makes you very hungry** (p. 101, l. 3).

Files 188–89 incorporate the corrections made in File 158-2, except for one change made in both Files 158-1 and 158-2: (p. 100, l. 14) **wholesome but not too original thoughts** is changed by Hemingway to **wholesome unoriginal thoughts**. Files 188–89 also introduce an error: **a boosted beast** is substituted for **boosted beasts** (p. 101, l. 20).

"EZRA POUND AND HIS BEL ESPRIT"

There are two manuscripts for this chapter: File 159 (six pages) begins with **Ezra Pound was always a good friend** (p. 107, l. 1) and ends with

It was a kinder and more Christian term than what I had thought about him myself (p. 110, l. 13); File 160 (seven pages) begins with **Ezra Pound was the most generous writer I have ever known** (p. 110, l. 17) and ends with **my original intention** (p. 113, last line). Both Files 159 and 160 are very clean manuscripts, and it appears as if Hemingway were uncertain which text to use since both manuscripts begin with page 1. There are a few deleted sentences or fragments of interest, such as: **although you always do in the end** is deleted after **criticize families** (p. 108, l. 3); a sentence is deleted after **stimulants** (p. 112, l. 20), which states that it was a long time after Bel Esprit that Ezra sent word one evening that Dunning was dying.

File 161 comprises three typescripts. File 161-1, the typescript of File 159, is headed with a large "**XI**" in pencil; it contains nothing but typographical corrections. File 161-3, the carbon copy of 161-1, is headed "**Chapter Eleven**" in pencil in the top right-hand corner and "**H**" and "**I**" in ink in the left-hand corner, with a crossed-out "**X**" in the middle. File 161-3 evidences some corrections and additions:

P. 107, l. 16: **Bjeskee** is corrected to **Brzeska**
P. 107, l. 22: **can be** is added
P. 108, ll. 14–15: **He was also irrascible but so, *I believe* have been many saints** is added (I.W.D.F.P.T.)
P. 108, ll. 24–26: **It was just . . . for the future** is added
P. 109, ll. 10–11: **sticking out . . . a few right hands** is added
P. 110, ll. 8–9: **goes back to London and** is added
P. 110, l. 13: the fragment **on the day that I first met him** is added and then crossed out after **myself**
P. 110, ll. 13–16: the sentences **Later I tried . . . Ezra's studio** are handwritten on a separate sheet of paper and headed "**5—continued.**"

File 161-2, an untitled typescript of File 160, bears few typographical corrections. The sentence **It turned out all right though we used the money to go to Spain** is added after the last sentence (p. 113). Files 188–89 transcribe File 161-3, incorporating the corrections and additions, and bear no corrections whatsoever.

"A STRANGE ENOUGH ENDING"

File 162 is a very clean manuscript without deletions or additions of interest. File 164, the original of the typescript, is titled in pencil "**XII**," and there are no corrections, while File 163, the carbon copy, is heavily corrected and headed by hand **"Chapter Twelve."** Among the corrections one should note:

P. 117, l. 6: **could ever wish to be** replaces **wished to be**

P. 117, l. 7: **great** is added before **women**

P. 117, l. 9: **usually** and **truly ambitious** are added

P. 117, l. 21: **a companion** replaces **her friend**; **Miss Stein's car** replaces **their car**

P. 117, l. 22: **Miss Stein** replaces **she**

P. 117, l. 22, to p. 118, l. 8: after an attempt at adding this whole section within the text, Hemingway finally wrote it on a separate page titled **"Chapter 12 insert."** It is heavily revised; in particular: **You had to learn early about the system of not visiting people** is revised to **we already knew a little about . . .** , and then to **You should know a little about . . .**

P. 118, ll. 21–22: **never, anywhere, ever** is added, crossed out, and re-added

P. 119, ll. 1–2: **It was bad to hear and the answers were worse** is added; the beginning of another sentence is crossed out: **She had written me many letters**

P. 119, l. 5: **I will write** is added

P. 119, l. 8: **stupidly enough** is added

P. 119, l. 10: **all the** is replaced by **most of** before **other men friends**

P. 119, l. 11: **new friends** replaces **fairies**; **like prancing lemmings** is crossed out after **moved in**

P. 119, ll. 14–15: **nearly** and **that were fond of her** are added

P. 119, ll. 16–18: **I am not sure . . . his paintings** is added, then crossed out; in the right-hand margin is a note: **"Betty ie leave in E.H."**

P. 119, l. 19: **new friends** replaces **fairies**

P. 119, ll. 22, 23: **had painted her** and **her** are added

P. 119, last line: the last sentence is added. Two more sentences are also added but crossed out. They say that it never occurred to him until much later that someone could hate someone else because she had learned to write from the novel that began with the quotation from the garage keeper, and that they had been great friends once.

On the back of the page bearing the handwritten insert is a sentence about their Paris not being Villon's. There is also a paragraph about Gide telling him how to punish a cat—never slap a cat, because he does not understand it; instead, one must hold him by the scruff of the neck, look at him straight in the eyes, and spit in his face. This page is titled "**3**."

Some fragments were lost in the typing of Files 188–89: (p. 118, l. 1) **can** was dropped after **naturally**; (l. 3) the sentence reads in File 163: **You had to learn it** *early and it was a necessary thing*. **We did not learn it** (italicized words dropped). On the other hand, Hemingway added **It was something that we never learned**. The last sentence, **But it was more complicated than that,** which Hemingway had added in File 163, has not been transcribed in Files 188–89.

"THE MAN WHO WAS MARKED FOR DEATH"

File 165 is a clean manuscript. Two deletions are of interest: (p. 123, l. 8) **black Irish unmistakably poetic** is changed to **faultlessly Irish, poetic**; (p. 129, l. 4) after **We left it at that** is a last sentence—**I cannot remember when Walsh finally died**—and a crossed-out passage, according to which, after Hemingway had written *The Sun Also Rises,* Walsh wrote to him asking to publish it as a serial. Hemingway declined because the quarterly that Walsh was publishing came out at irregular intervals, while his publisher had a definite publication date and needed galleys and page proofs on time. Hemingway then claims that, when the book came out, Walsh reviewed it in *New Masses* as the cheapest book he had ever read. One should also note that Hemingway could not remember the amount of the award, for he had written **a thousand or two thousand dollars,** with **check** above the **two** (p. 125, l. 5); he also could not remember whom the award had gone to, for the sentence read: **This was a huge sum for** *an honest* **writer to receive** *and the award had gone to* [   ] **and** [   ] **(I.W.D.F.P.T.)**; above the second blank Hemingway wrote, **"write and ask Malcom."**

File 166-1, the original, is unmarked except for two typographical corrections and some check marks in red pencil above some French words, such as **Pouilly Fuisée, Tournedos,** and **Chateauneuf du Pape.** File 166-2, the carbon copy, is heavily corrected and headed in pencil with a large "**XIII**" and titled. At the very top of the page are various annotations: "**H**," "**J**," and "**K**," the first two being crossed out. Other annotations include: "**Go over again,**" "**Went over Jan 25 61 E.H.,**" "**Check again,**" "**March 18,**" "**Chapter Thirteen.**" Errors were made in the typing, the most important being the transcription of **This Quarter** as **This quarterly** (p. 125, l. 11). Some faulty verb tense agreements are corrected—for example, **wishes he was there** to **wished he were there** (p. 126, l. 20) and **wants** to **wanted** (p. 127, l. 13). The following corrections are of interest:

P. 124, ll. 18, 19, 24, 25: Hemingway removed the girls' names: **Frances** is replaced by **Dear, the other girl**, and **the taller one of the girls**; **with Helen and with Frances** is replaced by **with them both**. Two crossed-out notes in the right-hand margin say: "**see if can eliminate names**" and "**Those were not their names of course.**"

P. 125, ll. 4–8: **edited by Schofield Thayer** is crossed out; **or two thousand** is crossed out; **I believe** is added; so are **in those days in addition to the prestige** and **various people; all deserving naturally; an honest** is replaced by **any straight**. Hemingway still wanted to put in the names of those who had received the award for in the blanks left for that purpose he had written **check and put in** and **leave open** before settling for **various people**

P. 125, l. 10: a sentence saying that no one had any idea that an honest writer could make $2000 a year is crossed out after **Vorarlberg**

P. 125, ll. 11–14: **co-editor** is changed to **one of the editors; offered two thousand dollars** is changed to **was alleged to be going to award a very substantial sum; year** is changed to **the first four issues**. Significantly, the error in the transcription of **This Quarter** is not corrected

P. 125, ll. 15–19: this paragraph is added in the margins

P. 125, l. 20: **that announcement** is replaced by **I heard . . . award**

P. 125, ll. 26–28: **appeared to be** replaces **was; from the boat and if they were . . . of course** are added

P. 126, ll. 2–3: **not the kind . . . it was** is added

P. 127, ll. 15–16: these two lines are added

P. 127, ll. 23–24: **you con man** replaces **you false professional Irishman**, which itself replaced **you con-ridden, con-riddled son of a bitch**

P. 127, l. 27: **good living out of it** is amended to **living out of your death**

P. 127, ll. 28–29: these four sentences are added

P. 128, ll. 11–12: **it was very legitimate** is added; **the son of a bitch would** is replaced by **that he would**

P. 128, ll. 14–17: **extremely** is added; **Also, I liked . . . well** is added;

Hemingway also added a sentence saying that Walsh was going to make them all rich, which was wonderful, and then crossed it out

P. 128, l. 18: **much later,** then **very much later** are added after **One day,** then crossed out and replaced by **years later**

P. 128, ll. 20–23: **although he could not see them** and **although you will . . . white wine** are added

P. 128, l. 25: **A son of a bitch but still alive** is crossed out and replaced by the published sentence

P. 129, ll. 4–7: **It was long before . . . story** is added

Files 188–89 are a typescript of File 166-2; File 188 bears only a few typographical corrections, mainly accents on French words, with some comments in Hemingway's hand, saying that the chapter is too dangerous and libelous to publish, as explained in a letter to Charles Scribner. Page 4 of File 166-2 has been so heavily corrected by Hemingway that a retyped page 4 is inserted for clarification. Files 188–89 follow the text of that new page which itself transcribes all the corrections made on the original page 4, except for two: 1) **edited by Scofield Thayer** is reintegrated with instructions for Scribner's to verify the spelling of the name; 2) **it meant, supplemented by loans and savings, a winter** is transcribed as **supplemented by loans and savings, it meant a winter . . . .**

"EVAN SHIPMAN AT THE LILAS"

File 167 is a rather clean manuscript with few deletions and additions, except on the first page. For instance, the first sentence, which says that if he had not read Dostoyevsky, Hemingway would not have been prepared for what happened to Shipman when he came of age, is crossed out. The sentence fragment **In Dostoyevsky** *everything was possible, true and human* [C] is revised to the published version (p. 133, ll. 14–15); **seductively** is crossed out after **purple dressing-gown** (p. 135, l. 21); **leaving the door open** is revised to **without closing the door** (p. 135, l. 22). Hemingway also wanted the spelling of Dostoyevsky, which he had spelt **Doestoevsky,** checked throughout, and he wanted to find the title of Evan Shipman's poem.

File 168-1, the carbon copy, is headed with a large "**XIV**" in pencil and bears only a few typographical corrections and check marks. File 168-2, the original, is annotated at the top of page 1: "**K bis,**" "**If include,**" "**If included necessary changes must be made in the Scott story as indi-**

cated; **Believe better not use E.H.,**" "**Jan 25 O.K. to use E.H.,**"
"**Chapter 14.**" In File 167 **everyone** is transcribed as **anyone** (p. 134, l.
4). A few corrections of interest are made in File 168-2:

P. 133, l. 4: **ever** is added
P. 133, l. 9: **great** is replaced by **good**
P. 133, ll. 11–13: **There were . . . ones too** is added
P. 133, ll. 16–17: **and the insanity of gambling** is added
P. 134, l. 1: **that** is replaced by **the wonderful Waterloo account by Stendhal**
P. 135, ll. 27–28: **He was a fine poet . . . painting** is added
P. 136, l. 2: **to not show** is corrected to **not to show**
P. 137, ll. 25–27: "**I'm sure it . . . translations**" is added
P. 138, l. 1: **again** is added
P. 138, ll. 10–11: **It was probably my fault** is added
P. 138, l. 12: **Most of it** is added
P. 138, l. 15: **and maybe . . . translation** is added
P. 139, ll. 7–8: **and his hair was slicked from one side across the bald top of his head** is crossed out and replaced by the published fragment
P. 140, l. 6: **of course** is added
P. 140, last two lines: **They are gardening together** is added.

One sentence was dropped in the typing of Files 188–89: "**Don't bring it, Jean**" before "*Entendu* **Messieurs**" (p. 139, l. 11). **Given** was also dropped between **certain** and **situations** (p. 134, l. 28). In File 188, the original, Hemingway corrected **translations** to **translators**—a correction not made in the published text.

"AN AGENT OF EVIL"

File 169 is an extremely clean manuscript, except for the first two and last two pages. It is headed "**Chapter 15**" and "**XV**" at the top of the first page and bears the following annotations: "**Study to see if include,**" and "**After Chapter 14 or before,**" "**15.**" There are also some indications for Betty, the typist, telling her to not capitalize **avenue** (de l'Opéra) and **terza rima**. There are no significant deletions or additions, but on a separate page are a couple of sentences saying that he cannot remember whether Ralph Cheever Dunning was in Ezra Pound's studio or in his own when Pound sent for Hemingway because Dunning was dying, and that the chicken gave him the same feeling of **absence** one gets when one goes to a gallery to see a picture which turns out to be away on loan.

There are no corrections to File 189, but **terza rima**, which had been transcribed as **terza riruce**, is corrected by hand four times on the first page of File 188. The accent on **monté** is added twice, while the accent on **catégoriquement** is missing. This chapter was typed only once, and the final version reflects almost exactly Hemingway's first draft.

"SCOTT FITZGERALD"

File 170 is a first draft typed by Hemingway, including many deleted words and sentences, a few of which are of interest; for instance: (p. 153, l. 17) after **drop it** is a sentence indicating that there might have been some British people present whom he had not noticed; (p. 155, l. 17) after **know** are two sentences indicating that it was spring and that Hadley and he had not been on any trip or spent any money except on necessities because they were trying to save enough money to go to Spain. He would have liked Hadley to go with him, but she wanted to stay in Paris because they had friends visiting from the States; (p. 172, l. 29) a new paragraph indicating that Hemingway had not cared whether Scott got through to Zelda is begun and then dropped; (p. 173, l. 4) after **spell**, a sentence saying that it was hard to take oneself seriously as one of Fitzgerald's minor heroes is crossed out.

Files 170-a and 170-b are typescript fragments; the first is an early draft of the temperature-taking episode, and the second an early draft of the first few lines of the chapter.

File 171 is headed in pencil with a large "**XVII**" and faithfully transcribes File 170, except in a few instances—for example: (p. 152, l. 30) **that** is dropped between **British** and **you**; (p. 163, l. 5) after **health** a sentence is dropped which states that Fitzgerald said that he was afraid that he was getting **congestion of the lungs**; (p. 169, l. 9) **at** is dropped between **sipping** and **his drink**; (p. 172, l. 19) **about** is dropped between **me** and **how**; (p. 171, l. 16) **could** is transcribed as **can**.

File 172 is a heavily corrected carbon of File 171, the first page of which bears some annotations: "**M**," "**G**," "**Chapter 17**," and "**Foreword to Scott**." The foreword is extensively revised; after **marred** the following sentence is crossed out: **He even needed some one as a con-**

science and he needed professionals or normally educated people to make his writing legible and not illiterate. Also crossed out is: **and could not fly any more . . . effortless.** Some positive comments are added and then crossed out: **In the meantime, thinking well and fully conscious of its worth, he had written The Great Gatsby. Tender Is the Night is a better book written in heroic and desperate confusion.** After an incomplete sentence, another sentence is added and not crossed out: **He was flying again and I was lucky to meet him just after a good time in his writing if not a good one in his life.** The revisions of that headnote clearly exemplify Hemingway's ambivalent feelings toward Fitzgerald: if he deleted a nasty comment, he also refused to replace it with one that made clear that Scott's career had by no means ended in failure. File 172 bears numerous corrections which are not important enough to be detailed exhaustively:

P. 149, l. 8: **Chaplin** is added after **Dunc**

P. 150, l. 14: **now** is replaced by **then**, which is in turn replaced by **at the time**

P. 150, l. 18: **too** is replaced by **overly** before **small**

P. 150, l. 27: **was** is replaced by **had been**

P. 152, l. 3: introduction of a new paragraph

P. 152, l. 9: **or death mask** is added

P. 153, l. 10: **with the phony title** is added

P. 153, l. 22: **about it in the old days** is added

P. 153, ll. 28–29: **even if you were . . . endearing** is added

P. 154, ll. 12–13: **It could only . . . been better** is added

P. 154, l. 13: **better** is added in the sentence **I believe it was much better later**

P. 154, l. 18: **gray blue light** is changed to **thin gray light**

P. 154, last line: **lovely** is changed to **at its best**

P. 155, l. 5: **a bad dream** is changed to **an unpleasant dream**

P. 156, l. 6: **and convince him** is added

P. 156, ll. 14–15: **though she did not take Scott's writing that she had read seriously** is revised to the published version

P. 156, l. 21: **to be** is crossed out and replaced by **that had been**, which is itself crossed out. Hemingway could not remember whether the book had been published, as evidenced by a note to that effect on the typescript

P. 156, l. 28: after **afterwards** a sentence which says that they had either

$200 or $400 in the bank, and about $800 coming in, is added and then crossed out

P. 157, l. 21: **on it that** is added

P. 158, ll. 6–7: **for a living** and **also** are added

P. 158, ll. 8–10: **His gums . . . métier** is added

P. 158, l. 17: **anything else** is added

P. 158, l. 20: **He said . . . place** is added

P. 159, l. 19: a rather meaningless sentence fragment about the chicken being as absent as the fleet when one is away is added and then crossed out

P. 160, l. 20: **I said** is added

P. 161, l. 7: **very much** is added

P. 161, l. 8: **more than** is replaced by **what it would have cost us**

P. 161, l. 27: **it had been damaged** is added

P. 162, l. 19: **Later I was to learn it was the key word** is added and deleted

P. 162, l. 26: **a wonderful** is replaced by **an excellent**

P. 163, l. 26: **and information** is added

P. 164, ll. 4–5: there is a crossed-out note by Hemingway: "**Ok to here EH 2/5/59**"

P. 164, l. 12: **I told him** is added

P. 166, l. 25: after **alcohol** a sentence saying that, at that time, they did not know anything about alcoholics is erased

P. 168, ll. 16–26: at this point, Hemingway hesitates: if he does not publish the chapter on Evan Shipman, this section is to read as it does in File 170: mainly a summary of the new rules at the Closerie and how they affected Jean. If he publishes the Shipman chapter, then this section is to be revised as it would eventually be published. This is a very messy section with several notes to Betty, telling her first to leave it as it is, then to fix it if the story of Shipman and the waiter is included, and finally to put it back as it was if that story is not included, and so on

P. 168, l. 28: **whom he did not understand** is added

P. 169, l. 5: **then or any Swiss** is added

P. 172, l. 6: **by** is added before **now**

P. 173, ll. 10–11: **single seater sea** is added before **plane**

P. 173, ll. 27–28: **garlic and parsley** is added

P. 176, ll. 11–12: **on** before **wood** and **nor on marble as this café table was** are added.

A few changes were also made in paragraphing File 172—that is, the introduction of new paragraphs (p. 152, l. 3; p. 154, l. 16; p. 159, l. 15; and p. 163, l. 1) and the running-in of a paragraph with the preceding one (p. 157, l. 6).

Files 188–89 are a faithful transcription of File 172, the only real change being in the spelling of **Tatie** (**Taty** in File 172). File 188, the original, bears a few handwritten corrections: some accents on French words are added; the spellings of **alcoholic** and **parsley** are corrected; indications to print the foreword in italics are added; and on page 154, line 18, **thin gray light** is transcribed as **then gray light**.

"HAWKS DO NOT SHARE"

File 173 is a reasonably clean manuscript with a few deletions of interest: (p. 184, l. 3) after **stairs** is a crossed-out sentence saying that Fitzgerald held Scotty so that she could go to the potty; (p. 186, l. 4) after **hair** is a crossed-out fragment saying that it made you want to stroke it or touch it; (l. 7) **revealing something of true importance** is crossed out after **said to me**. The last three sentences of the chapter were reworked extensively, and much was crossed out. The main change is one of emphasis: in the early draft, it is Hemingway who cannot share with a hawk, rather than the other way around.

File 174 is headed in pencil "**XVIII**" and bears no corrections except for a red-pencil check mark over **Tilsitt**. It is an accurate transcription of File 173, except for a few typographical errors and the dropping of **had** before **told** (p. 181, l. 9) and of **that** before **they** (p. 181, l. 28). File 175, the carbon copy, bears corrections and additions in blue ink and includes a one-page insert. It is headed in pencil "**H**," "**Chapter 18**," with an "**R**" and an "**M**" crossed out in the top left-hand corner and an "**N**" (not crossed out). Among the changes one should mention:

P. 179, l. 15: **There was no view** is added
P. 181, l. 9: **many times on our walks** is added
P. 181, l. 10: **very** and **starting on the trip** are added
P. 182, l. 11: **small** is crossed out before **mountains**
P. 182, l. 16: **that was not expensive** is added
P. 183, ll. 6–7: **she said** is added
P. 183, l. 8: **to the places** is added
P. 183, ll. 19–20: **and I was sure . . . later** is added in two stages: first in pencil up to **that** (l. 20), then in ink, suggesting a second thought

P. 184, l. 19: above **1925** are two crossed-out words: **"check, OK"**

P. 184, l. 23: **first** is added

P. 184, l. 28: **after** is added

P. 184, l. 29: **rewritten and cut** is added (a very important revision)

P. 184, l. 30: **at the end of April** is added; the next sentence is revised by adding **that summer** after **proofs**, and putting **made** in the past perfect (thus suggesting that the cuts had been made before he showed Fitzgerald the first proofs that summer), and then the sentence is crossed out. There are several more crossed-out sentences saying that he remembers showing Fitzgerald the proofs when they came back from Scribner's, that he probably showed him the manuscript after he sent it to Perkins, and that the cuts were his own suggestions, showing that Hemingway was struggling with both his conscience and his memory. The one-page insert is meant to be added here: it indicates that Hemingway does not remember when he first showed **finished things** to Scott that year, or when he saw the proofs or the rewritten and cut version of *The Sun Also Rises*. They discussed them, but Hemingway made the decisions. Then follows the draft of the two sentences on page 184, last line, and page 185, lines 1–3, with a couple of crossed-out sentences saying that Fitzgerald saved the letters and that he met him first in June, probably in Juan les Pins

P. 185, l. 5: after **novel** a description of how he wrote the book—in six weeks, starting on his birthday in Valencia, continuing in Hendaye, and finishing the first draft in Paris on 6 September—and how he did the rewriting in two stages in the mountains, except for the final cuts, is added and then deleted

P. 185, l. 8: **which** is added

P. 185, l. 9: **really** is added after **wanted us**

P. 185, l. 10: **an inexpensive** is added

P. 185, l. 21: **stupidly** is added

P. 185, l. 23: **fine villa** is changed to **nice villa**, and **nice house** to **fine house**

P. 186, l. 10: **except Pauline** is added after **nobody**

P. 186, l. 11: **her** is replaced by **Zelda's** before **secret**

P. 186, l. 13: **after** is added

Files 188–89 transcribe accurately File 175, incorporating the corrections. Neither bears any corrections. File 188 is the original and File 189 the carbon copy.

"A MATTER OF MEASUREMENTS"

File 176 is a pencil manuscript of a short fragment describing how, before Scott knew that Zelda was crazy, he and Hemingway had lunch together at Michaud's, despite the fact that Scott did not like to eat on the Left Bank. Hemingway was able to convince him to eat there because Joyce used to. The restaurant was usually crowded, but they arrived late, when other people were already leaving. File 177 is a first draft of the chapter, the first two pages typewritten by Hemingway and the next five pages drafted in pencil (the typescript ends with **We went . . . himself** [p. 191, ll. 4–5]). Page 1 is headed in pencil "**O**," "**I**," and "**Chapter 19**," with "**18**" crossed out. There are no deletions or additions to speak of in either the manuscript or the typescript, except for the first sentence, which begins **Once . . .** , with the **much later** added by hand. On the back of page 6 of File 177 is a sentence in pencil saying that Fitzgerald had the happy faculty of changing everything.

Files 188–89 are an accurate, uncorrected transcript of File 177. Strangely enough, pages 1–6 of File 188, the original, bear an alternative pagination of 9–14. Included with this typescript is also a large, brown envelope with the name of the Union Pacific Railroad Company on it and, on the reverse, in Hemingway's hand, "**Chapters 5 and 6 (if include) to correct from first copy**," and in Mary Hemingway's hand, "**Carbon of Typed copy Paris MSS.**" There are also some notes in Hemingway's hand about things to do and about asking Alfred Rice not to burden him.

"THERE IS NEVER ANY END TO PARIS"

This is by far the messiest chapter of the whole book. Clearly, Hemingway was dealing with material that still evoked in him a strong emotional response. His self-revelation is much more intimate in this than in any other chapter. It has been much rewritten and much material has been deleted, especially descriptions of Hemingway's uncertainty at the time he loved both Hadley and Pauline, of his lying and pretending, and of his remorse. File 121 is a twenty-page pencil manuscript of the first section of the published chapter, up to page 207, line 6. It is clean in parts but very messy in others, with many additions and deletions, among which one should note:

P. 198, l. 19: Hemingway was unsure whether the pension was $3.00 or $2.50. He eventually left $2.00, after crossing out the other two figures

P. 201, l. 14: **was next to the public bar** is crossed out after **alley that**

P. 202, l. 6: **in the sleigh** is crossed out after **nurse**

P. 202, l. 9: a sentence saying that he could not remember what stories he wrote there is crossed out after **1926**

P. 202, l. 14: the sentence is reworked as follows: **I remember the** *cold nights climbing stone houses* [C] **snow in the village on the road . . .**

P. 203, l. 24: **Austria** is crossed out after **Germany and**

P. 204, l. 6: **Germans** is crossed out and replaced by **Berliners**

P. 204, l. 14: **One man who was dug out dead** is crossed out after **dead**

P. 205, l. 18: **in the shelter of** is crossed out after **built**

P. 206, l. 8: **and they wished us** is crossed out after **devils**

P. 207, l. 6: after **possible** the last few lines of the manuscript are different from the published text. These lines tell us that the following year the rich came and that nothing was ever the same again. He and Hadley were **infiltrated** because they had become too confident in each other and careless in their confidence, and because they trusted people too much. They were overrun, and nothing was ever the same again. The story of how two people's happiness can be destroyed by the **relentlessly determined and the well meaning** is an instructive one, but Hemingway never tried to apportion the blame, except to take his own share. Hadley, the only one who was blameless, came well out of it, and that was the only good thing that came out of that year.

File 123 is composed of some twenty-seven pages of drafts and rewritings and of a thirteen-page coherent manuscript, dated 16 December on page 1 and 17 December on page 2. Some of the drafts are dated as follows: "**Still work on it Feb. 16**," "**March 26**," "**March 28**," and "**March 28, 29, 30, April 1**,"[10] and "**Continued 27th, March 27**." The thirteen-page manuscript is the manuscript for the last section of chapter 16 (chapter 20 in the published book). It is a pencil manuscript, quite messy in sections, with major additions and deletions: in particular, a long section is crossed out by Hemingway with a note in the margin for **Val** to copy out and then cross it over lightly in pencil. It begins with **It sounds very simple** and dramatizes how difficult it is to truly love two women at the same time, and how the most destructive and terrible thing that can happen to a married man is for the unmarried woman to decide to marry him. The wife does not know about the affair and trusts her husband. They have been through very difficult times together, and they have loved each other despite the difficulties, and she finally trusts her husband completely. The mistress (Hemingway is too puritan to use that word) says that if he loves his wife, he cannot love her, although she does not say that at the beginning. She says that only when it is too late and he already loves them both, and he has begun lying to everyone. He does things that are impossible, and when he is with one of them, he loves her; and when he is with the other, he loves her, too; and when they are all together, he loves them both. He breaks all the promises he has ever made, and he does things he would never have dreamt he could do. But the woman who is relentless wins. In the long run, though, it is the one who loses who wins, and that is the luckiest thing that ever happened to him. That was how his last winter with Hadley was, and these are the things he remembers about it. Then they returned to Paris.

The more disconnected drafts of File 123 deal with several topics and are reminiscent of the drafts of the Preface. Hemingway talks about giving his readers an account of the people and the places at the time Hadley and he believed that they were invulnerable. But they were not invulnerable, and their happiness was destroyed because they had become overconfident and careless. It is a long and complicated story, and he does not want to apportion the blame, except his own. He remembers everything, the magic, and the places, and all the blame was his to take and understand for how things finally ended. He keeps repeating that Hadley, who was blameless, came well out of that last **murderous year.** He also writes some long passages about skiing, and about there being different bindings now, and nobody having to climb on seal skins any longer. People ski much better now; they come down very fast and drop like birds, and they all know as many secrets as Hemingway and his friends knew in their time. But although things are much better now with ski patrols and motors to start avalanches, one can never be sure that one will not break a leg.

Hemingway also talks about breaking one's heart and about the impossibility of breaking it unless one has one. He also mentions that one never possesses anything unless one has given it away or thrown it away if one is in a hurry. He also talks about there being **remises** or storage places where one can leave things, such as a trunk or a bag containing personal effects or the poems of Evan Shipman, or maps or weapons, and this book contains materials from the **remises** of his memory and his heart. Sometimes things are stolen or lost, but he explained to Edward O'Brien that nothing is ever lost, no matter how it seems at the time. What is left out will always show and make the strength of what is left in. A writer must learn from other writers, but he must also have something of his own that is new, and that no other writer has. Gertrude Stein stated that fact clearly when she said that no classic resembled a previous classic, but he feels that she did not go all the way.

File 123 also includes some drafts of the passage about there never being any end to Paris, and about Picard telling him of a system for dealing with the rich: always accept invitations because it makes the rich happy, but never actually go. Hemingway also talks about remembering the last time Shipman visited him in Cuba, when he was suffering from cancer of the pancreas, and how he was dressing it himself and had forgotten to bring morphine.

File 126 includes two typescripts: 126-1, which is a basically accurate typescript of the thirteen-page manuscript of File 123, and 126-2, headed in pencil with a "**XVI**," which is the carbon copy of the typescript of File 121. File 126-2 bears only typographical corrections and some check marks over foreign words. At the top of File 126-1 are the following annotations in Hemingway's hand: "**Go over EH Jan 26**," "**Don't use until I'm dead. Maybe not then! Not in Hadley's lifetime.**" File 127 is the original of the typescript of File 121. It is basically accurate, except in two minor instances: (p. 205, l. 8) **was** is corrected to **were** in **So were the table and chairs**; and (p. 206, l. 14) **of** is added before **skiing**. File 127 is quite heavily corrected in pencil and in ink, with many additions, and is headed "**L**" and "**Chapter 16**" after "**15**" was crossed out.

P. 198, l. 10: **beautiful** is replaced by **pebbly; lovely** before **valley** is deleted after having been replaced by **open**, which is also crossed out
P. 199, l. 13: **north** is replaced by **lower** and then by **far** before **edge**
P. 199, ll. 17–18: **dark haired** is added between **very** and **beautiful**
P. 199, l. 27: **a racket** is crossed out and replaced by **the way . . . common**
P. 199, last line: after **run down with** Hemingway adds and then crosses out a couple of sentences which say that then the bindings had not been perfected, so that when a skier fell he would lose his ski rather than break a leg; everyone also knew the different snow conditions, and how to ski in deep snow
P. 200, ll. 15–16: **and absolutely controlled running** is added
P. 200, ll. 17–19: **We all knew . . . powder snow** is added
P. 202, l. 2: **sheep dog** is added and then crossed out before **dog**

P. 202, ll. 12–13: **There were . . . well** is added

P. 202, l. 18: Hemingway wants to check the spelling of **Gruss Gott**

P. 203, l. 10: **and scars** is added

P. 203, l. 17: Hemingway writes above **wein-stube**: **"Should put in German EH? yes"**

P. 205, l. 8: **was** is corrected to **were** before **silky**

P. 207, l. 6: Hemingway revises the last few lines of this typescript, in particular deleting **the relentlessly determined and well meaning** and adding some comments on the complications of loving two women at the same time, and on how it is the most instructive and complicated thing a man can learn. The paragraph is then crossed out, with some instructions to Betty, asking her to continue on **next page of pencilled writing.** On that next page is the text as transcribed in Files 188–89, which ends at what would be page 207, line 12. At the top of that last handwritten page is the following annotation in Hemingway's hand: **"Last version March 15,"** and at the bottom, **"Betty: please end here."**

Files 188–89 are an accurate transcription of File 127, except in two main instances: (p. 203, l. 10) after **lecture** a portion of the sentence has been dropped: **with lantern slides on the great and unappreciated German victory**; and (p. 205, l. 12) **with the stars still bright** has been transcribed as **with the stars close and very bright**. Neither bears any correction.

CHAPTER EIGHT

The Editing of A Moveable Feast *After Hemingway's Death*

JN "The Making of the Book: A Chronicle and a Memoir," Mary Hemingway defines the editing that was done after Hemingway's death as follows:

> . . . I went over the book and gave it the same hard-headed editing I would have done if I had been copying from Ernest's original typing and hand script as I used to do in Cuba. Working toward lucidity I put in or removed commas, checked spelling, sometimes but rarely cut out repetitive words or phrases which I felt sure were accidental rather than intentional or for phonetic or poetic effect. With Harry Brague, Ernest's editor at Scribner's, I made a few further cuts when we went over the manuscript together, and we switched about a couple of the chapters for continuity's sake. No one added any word to the book.

Mary Hemingway thus downplays the intervention of Hemingway's editors after his death, and wisely so, since the specter of outside and ill-advised interference in a major author's work published posthumously always looms large in the imagination of an educated reading public. Indeed, Hemingway had no hand in the final editing of his own autobiography, and the extent to which his editors changed his original text, therefore, becomes an important concern.

An examination of the manuscripts, however, reveals that the editing done by Mary Hemingway and Harry Brague was far more extensive than acknowledged by Mary in either her review of the book or in *How It Was*.[1] Much was changed, deleted, and added, but the additions were generally culled from passages that Hemingway had decided against using. Thus, one cannot say that much that was not Hemingway's was added, but one might well say that the book published is not really the book Hemingway had written or wanted published.

The changes that were made to Hemingway's manuscript range from warranted, to unwarranted, to ill-advised. A few complex, run-on, and poorly structured sentences were shortened and clarified by the editors. For instance, "Miss Stein Instructs" contained a paragraph reading:

> But for her to continue to write each day without the drudgery of revision nor the obligation to make her writing intelligible and continue to have the true happiness of creation, it was beginning to become necessary for her to have publication and official acceptance, especially for the unbelievably long book called *The Making of Americans.*

This paragraph was wisely simplified to the published version which reads:

> But she disliked the drudgery of revision and the obligation to make her writing intelligible, although she needed to have publication and official acceptance, especially for the unbelievably long book called *The Making of Americans.* (17)

A similarly long, convoluted, and ineffective sentence was edited down in "Shakespeare and Company." The three sentences which form the first long paragraph on page 37 were originally one long sentence. Only about ten of Hemingway's words were not published, but the published words were somewhat reorganized, and twelve words were added. In both cases, the editors used Hemingway's sentences as a rough draft, and turned out a different, less awkward text.

Such simplification of awkward sentences is good editing—not only warranted, but necessary. Other forms of editing, such as the correction of spelling and grammatical errors, as well as the correction of the spelling of foreign names and words, were also necessary. For instance, in the first chapter, "*povrottes*" and "Cardinale Lemoine" were corrected to "*poivrottes*" and "Cardinal Lemoine." Unfortunately, not all of Hemingway's errors in the spelling of foreign names and words were corrected as Hemingway had himself requested. Some were even corrected inaccurately, changing, for instance, "Place de la Verte Galante" to "Place du Verte Galente," thus correcting one error, leaving three, and adding one. (The correct spelling is of course "Square du Vert Galant.") In *A Moveable Feast*, as in his other books, foreign names and sentences are usually inaccurate, thus evidencing not only Hemingway's lack of true knowledge of these languages, in particular French and Spanish, but also his editors' carelessness in such matters. But perhaps the most startling case of poor copy editing done by omission can be found in chapter 16, "An Agent of Evil." Betty, who typed some of the manuscripts, clearly found it hard to read Hemingway's handwriting, in this particular case at least, and transcribed "*terza rima*" as "*terza riruce*" four times in a row. Hemingway read the typescript and corrected the error by hand four times on the original but not on the carbon copy. After Hemingway's death, his editors obviously used the uncorrected carbon instead of the corrected original to set type and unquestioningly published "*terza riruce*" once on page 143 and three times on page 144 of the book. That a typist might be unfamiliar with literary terminology is understandable. But that editors for Scribner's under the guidance or, at least, with the help of Mary Hemingway not know that "*terza riruce*" does not exist, and not check in a dictionary or search for possible error in the transcription of the manuscript or for Hemingway's corrections on the original of the typescript, is unforgivable.[2] Hemingway corrected at random either the original or the carbon copy of his typescripts. Thus, any serious editor, working with the entire array of manuscripts and typescripts, might be expected to check for possible corrections of such errors on the other copy of the typescript or, even more simply, refer to the manuscript. However, the British edition published by Jonathan Cape (London, 1964), pages 123–24, correctly prints "*terza rima*," suggesting that Jonathan Cape either used the corrected typescript to set type or had an editor who could recognize nonsense.

Many instances of copy editing appear to have been gratuitous, perhaps made simply because the editors did not like some of the words used by Hemingway. For instance, Hemingway used "wonderful" and "wonderfully" repeatedly in the manuscript. Most of these repetitious adjectives and adverbs were deleted by the editors and replaced with more or less felicity by other adjectives and adverbs. A striking example of editing done for its own sake can be found in chapter 2, "Miss Stein Instructs," where the adjective "beautiful" is replaced by "sculpture" in the sentence: "The trees were sculpture without their leaves when you were reconciled to them. . . ." It may be a matter of taste, but "beautiful" seems much more satisfactory than "sculpture." But what is more important is that Hemingway had chosen "beautiful," and that the editors really had no valid justification for making the change. Other changes, while apparently warranted, create confusion for the well-informed reader. For instance, in "The End of an Avocation," "Pauline and I" was replaced by "we" in the sentence ". . . the wickedest track of all where we saw that great rider Ganay fall and heard his skull crumple . . . ," thus suggesting that Hemingway and Hadley were still living together when Ganay was killed in August 1926, which was no longer the case.

A more pervasive form of unjustified editing is the fact that, throughout the text, the editors deleted the indeterminate pronoun "you" used as subject and replaced it by the determinate pronouns "I" and "we," thus clearly modifying Hemingway's diction. This is done at least thirty times in the published text, excluding the times when "you" was changed to "it" and when "your" was changed to "my," in particular in "A Good Café," "Miss Stein Instructs," "The End of an Avocation," and "There Is Never Any End to Paris." Moreover, numerous passages using "you" as subject were deleted, especially in the last chapter. Such editing is double-edged, for it removes the psychological link Hemingway was trying to establish with his reader by making the reader part of his personal experience in such sentences as "Finally towards spring there was the great glacier run, smooth and straight, forever straight if *your* legs could hold it, *your* ankles locked, *you* running so slow, leaning into speed dropping forever and forever in the silent hiss of the crisp powder" (206–7; I.W.D.F.P.T.). The use of "I" or "we" instead of "you" isolates Hemingway within his own experience and from the reader, who no longer participates in his life.

While it would be tedious to discuss here every change made to Hemingway's text, it is nevertheless important for the dedicated reader to be given the chance to recapture Hemingway's original *Feast*. To this effect, a comprehensive list of the changes made is included at the end of this chapter. In order to determine the copy editing done for publication by Mary Hemingway and Harry Brague after Hemingway's death, the text of Files 188–89 was compared with the published text, since the typescript in these files is the last one seen and occasionally corrected by Hemingway. There is at the Beinecke Library another typescript which was presented to the Book-of-the-Month Club in 1964, and reported on by Clifton Fadiman. This typescript includes most of the editing done for publication and is by far the closest to the published version. Since it bears no correction whatever in Hemingway's hand and since there seems to be no record of Hemingway's desire for further copy editing after the typescript of Files 188–89, it is wise to assume that the editing on this Book-of-the-Month Club typescript was done after Hemingway's death.

The few changes not made in this typescript will be identified by an asterisk. Because of the reluctance of the Hemingway estate to allow long quotations from unpublished manuscripts, the deleted sentences have been paraphrased and transposed into indirect discourse. However, some very substantial changes, additions, and deletions were made by the editors, which should be discussed at length. They involve mainly the order and the titles of the chapters, and the following chapters: "Birth of a New School," "Ezra Pound and his Bel Esprit," "There Is Never Any End to Paris," the Preface, and the Fitzgerald epigraph.

In Files 188–89 the chapters are numbered but not titled, suggesting that the titles were the work of Hemingway's editors and not of Hemingway himself. Only two chapters were actually titled by Hemingway on the manuscripts or typescripts: "Ford Madox Ford and the Devil's Disciple" is titled in pencil on the manuscript and in type on the typescript. "Birth of a New School" is titled in pencil on the manuscript with two crossed-out titles: "A Non Friend in Full Cry" and "The Work Destroyers." The other chapters are only numbered numerically or alphabetically. Moreover, the order of the chapters was different. Chapter 3, "Une Génération Perdue," was chapter 7 in Files 188–89, situated between "The End of an Avocation" (chapter 6) and "Hunger Was a Good Discipline" (chapter 8). The existing chapter 10, "Birth of a New School," was not included in Files 188–89, thus diminishing by one the total number of chapters. The current chapter 20, "There Is Never Any End to Paris," was chapter 16 in Files 188–89, situated after "An Agent of Evil" (chapter 15) and before the three Fitzgerald chapters (chapters 17, 18, and 19). Finally, although Hemingway had qualms about publishing it because of its libelous nature, "The Man Who Was Marked for Death" (chapter 13 in Files 188–89) was eventually published. In the Book-of-the-Month Club typescript, however, the chapters are titled as they are in the published book, they are organized in the same order as published, and chapter 10 is included.

The shuffling of the sequence of the chapters negatively affects the thematic patterns Hemingway established, especially the pattern of despotic women versus nurturing women. Indeed, in the chapter order Hemingway settled upon, "Shakespeare and Company," dramatizing Sylvia Beach as the tolerant and nurturing mother, follows "Miss Stein Instructs," which dramatizes Gertrude Stein as the high-handed bad mother. The same coupling occurs with chapters 7 and 8: "Hunger Was a Good Discipline" dramatizes Beach as the good and supportive mother, while the preceding one, "Une Génération Perdue," dramatizes Stein as the critical and negative mother. The pattern climaxes with the three final chapters which portray not only Scott Fitzgerald but also Zelda Fitzgerald, whom Hemingway saw as the epitome of the destructive, castrating woman. On the other hand, using the former chapter 16, "There Is Never Any End to Paris," as the final chapter does not in itself affect the nurturing/destructive-women pattern, since the three Fitzgerald chapters are still grouped together as chapters 17, 18, and 19; moreover, it has the important advantage of functioning as a parallel chapter to "A Good Café on the Place St.-Michel," thus framing the other chapters perfectly and establishing yet another pattern: perfect happiness versus the end of happiness, the going to a place that will be fine, clear, and cold versus the coming back from a place that was fine, clear, and cold.[3]

The three chapters "Birth of a New School," "Ezra Pound and his Bel Esprit," and "There Is Never Any End to Paris" were all expanded by the editors. In fact, it seems that Hemingway had decided not to include "Birth of a New School" in the book since it was not retyped as part of Files 188–89 and since he had selected neither of the two endings he had written for that chapter. His editors decided to reinsert it in the book, chose the second ending rather than the first, revised the transition to that ending, and added a last paragraph that was a hodgepodge of passages culled from the first ending, including an almost exact transcription of the last paragraph of that first ending. Thus, to determine the changes that were made to Hemingway's draft of that chapter for publication, one must compare File 155 with the book. Hemingway had two different manuscripts and two different typescripts for "Ezra Pound and his Bel Esprit," but it seems that he had decided to use only the first one (Files 159, 161-1, 161-3) since it was the only one that was retyped as part of Files 188–89. It is also the only one that was given a chapter number. Thus, his editors again made a major editorial decision and decided to use the second one (Files 160, 161-2) as a follow-up to the first. Therefore, as of page 110, line 17, one must compare the book with File 161-2 to determine the use made of Hemingway's text.

The expansion of these two chapters and the reinsertion of one seem justified to a certain extent, as it makes use of valid Hemingway material that had been rejected for nonliterary reasons. Hemingway may have decided against using "Birth of a New School" for the same reason he had rejected "The Man Who Was Marked for Death" (its libelous nature), which may also be why his editors changed the name of the "work destroyer" from Harold to Hal. On the other hand, the editing that was done to "There Is Never Any End to Paris" is far from being as justified. Indeed, this last chapter was both expanded and reduced by the editors to the extent that we no longer have, by any stretch of the imagination, the chapter Hemingway wrote. We have an extensively reworked chapter which shows Hemingway at his worst as a human being.

As seen previously, Hemingway had great difficulties with this chapter. There are two main manuscripts and typescripts as well as a mass of drafts and rewrites. Again, Hemingway had decided to use only one of the two typescripts, as evidenced by the fact that only one of them (Files 126-2, 127) was retyped in Files 188–89 and by his handwritten note on the other typescript (126-1)—"Don't use until I'm dead. Maybe not then! Not in Hadley's lifetime"—dated 26 January. The editors used the Files 188–89 typescript for the first part of the chapter, and the other one, after extensive cutting, for the second part of the chapter, finally borrowing the last paragraph from the numerous drafts and rewrites in File 124.

The editing done to the first part of the chapter is of the same order as that done to the rest of the book. Only a long paragraph was deleted, which, had it been left in, would have continued page 207, line 12, after "to follow." In this revealing paragraph, Hemingway writes that Hadley and he had become too confident in each other and careless in their confidence and pride. In the mechanics of how their happiness was penetrated he never tried to apportion the blame, except his own share, and that was clearer all his life. "The bulldozing of three people's hearts to destroy one happiness and build another," and the love, and the good work, and all that came out of it, Hemingway does not feel is part of this book. He wrote it and he left it out. "It is a complicated, valuable and instructive story." How it all ended, finally, has nothing to do with this book, either. Any blame was his "to take and possess and understand." Hadley could not possibly be blamed, came well out of it eventually, and married a much finer man than he ever was or could ever hope to be. She is happy and deserves it, and "that was one good and lasting thing that came out of that year."

The cuts made in the second typescript which Hemingway had decided not to use for fear of hurting Hadley, and perhaps, subconsciously, because he realized that it revealed much about him that he did not want advertised, removed much about Pauline and the way Hemingway saw her role in the breakup of his first marriage. In three deleted paragraphs, which would have been on pages 210 and 211, Hemingway rather damns Pauline. As the relationship progressed, "the new one," Pauline, was not happy because she could see he loved them both, although she was still settling for that. "When you are alone with her she knows you love her." She was a fine girl, and she believed that if a man loves someone he cannot love anyone else; and he never spoke about his wife to help her and to help himself, although he was past help. He never knew, and maybe she did not know herself, when she made her decision, but sometime in "the middle of the winter she began to move steadily and relentlessly toward marriage," never breaking her friendship with his wife, "never losing any advantage of position, always preserving an appearance of complete innocence." She went away elaborately, but was away at any time only long enough for him to miss her badly. There was no evil in her intent ever, only an aim; she loved him truly, and they were happy together in their heads and in their hearts. Hemingway felt that the winter of the avalanches had been like a happy day in childhood compared to the previous winter. The new and strange girl who now owned half of him, once she had decided to marry ("you could not say break up the marriage because that was only a necessary step," a regrettable one, but not an end, probably passed over or avoided in thinking), made only one grave mistake: "She under valued the power of remorse." (Hemingway hesitated between "under valuated" and "under rated/under valued.") These three paragraphs were written in the indeterminate "you" form which clearly made the reader a party to Hemingway's guilt or, rather, in his own view, victimization. After all, it could happen to anyone is the hidden message. In the other deleted paragraph, Hemingway accepts a portion of the blame, however reluctantly and underhandedly:

> For the girl to deceive her friend was a terrible thing but it was my fault and blindness that this did not repel me. Having become involved in it and being in love I accepted all the blame for it to myself and lived with the remorse.

Of course, it is obvious that if Hemingway accepted all the blame with respect to Hadley, he certainly blamed Pauline for having seduced his innocent self. He is guilty not of cheating on his wife, but of loving too much!

Removing such explicit references to Pauline may have reinforced the artistic unity of the book, but was in no way necessary for, despite these cuts, Pauline still has to be present in the book as the unmarried young woman he was in love with to justify his betrayal of Hadley.[4] Removing Pauline as a living presence from the book also entailed leaving out much of Hemingway's agony and remorse. Indeed, the editors removed five groups of sentences which expressed Hemingway's guilt, thus making the book less human and Hemingway's persona more callous. Several deleted sentences and a paragraph that would have been on page 210 dramatize that remorse. He felt that everyone was still happy except himself when he woke up in the night. He loved both women now and he was gone. Everything was split inside of him and he loved two people instead of one. When he was with the one, he loved her and also the one who was away. When he was with the other, he loved her and also the other who was away. When he was with them both he loved them both, and the strange part was that he was happy. When he was in Paris, after having returned from New York, with Pauline who was still writing to his wife, the places they went to and the "unbelievable wrenching, killing happiness, selfishness and treachery" of everything they did gave him "such a bad remorse, and dreadful strange happiness" that the "black remorse came, and hatred of the evil, and no contrition." In a deleted sentence and a paragraph which would have been on page 211, Hemingway writes that the remorse was a fine and good thing and that with a little luck and if he had been a better man it might have saved him from something worse, instead of being his true and constant companion for the next three years. After commenting on the rich and on how terrible it was for Pauline to deceive Hadley, Hemingway writes:

> The remorse was never completely away day or night until my wife had married a much finer man than I ever was or ever could be and I knew that she was happy. Then I was happy and without remorse and I never worked better nor was I happier and I loved the girl truly and she loved me truly and well and we had as good a life together for many years as early Paris had been.

Not only were Hemingway's expressions of guilt and remorse removed from the text, but also the measure of compassion and honesty present in his discussion of the rich, and of maturity in his acceptance of personal responsibility for his own actions. In a long paragraph that would have been on page 211, had it not been deleted, Hemingway writes:

> Maybe the rich were fine and good and the pilot fish *that brought them* [A] was a friend. Certainly the rich never did anything for their own

ends. They collected people then as some collect pictures and others breed horses and they only backed me in every ruthless *and evil* [C] decision that I made *after I had made it* [A]. All of the occasions seemed so inevitable and logical and fine and all had been brought about by deceit. It wasn't that the decisions were wrong, although they all turned out badly finally *and* [A] from the same fault of character that made them *but not until many years later and then from bad luck* [A]. If you deceive and lie with one person against another you will eventually do it again. If some person is able to do it to you once another person will do it again. I had hated these rich *at one time* [A] because they had backed me and encouraged me when I was doing wrong. *They had not, really, they had only accepted my decision* [A]. *But how could they know it was wrong and had to turn out badly, when they had never known all the circumstances?* [C] It was not their fault. It was only their fault for coming into other people's lives. They were bad luck for people but they were worse luck to themselves and they lived to have all their bad luck finally to the very worst end that all bad luck could go.[5]

When Carlos Baker published most of this long passage, he clearly used as a source Hemingway's uncorrected carbon copy of the typescript. It is indeed a pity that this revealing passage was not included in *A Moveable Feast.*

Finally, several explicit descriptions of Hemingway's happiness with Hadley were also deleted from the text. A paragraph that would have been on page 210 tells the reader that the husband and wife have shared in everything, that they are never bored together, and that they have something that seems unbreakable. They love their child and they love places such as Paris and Spain, parts of Switzerland, the Dolomites, and the Vorarlberg. "They love their work and she has sacrificed hers to his and never mentioned it." In another paragraph that would have been on page 211, he writes that they had a lovely time in Schruns that winter before he knew that he would ever get back into "the badness" (crossed out on original and replaced by "what happened that summer"), and he remembers all of it, and the coming of spring in the mountains, and how much he and his wife loved and trusted each other truly, and how happy they were that all the rich were gone, and how Hemingway thought that they were invulnerable again. But they were not invulnerable, "and that was the end of the first part of Paris."

Indeed, the editing done to the Schruns material by Mary Hemingway, since it is by her own acknowledgment she who did most of that work, presents a less flattering picture of Hemingway than would have been the case had she abided by his decision not to use the File 126-1 typescript or had she used that typescript in its entirety. By deleting much about Pauline and Hadley and much about Hemingway's expressions of guilt, pain, and acknowledgment of personal responsibility, and by keeping, and in fact indirectly emphasizing, the disingenuous self-deprecation, the sentimentality, the melodrama, and the self-pity, she presents her own version of the breakup of Hemingway's marriage to Hadley. On the other hand, it seems that she was wise to change the last paragraph and not use the one written by Hemingway at the end of File 126-1, as it was awkward and somewhat irrelevant. In that closing paragraph Hemingway wrote that nobody climbed on skis and that most people broke their legs, and that maybe it is "easier in the end to break your legs than to break your heart. . . ." In fact, the only sentence from this paragraph that was used in the book is: "but this is how Paris was in the early days when we were very poor and very happy."

The editing done to the Fitzgerald epigraph is puzzling and tends to show Hemingway in a far more negative light than was necessary. As was seen in chapter 7, Hemingway had revised his foreword to include a last sentence later deleted by the editors, which read: "He was flying again and I was lucky to meet him just after a good time in his writing if not a good one in his life." Moreover, Hemingway had deleted the last and more negative part of the sentence which was published and reads: "and could not fly any more because the love of flight was gone and he could only think ["remember" in the published text] when it had been effortless." It is unfortunate that the sentence Hemingway wanted was deleted and a sentence fragment he had rejected eventually published in its place, thereby discarding Hemingway's implicit acknowledgment of the excellence of *Tender Is the Night* and of Fitzgerald's ability to write magic prose once more—a measure of honesty that would have been welcome, given the condescending and disparaging portrayal of Fitzgerald which follows in the next three chapters.

As was also seen in chapter 7, there is no coherent manuscript for the Preface. The only manuscripts existing in Hemingway's hand are the various attempts at introductory or concluding sentences found in Files 122 and 124 and in the notes and fragments of Files 186 and 187. Moreover, there is no typescript for the Preface which can be attributed to Hemingway. The likelihood that a manuscript or a Hemingway typescript of the Preface was lost or withheld is small, since Hemingway tended to keep everything he wrote, particularly, one would expect, recent manuscripts. The one reason Gerry Brenner advances in favor of such a loss—that another manuscript, a portrait of Hemingway's son Bumby, of which we know the existence thanks to Carlos Baker, is also missing—is no longer valid since that manuscript has been found. Of course, the manuscript of the Preface could also be found at some later date, but the chaotic quality of the manuscripts we now have suggests that Hemingway never settled on a Preface that was coherent and satisfied him.[6] One might then conclude that the published Preface, despite the fact that it is signed in the book as Ernest Hemingway's and dated 1960, is in fact the work of Mary Hemingway and/or the editors at Scribner's. It made use of some of Hemingway's sentences from Files 122 and 124, with heavy editing, but discarded most of the material in these files. The nature of the editing done falls in the following main categories: 1) It softens Hemingway's affirmation that the book *is* fiction. Nowhere does Hemingway write that, if the reader prefers, the book may be read as fiction. Instead he states at least nine times in File 122 that the book *is* fiction, and once in File 187 that it cannot be any other way. 2) It discards Hemingway's statements that he wrote little about Pauline because their relationship was a beginning rather than an ending. 3) It discards Hemingway's repeated and concerned apologies to Hadley for any misrepresentations or mistakes, and for having written the book as fiction. 4) It deletes the various statements that Hadley is the true heroine of the book.[7] 5) It deletes all expressions of self-doubt, such as the following: "It seemed so easy when it started. Then you found mistakes and errors" (File 122). 6) It removes all notations concerning his fear of being sued by such people as Miss Moorehead and others whose names begin with Miss. 7) It deletes mention of a variety of people, such as André Gide and Harold Stearns. 8) It also eliminates mention of some places, such as Menilmontant. Indeed, Hemingway provided only the rough material for this Preface from which his editors picked and chose and created something coherent which, however, is not truly Hemingway's.

Thus, *A Moveable Feast* is not entirely Hemingway's. Sections of it, especially the Preface and the last chapter, are Mary Hemingway's as much as Hemingway's. The tone of both has been drastically affected by Mary's editing, which was perhaps misguided rather than ill-intentioned. There was no need to be worried when Hemingway expressed doubt or acknowledged that there were errors. No one's memory can be expected to be perfect, even that of Hemingway, who was supposed to be the best at everything, and it is better to acknowledge forgetfulness than to be caught lying, as is the case with Hemingway's claim that Fitzgerald had not helped him with *The Sun Also Rises*. It would indeed have been wiser for Mary to leave in Hemingway's hesitations in that respect—not that they would have entirely concealed the lie, in any case. But her excision of material where Hemingway acknowledged weakness or fallibility is on a par with her excision of material that would show Fitzgerald in a better light, Hadley as blameless, Pauline as having a real personality—all of which eventually backfires in that, rather than building up Hemingway's positive qualities, it diminishes him as a human being.[8] On the other hand, much editing that needed to be done was done properly; but much that also needed to be done was either left undone or done inadequately. In general, one might say that it would perhaps have been better for Mary Hemingway (since she is the one who did most of the work) to leave her own feelings out of the book and to concentrate more on technical details. By selecting and deleting, one can indeed re-create a text.

A listing of the significant changes from Files 188–89 to the published version of *A Moveable Feast* follows. Minor corrections and changes, such as corrections of spelling and punctuation errors, italicizing of foreign names and titles, and the like are not listed here. The asterisks indicate changes not made in the Book-of-the-Month Club typescript.

"A GOOD CAFE ON THE PLACE ST.-MICHEL"

P. 3, l. 2: **You** is changed to **We**
P. 3, l. 22: **the** is added before **two cleated**
P. 4, l. 1: **you** is changed to **we** (*)
P. 4, l. 14: **you** is changed to **I** (*)
P. 4, l. 15: **you** is changed to **I** (*)
P. 5, l. 17: **wonderfully** is changed to **wonderful**
P. 7, ll. 9–11: Two sentences which Hemingway crossed out in File 130 and which do not appear in Files 188–89 are reintegrated after some revisions. They are the last two sentences of the paragraph
P. 7, l. 27: **lovely** is changed to **gently**

"MISS STEIN INSTRUCTS"

P. 11, ll. 11–12: **beautiful** is changed to **sculpture**
P. 11, l. 14: **were blowing** is changed to **blew**

P. 12, l. 5: **I put the notebook, or the paper away in** is changed to **I put away the notebook, or the paper in**

P. 12, l. 23: **you** is changed to **I**

P. 13, l. 8: **you** is changed to **I**

P. 13, l. 9: **though** is deleted after **feeling**

P. 14, l. 8: **your tongue** is replaced by **it**

P. 14, l. 18: **Boutet de Monville** is corrected to **Boutet de Monvel**

P. 14, l. 26: the sentence that reads **But we liked Miss Stein and her friend, although the friend was** *frightening,* **and the paintings and the cakes and the eau-de-vie were truly wonderful** is changed to the present two-sentence version (I.W.D.F.P.T.)

P. 15, l. 7: **some of them** is changed to **them**

P. 15, ll. 20–21: **She told me and she would be** is an independent sentence in Files 188–89. It is now integrated within the preceding sentence after a comma

P. 15, l. 28: **That afternoon, too, she told us** is changed to **That afternoon she told us, too,**

P. 16, l. 4: **and** is deleted before **money**

P. 16, l. 5: **even** is deleted after **But** (*)

P. 16, l. 18: **come in to** is changed to **come to**

P. 16, l. 23: **the** is added before **cafés**

P. 17, l. 1: **wonderful** is changed to **exciting**

P. 17, ll. 8–10: the sentence fragment **it was necessary for** *this daily output, which varied with her energy,* *but was regular, and therefore became huge,* **be published and that she receive** *official recognition* is changed to the published version (I.W.D.F.P.T.)

P. 17, l. 17: **could** is changed to **would**

P. 17, l. 19: **on trust** is moved from after **understand** to after **took**

P. 17, ll. 20–21: **because of** is added after **and**

P. 17, l. 22: **things** is changed to **truths**

P. 17, ll. 25–28: the paragraph that reads **But for her to continue to write each day . . . and official acceptance, especially for the unbelieveably long book called *The Making of Americans*** is changed to the published version (see p. 172)

P. 17, last line: **great** is added before **stretches**

P. 18, l. 3: **—forced, perhaps would be the word—** is moved from after **serially** on line 5 to its present position

P. 18, l. 5: **Revue** is changed to *Review*

P. 18, l. 6: **I was overly familiar with the revue's finances, and** is replaced by **For publication in the** *review*

P. 18, l. 11: The first two sentences on lines 9–12 are one in Files 188–89 and read, **. . . ahead; and on this day . . .**

P. 18, l. 13: **some time before** is deleted after **learned**

P. 18, l. 15: **what we would call now a square** is changed to **too uneducated**

P. 18, l. 27: **That was the term that was** *accrochable* is changed to **That term was** *accrochable*

P. 19, l. 9: **such** is deleted after **world**

P. 19, l. 10: **but some of them** is changed to **although some of them**

P. 19, l. 14: **me** is added before **a bottle**

P. 19, l. 15: **you** is changed to **I**

P. 19, l. 15: **to never let** is changed to **never to let**

P. 20, l. 17: **They drink, take drugs** is changed to **They drink and take drugs**

P. 21, l. 6: **very** is changed to **so** before **brightly**

P. 21, l. 8: **it** is deleted before **now**

P. 21, l. 9: **I believed** is changed to **I decided**

P. 21, l. 11: **I** is deleted before **told**

P. 21, l. 12: the last two sentences are one in Files 188–89 and read, **. . . I told my newly acquired knowledge to my wife** *and we were happy in the night* **with our own knowledge . . .** (I.W.D.F.P.T.)

"UNE GENERATION PERDUE"

P. 25, l. 5: one sentence is deleted after **affectionate: She loved to talk about people and places and things and food.**

P. 25, l. 6: **political** is added before **conferences**

P. 25, l. 8: **did work** is changed to **worked**

P. 25, l. 9: **things that had happened** is changed to **details**

P. 25, l. 9: **things** is changed to **parts** before **always**

P. 25, l. 11: one sentence is deleted after **stories.** It says that Stein **did not like to hear really bad nor tragic things,** but that no one else does, and that, having seen them, Hemingway did not want to talk about them unless she asked him how the world was going

P. 25, l. 11: **about** is changed to **of** before **how the world**

P. 25, l. 15: **things** is deleted after **these**

P. 25, l. 20: a sentence fragment is deleted after **written: , to keep my mind from going on with the story I was working on.**

P. 25, l. 23: **my** is changed to **the** before **body**

P. 26, l. 9: **you** is changed to **I** before **could get**

P. 26, l. 9: **, by now,** is deleted before **find**

P. 27, l. 6: a sentence fragment is deleted after **book: , the title of which I cannot remember,**

P. 27, l. 17: **talk** is changed to **speak**

P. 27, l. 25: **well** is deleted after **speak**

P. 28, l. 23: **Pound** is added after **Ezra**

P. 28, l. 26: **That finished Ezra at 27 rue de Fleurus.** is deleted after **broken it.**

P. 29, l. 1: **while we** is deleted before **were**

P. 29, l. 8: a sentence is deleted after **Miss Stein's Ford.: Perhaps he had not realized the importance of Miss Stein's vehicle having the right of immediate repair.**

P. 29, l. 30: **published** is changed to **wrote**

P. 30, l. 5: **when** is changed to **and** before **braking**

P. 30, l. 15: **a balls-up** is changed to **a fiasco**

"SHAKESPEARE AND COMPANY"

P. 35, l. 1: **Books you borrowed** is changed to **I borrowed books**

P. 35, l. 4: **lovely,** is deleted before **warm**

P. 35, ll. 9–10: **very sharply cut face** is changed to **sharply sculptured face**, which ignores Hemingway's correction in File 138 and returns to the File 136 version

P. 36, l. 2: **the shelves on shelves** is changed to **shelves and shelves**

P. 36, l. 3: **richness** is changed to **wealth**

P. 36, l. 10: **by** is changed to **back** (★)

P. 36, l. 20: **someone** is changed to **people**

P. 37, ll. 6–13: in Files 188–89 the paragraph reads: *At home in our* **two-room flat that had no hot water and no inside toilet facilities except an antiseptic** *portable* **container** *that was* **not uncomfortable to anyone who was used to a Michigan outhouse,** *but which was a cheerful gay flat* **with a fine view and a good mattress and springs for a comfortable bed on the floor,** *well and tastefully* *covered,* and pictures that we liked on the walls, I told my wife about the wonderful place I had found. (I.W.D.F.P.T.)

"PEOPLE OF THE SEINE"

P. 41, l. 2: **where we lived** is deleted after **Lemoine**
P. 41, l. 6: **dull** is changed to **bleak**
P. 41, l. 18: **cheaply** is changed to **cheap**
P. 42, l. 22: **past** is changed to **beyond**
P. 43, l. 12: **elms** is changed to **chestnut trees**
P. 43, l. 12: **some** is deleted before **huge**
P. 43, ll. 18–19: **expertly** is moved from after **fished** to before **baited**
P. 44, l. 9: **the** is added before **men**
P. 44, l. 18: **would rather** is changed to **preferred to**
P. 44, l. 24: **good** is changed to **sound**
P. 44, last two lines: the sentence fragment in Files 188–89 reads, . . . *the great plane trees on* the stone banks of the river, *the elms and sometimes the poplars* . . . (*) (I.W.D.F.P.T.)

"A FALSE SPRING"

P. 49, l. 7: **morning** is changed to **mornings**
P. 49, last line: **I thought I would** is changed to **I decided to**
P. 50, l. 8: **work** is added after **started**
P. 50, l. 8: **first** is deleted after **paper**
P. 50, ll. 9–10: **the small, pretty and larcenous track that was the home of the outsider** is added after **Enghien**
P. 50, l. 17: **keep us six months** is added to replace **have paid for a trip**, which was crossed out in File 142 and had not been replaced in File 144
P. 50, l. 18: **to do what** is changed to **of that**
P. 50, l. 18: **but chevre d'Or would have** is changed to **until Chèvre d'Or; We didn't think about Chevre d'Or. We went out to Enghein; the small, lovely and larcenous track that was the home of the outsider** is deleted at the end of the paragraph
P. 50, l. 29: **is hard on** is changed to **bothers**
P. 51, l. 13: **later on** is deleted after **strange to me**

P. 52, l. 8: **to find someone** is changed to **and found someone**

P. 52, l. 12: **with one** is changed to **the first**

P. 53, l. 9: **and there was racing at some track every day** is deleted after **all other capital**

P. 53, l. 14: **afterwards** is deleted after *Mexicaine*

P. 56, l. 24: **Norah** is changed to **Nora** (*)

P. 57, l. 4: **being** is added after *tournedos*

P. 57, l. 13: **was** is changed to **were** before **riding**

P. 57, last line: **first** is deleted before **morning**

"THE END OF AN AVOCATION"

P. 61, l. 10: **it** is added before **stayed**

P. 61, l. 11: **speak** is changed to **think**

P. 61, l. 13: **one** is changed to **friend** after **this**

P. 61, l. 16: **I wrote about it.** is changed to **wrote it,** (*)

P. 61, l. 17: **Though in the end** is changed to **even though in the end**

P. 61, l. 18: **the one racing story that was out in the mails that survived** is changed to **one racing story that survived, because it was out in the mails**

P. 61, last line: **paper** is changed to **newspaper**

P. 62, l. 4: **or at least how,** is deleted after **why**

P. 62, l. 11: **that** is changed to **when**

P. 62, l. 16: **You only, in principle, bet when you had a horse to bet on but you** is changed to **In principle I only bet when I had a horse to bet on but I**

P. 62, l. 19: **you** is changed to **me** before **betting**

P. 62, l. 19: **You had to follow it very closely to really know anything.** is deleted after **them.**

P. 62, l. 24: **you** is changed to **it** after **stopped**

P. 64, l. 15: **that is as good as it is both** is changed to **that is as good as the races are both**

P. 64, l. 16: **All that and the six day races are still to come** is deleted after **roads**

P. 64, l. 29: **a shelter from the air resistance** is changed to **shelter**

P. 64, l. 30: **any racing** is changed to **anything**

P. 65, l. 4: the two sentences are one, linked by a comma after **racing**

P. 65, l. 16: **The Sioux** is changed to **"the Sioux"** (*)

P. 65, l. 23: **Pauline and I** is changed to **we**

P. 65, l. 29: **But** is deleted before **Mike**

P. 65, last line: the two sentences are one: **. . . no need to bet, and it comes at another time in Paris (and** changed to **But)**

"HUNGER WAS A GOOD DISCIPLINE"

P. 69, l. 4: **When you were at a time** is deleted before **When you had given up**

P. 69, l. 7: **the best place to do it was in the Luxembourg** is changed to **the best place to go was the Luxembourg**

P. 69, l. 11: **heightened** is changed to **sharpened**

P. 69, l. 15: **was** is changed to **were** before **hungry**

P. 69, ll. 15–16: **it was possibly only that** is changed to **possibly it was only that**

P. 70, l. 8: **bookshop** is added after **Sylvia Beach's**

P. 70, l. 15: **before** is added after **seen**

P. 72, l. 1: **You** is deleted before **Forgive**

P. 73, l. 15: **'s** is added after **O'Brien**

P. 73, l. 25: **so I could work on them on our holidays in the mountains** is a separate sentence in Files 188–89

P. 73, l. 27: **these** is deleted before **manila**

P. 73, l. 28: **because** is changed to **that** before **Lincoln Steffens**

P. 74, l. 2: the two sentences are one and read: **. . . before Miss Stein had come to our flat that I had never had . . .**

P. 74, l. 4: there is no new paragraph in Files 188–89; paragraphing is added

P. 74, l. 9: **it** is changed to **the story**

P. 74, l. 12: **and make some joke about it** is moved from after **crash** to after **foot**

P. 74, l. 20: **had** is deleted before **told me**

P. 74, l. 22: the two sentences are one and read: **. . . newspaper job, I was making good money . . .**

P. 74, l. 27: **badly** is changed to **bad**

P. 75, l. 2: **badly** is changed to **bad**

P. 75, l. 21: **;but you can work something out.** is deleted after **you learn from it**

P. 76, l. 19: **across** is changed to **up** after **d'Assas** (★)

P. 77, last line: one sentence is deleted at the end: **In those days we never thought that any of that could be different.**

"FORD MADOX FORD AND THE DEVIL'S DISCIPLE"

P. 81, ll. 2–3: the sentence has been reworked; Files 188–89 read: . . . **when we lived** *down the rue Notre Dame des Champs in the top floor of the pavilion in the courtyard with the sawmill,* **and it was one of the** *nicest* **cafés in Paris.** (I.W.D.F.P.T.)

P. 82, l. 16: **to notice** is deleted after **watched** (★)

P. 82, l. 17: **or at** is changed to **and saw** (★)

P. 82, l. 27: **, our only poet,** is deleted after **Cendrars**

P. 84, l. 29: a comma is replaced by a period after **correcting him** (★)

P. 86, l. 18: **to have known** is changed to **to know**

P. 88, ll. 8, 12: **Emil** is changed to **Emile** (★)

P. 88, l. 18: **Aleister** is changed to **Alestair** (★)

"BIRTH OF A NEW SCHOOL"

P. 91, l. 3: **the smell of café cremes,** is deleted after **tables**

P. 91, l. 17: **the** is added before **sweat-salted** (★)

P. 92, l. 15: **your** is changed to **my** before **home café**

P. 92, l. 16: **You** is changed to **I** before **had to make**

P. 93, l. 9: **feel** is changed to **felt**

P. 94, l. 9: **muck** is changed to **hell**

P. 94, l. 15: this is the last line before a choice had to be made by the editors as to which of two possible endings to choose (see Files 154–56). The published text uses the ending labeled "(p.) '(5a) **Second ending**"

P. 94, ll. 16–18: these three lines do not appear in File 155, in either one ending or the other. Line 16 can be found in a crossed-out portion of File 154. The origin of lines 17 and 18 cannot be found in the manuscripts. They were probably added by the editors. On the other hand, the two lines that should follow line 15 in the second ending—**"I have to write"** and **"I have to write too"**—are deleted in the published text

P. 96, l. 10: **Harold** is changed to **Hal**

P. 96, l. 20: **for him** is deleted after **hopes**

P. 96, l. 20: is the last line of the second ending

P. 96, ll. 21–30: this paragraph has been culled from the first ending, with some changes (see File 154). **The next day . . . a day's rest** has been added by the editors

"WITH PASCIN AT THE DOME"

P. 99, l. 2: **where we lived** is deleted after **flat**

P. 99, l. 2: **at 113 rue Notre Dame des Champs,** is deleted after **sawmill**

P. 100, l. 14: **too** is deleted after **not**

P. 100, l. 17: one sentence is deleted after **badly.**: **It was necessary to give up going racing in the time of our real poverty and I was still too close to that poverty to risk any money.**

P. 100, ll. 17–27: the remainder of the paragraph after **badly.** appears in Files 188–89 two paragraphs later, after **and have luxuries** (that is, p. 101, l. 16)

P. 100, l. 18: **good** is deleted before **money**

P. 100, l. 28: **By any standards** follows the deleted sentence on line 17 without a new paragraph in Files 188–89

P. 101, l. 20: in Files 188–89 the sentence reads: . . . as *a boosted* beast that I had just foresworn *at Enghein to work on this day as a serious writer; now full* of my evening virtue . . . (I.W.D.F.P.T.)

P. 101, l. 21: **of** is changed to **at** after **inmates**

P. 102, l. 7: one sentence is deleted after **depravity.**: **She was a lesbian who also liked men. (★)**

P. 104, l. 16: **the dark sister said promptly.** is changed to **the dark girl said.**

P. 104, l. 16: Two sentences are deleted: **"You want to contrast me with all the beautiful Nordic Types. No." "I like it very much *Chez Viking*,"** the dark girl said.

P. 104, l. 29: **that** is changed to **who** after **those**

"EZRA POUND AND HIS BEL ESPRIT"

P. 108, l. 3: **could** is changed to **can**

P. 108, l. 14: **, I believe,** is changed to **perhaps**

P. 108, l. 22: **fencing** is changed to **boxing**

The following items in this section show the differences between File 161-2 and the published text.

P. 110, l. 18: **He was always doing something practical for** is changed to **He helped**

P. 110, last line: **have** is changed to **had** before **salons**

P. 111, l. 10: **gotten** is changed to **got**

P. 111, l. 14: in File 161-2 **about** is at the end of the sentence: **whose ideas Ezra was very enthusiastic about.**

P. 112, l. 5: **revue** is changed to **review**

P. 112, l. 13: **fine laurel that I could ride out and get on my bicycle and I thought . . .** is changed to **fine laurel that I could gather, riding out on my bicycle to get it, and I thought . . .**

P. 112, l. 19: **betted** is changed to **bet**

P. 113, l. 4: **was** is added after **than**

P. 113, last line: the last sentence in File 161-2 is deleted: **It turned out all right though as we used the money to go to Spain.** (★)

"A STRANGE ENOUGH ENDING"

P. 117, l. 23: **me** is changed to **us** after **asked**

P. 117, l. 24: **hotel before and after this trip and we had written many letters. But Hadley and I** is shortened to **hotel, but Hadley and I**

P. 117, last line: **that** is changed to **where** after **places**

P. 118, ll. 1–3: Files 188–89 read: **Naturally you say nothing about this but you *can hope to come* and then it is impossible. *You should know a little* about the system of not visiting people. *It was something that we never learned. You* had to learn it. Much later Picasso . . .** (I.W.D.F.P.T.)

P. 118, l. 9: **very** is deleted before **lovely**

P. 118, l. 26: **it** is changed to **the glass** (★)

P. 119, last line: one sentence is deleted after **worst**; it says that it never occurred to him until many years later that one could hate another because one had learned to write conversation from the novel that started off with the quotation from the garage keeper

P. 119, last line: **really much** is deleted before **more**

"THE MAN WHO WAS MARKED FOR DEATH"

P. 125, l. 3: **At that time** is changed to **At the time**

P. 125, l. 10: one sentence is deleted after **travel**; it says that the advance he had received from an American publisher on his first full-length book of short stories was $200, and that, supplemented by loans and savings, **it meant a winter to ski and write in the Vorarlberg.**

P. 125, l. 18: **in any way** is deleted after **imputed**

P. 125, l. 19: **ever** is deleted after **co-editor**

P. 127, l. 21: **I was embarrassed and it made me feel** is shortened to **It made me feel**

P. 127, l. 26: **was** is deleted after **the dust**

P. 127, l. 28: **lest** is changed to **that** before **thou** (*)

P. 128, l. 17: **I am sure** is deleted after **well**

P. 128, l. 24: **Now about Walsh,** is changed to **How about Walsh?**

P. 129, l. 4: two sentences are deleted after **at that.**: **I cannot remember when Walsh died. It was long before that evening with Joyce.**

P. 129, l. 4: **But I can remember telling Joyce** is shortened to **I told Joyce**

P. 129, l. 6: **and how very happy it made him to hear** is shortened to **and it made him happy to hear**

"EVAN SHIPMAN AT THE LILAS"

P. 134, ll. 4–5: the sentence fragment in Files 188–89 reading **living well then for anyone who worked, no matter how poor they were** is changed to **living well and working, no matter how poor you were**

P. 134, ll. 11–14: the sentence in Files 188–89 reads: **. . . your high shelter *or your pension* in the Hotel Taube in the village at night; *and* you could . . . Russian writers *had given you.* (I.W.D.F.P.T.)**; **in the day time, and** is added before **at night**

P. 135, l. 5: **where we now lived in the courtyard of** is deleted before **the sawmill**

P. 135, l. 8: **Place and the** is deleted before **Boulevard**

P. 135, l. 8: **of the sawmill** is deleted after **gate**

P. 139, l. 10: **softly to us** is added after **he said**

P. 139, l. 11: **"Entendu, Messieurs"** begins a new paragraph in Files 188–89 and is fully italicized. It is followed by **Jean said** instead of **he said**

P. 139, l. 12: **aloud** is added

"AN AGENT OF EVIL"

P. 143, ll. 12–16: the two sentences are one and read: **The Hole in the Wall was a very narrow bar, *almost* a passage way, *on the rue des***

Italiens with a red painted facade which had, at one time, a rear exit into the sewers of Paris from which you were supposed to be able to reach the catacombs. (I.W.D.F.P.T.)

P. 143, l. 19, p. 144, ll. 5, 6, 7: **terza rima** is changed to **terza riruce** and italicized

P. 144, l. 13: **what** is replaced by **which** before **lovers**

P. 144, l. 13: **in** is replaced by **on** before **behalf**

P. 144, l. 24: **who was** is deleted before **very excited**

P. 145, l. 19: **yet** is added before **another milk bottle**

P. 146, l. 4: the sentence in Files 188–89 reads: **I do not know** *the date of Dunning's actual death, nor if he ever died, nor why he* **threw the milk bottles . . .** (I.W.D.F.P.T.)

P. 146, last line: the last sentence of the paragraph saying that Hemingway had never seen anything written about Evan Shipman and this part of Paris, nor about Shipman's unpublished poems, and that he feels it is important to include him in this book, was deleted.

"SCOTT FITZGERALD"

P. 147: the last sentence of the foreword is deleted: **He was flying again and I was lucky to meet him just after a good time in his writing if not a good one in his life.; and could not fly any more . . .** is restored after **to think** (see File 172)

P. 150, l. 4: **also** is deleted before **ordered**

P. 150, l. 9: **as his face was faintly puffy** is changed to **his face being faintly puffy**

P. 150, l. 13: **in fact** is deleted before **there were**

P. 150, l. 18: **overly small** is replaced by **too small**

P. 150, l. 26: **over** is replaced by **ending** after **speech**

P. 151, l. 3: **un-pardoning** is replaced by **inescapable**

P. 152, l. 6: **sunk** is corrected to **sank** (*)

P. 152, l. 9: **nor have I exaggerated in describing it** is deleted after **imagination**

P. 152, l. 10: **your eyes** is replaced by **my eyes**

P. 154, l. 2: **and** is added between **last** and **only**

P. 154, l. 13: one sentence is deleted before **Scott was: I believe it was much better later.**

P. 154, l. 18: **then** is deleted before **grey light**

P. 155, l. 10: **I believe** is changed to **as I recall**

P. 155, l. 13: the following sentence is deleted at the end of the paragraph: **We set a tentative date for leaving and I saw him again twice, we made a final date, and checked it the night before.**

P. 155, l. 14: **and my wife thought it was a splendid idea** is deleted after **trip**

P. 155, l. 20: **who had written a very silly, badly written and collegiate book followed by another book I had been unable to read** is deleted after **older writer**

P. 156, ll. 1–2: **they could write** and **their talent** is changed to **he could write** and **his talent**

P. 156, ll. 2–4: this sentence is condensed from two sentences that read: *He said he had learned to write the stories for the* **Post** *so that they did him no harm at all. He* **wrote the real story first, he said,** *and* **the destruction and changing of it that he did at the end did him no harm.** (I.W.D.F.P.T.)

P. 156, l. 7: **started to break all my writing down** is changed to **started to break down all my writing**

P. 156, l. 26: **in order** is added before **to save**

P. 157, l. 5: **, by now,** is deleted after **only**

P. 157, last line: **had** is deleted before **left**

P. 159, l. 24: **heavy** is deleted before **luxury**

P. 159, l. 26: **back** is replaced by **shoulders**

P. 161, ll. 25–26: **it was astonishing to** is replaced by **I was astonished to**

P. 161, l. 28: **—Scott explained it a little vaguely—** is deleted after **some manner**

P. 162, l. 3: **just** is deleted before **charges**

P. 162, l. 10: **if it was cared for at all** is deleted after **built for**

P. 162, l. 23: one sentence is deleted after **others.** It says that if they had had a top **it would only have meant driving with the annoyance of the windshield wiper sweeping**

P. 165, l. 9: **a** is deleted before **cold**

P. 167, l. 7: **that** is replaced by **one whisky**

P. 167, l. 9: **Driving in an open car,** is deleted before **The alcohol**

P. 167, l. 14: **when you live in France** is at the beginning of the sentence—that is, on line 12

P. 167, l. 19: **passing** is replaced by **traveling**

P. 167, l. 22: **from time spent in a café** is replaced by **from reading about them in a café**

P. 169, l. 1: **even** is moved from before **talk** to after **calmly**

P. 170, l. 17: **again** is added after **pulse**

P. 173, l. 6: **many** is deleted before **more**

P. 174, l. 20: **This was untrue and my training was** is changed to **This was not true. My training was**

P. 176, ll. 10–11: **he, nor no one else, nor** is changed to **not he, nor anyone else, nor**

P. 176, l. 11: **nor on marble** is changed to **or on marble** (★)

P. 176, l. 12: **top** is added after **table**

P. 176, l. 23: **preposterously** is deleted after **how**

"HAWKS DO NOT SHARE"

P. 180, l. 1: **where** is changed to **when** before **the rain**

P. 180, l. 19: **cat's eyes** is changed to **hawk's eyes** (★)

P. 180, l. 28: **very** is deleted before **jealous**

P. 181, l. 10: one sentence is deleted after **pilot.**: **He had told me the story very many times by now starting on the trip and it was his best story no matter how he told it.**

P. 181, l. 28: **that** is added before **they went to.** (★) (see File 173)

P. 182, l. 22: **wonderful** is changed to **disciplined**

P. 184, l. 6: **very politely** is deleted after **said**

P. 184, l. 8: **too** is deleted before **careful** (it had been a typist's error in Files 188–89)

P. 184, l. 11: **would be** is corrected to **was**

P. 184, l. 25: **finishing** is changed to **finished**

P. 184, last line: four sentences are deleted after **April**, which say that he does not remember when he first showed **finished things** to Scott that year, or when Scott first saw the galley proofs on the **rewritten and cut version**. They discussed them, but Hemingway made the decisions. **Not that it matters.**

P. 185, l. 1: **them** is replaced by **it** after **about**

P. 185, l. 3: **trying to do it** is replaced by **rewriting**

P. 185, l. 9: **, really,** is deleted after **wanted us**

P. 185, l. 18: **wonderful** is changed to **disciplined**

P. 186, l. 10: **except Pauline** is deleted after **Nobody**

"A MATTER OF MEASUREMENTS"

P. 189, l. 1: the first word, **Once,** is deleted before **Much later**

P. 189, l. 7: **him** is deleted after **answer**

P. 189, l. 8: **For a long time** is deleted before **When he would**

P. 189, l. 10: **the thing that** is replaced by **what** before **I said**

P. 189, l. 12: **would brood** is replaced by **had brooded** before **on it**

P. 189, l. 12: there is only one sentence in Files 188–89: **and it would be something** is replaced by **My words would become something**

P. 189, l. 14: **it** is replaced by **them** to agree with the change on line 12

P. 189, l. 18: **that we had been out of touch with** is replaced by **that we had not seen lately**

P. 190, l. 12: one sentence is deleted after **I said.: "Or you go out first."**

P. 190, ll. 24–25: **in the world** is at the end of the sentence after **out of business,** instead of after **the oldest way**

P. 191, ll. 24–25: **end of the last war** is replaced by **end of the World War II**

P. 191, l. 25: **bar man** is replaced by **bar chief**

P. 192, l. 3: a sentence is deleted after **please them.: "What do you wish?"**

"THERE IS NEVER ANY END TO PARIS"

P. 197, l. 3: **really** is deleted after **problem**

P. 197, l. 4: **were** is replaced by **got** before **used to it**

P. 197, l. 13: **wonderful** is replaced by **loving** before **cat**

P. 197, l. 22: **really** is deleted before **poor**

P. 197, l. 22: **truly** is replaced by **really** before the second **poor**

P. 197, last line: there is only one sentence which reads in part: . . . **Paris in the winter; even with Mr. Bumby who at three months had crossed . . .**

P. 198, l. 2: again, only one sentence in Files 188–89 which reads in part: . . . **January, and never cried once . . .** ; basically one long sentence is broken into three by the editors

P. 198, l. 5: **But our Paris was too cold for him.** is added

P. 198, l. 21: **it was less all the time** is replaced by **our room and food were less all the time**; the Book-of-the-Month Club typescript reads: **our room and food was less all the time**

P. 198, l. 23: **longer** is added before **course**

P. 198, l. 30: **the** is deleted before **mountain** (*)

P. 199, l. 8: **Hotel** is deleted after **Taube**

P. 199, l. 11: **wonderful** is replaced by **excellent** before **collection**

P. 199, l. 17: **wonderful** is replaced by **healthy** before **place**

P. 199, l. 17: **very** is deleted before **dark-haired**

P. 199, l. 25: **were** is deleted before **enrolled**

P. 199, last two lines: the last two sentences in Files 188–89 read: **Anything you ran down from you had to climb up** *to first, and you could run down only as often as you could climb up.* **That** *made you have* **legs that were fit to run down with.** (I.W.D.F.P.T.)

P. 200, l. 10: **done it** is replaced by **tried it**

P. 200, l. 17: one sentence is deleted after **not fall.**: **She would not fall any more than she would have fallen in un-roped glacier skiing.**

P. 200, ll. 22–23: the sentence in Files 188–89 reads: **There was always the skiing although, because Schruns was not high enough for a ski resort except in a heavy snow winter, you had to climb for it.**

P. 201, l. 4: **wonderful** is deleted before **Kirsch**

P. 202, l. 1: **wonderful** is replaced by **good** before **ham**

P. 202, l. 11: **But** is deleted before **I cannot**

P. 202, l. 15: **you walked** is changed to **we walked**

P. 202, l. 15: **your skis** is changed to **our skis**

P. 202, l. 16: **your shoulders** is changed to **our shoulders**

P. 202, last line: **the** is deleted before **wool**

P. 203, l. 10: **of** is changed to **on** before **the battle**

P. 203, ll. 22–23: **I believe** is changed to **I heard**

P. 204, l. 15: **after it** is changed to **afterwards**

P. 204, l. 16: the beginning of the sentence before **We became** is deleted: **There were many people killed by avalanches that year in the Arlberg and we became . . .**

P. 204, l. 24: **it** is added before **took** (★)

P. 205, l. 1: the beginning of the sentence before **He was refused** is deleted: **But there was no problem because he was refused . . .**

P. 205, l. 4: **I remember the long trip** is changed to **we used to make a long trip**

P. 205, l. 7: **you ate** is changed to **we ate**

P. 205, l. 9: **the** is deleted before **chairs,** and a sentence is deleted after **chairs.**: **The food was always good and you were always hungry.**

P. 205, l. 9: **You slept** is changed to **We slept**

P. 205, l. 11: **you** is changed to **we** before **all loaded**

P. 205, l. 13: **your skis on your shoulders** is changed to **our skis on our shoulders**

P. 205, l. 23: **There was a wonderful German girl** is changed to **One of our friends was a German girl**

P. 205, last line: one sentence is deleted at the beginning of the paragraph: **The peasants of the end of the upper valley were very** different from the lower and middle valley, and those of the Gauertal were as friendly as these were hostile. (*)

P. 206, l. 1: **your face** is changed to **my face**

P. 206, l. 1: **did not have a hair-cut** is changed to **did not bother having a haircut**

P. 206, l. 2: after **hair-cut** the sentence in Files 188–89 continues: . . . **hair-cut, and running on skis late in the evening down the logging trails Herr Lent** . . . (the sentence structure is changed, and the long sentence is broken into two)

P. 206, l. 14: **and of skiing** is changed to **and the skiing**

P. 206, l. 19: **on** is deleted before **carefully**

P. 206, l. 25: **you had** is changed to **we had**

P. 206, l. 27: **You had** is changed to **We had**

P. 206, l. 28: **towards spring** is added

P. 206, l. 29: **your legs . . . your ankles** is changed to **our legs . . . our ankles**

P. 206, l. 30: **you running** is changed to **we running**

P. 207, l. 3: **you built** is changed to **we built**

P. 207, l. 4: **You could not buy it** is changed to **We could not buy the trip**

P. 207, l. 5: **we worked all winter for** is changed to **we worked for all winter**

P. 207, l. 7: **The last year** is changed to **During our last year**

P. 207, ll. 10–11: **that winter** is changed to **the next winter**

P. 207, ll. 10–11: **, a nightmare winter disguised as the greatest fun of all,** is added

P. 207, l. 12: after **to follow.** the text of Files 188–89 is different from that of the published version. A deleted paragraph says that Hadley and he had become too confident in each other, and so on (see *MM*, p. 177).

Files 188–89 end here. The remainder of the chapter was taken from File 126-1, which Hemingway had decided not to include, for fear of hurting Hadley. The editors reinstated this portion, with major cuts in the text.

P. 207, l. 12: the first paragraph of File 126-1 is not used in the book, except for the last sentence, and reads: **The first year in the Voralberg was an innocent year. The year of the great killing by avalanches was a different kind of year and you began to know** people and the places very well. You knew some people too well and you were learning the places for survival as well as for pleasure. The last year was a nightmare and a murder year disguised as the greatest fun of all. It was that year that the rich showed up.

P. 207, l. 18: **(giggle)** is deleted after **mean**

P. 208, l. 1: **that** is replaced by **who** before **are caught**

P. 208, l. 7: the last sentence is deleted from the paragraph: **They could tell that through all the then true sincerity of his politics it was a passing sham and that he was one of them although he did not know it then.**

P. 208, l. 10: **badly** is changed to **surely**

P. 208, l. 11: **light or** is deleted before **beacon**

P. 208, l. 12: **as experienced or** is deleted after **were**

P. 208, l. 15: after **inexperienced** the sentence in File 126-1 continues as follows: **but they learn quite rapidly how not to be over-run and they learn how to go away.** The meaning of this passage is reversed and made into the next sentence of the published version

P. 208, l. 16: the beginning of the sentence in File 126-1 reads: **But they have not learned about the good . . .**

P. 208, l. 20: **nouriture** is changed to **nourishment**

P. 208, l. 23: **That year** is deleted before **The rich**

P. 208, last line: two sentences are deleted after **Many others.**: **But this was the one they had taken up *completely and solidly.* He was a good enough painter too if you liked it and no one's fool.** (italicized words added in pencil)

P. 209, l. 5: the first sentence of the paragraph is dropped: **It gives me the horrors to remember it.**

P. 209, l. 5: **, in those days,** is deleted after **would trust**

P. 209, l. 12: **wonderful** is changed to **marvellous** before **discovery**

P. 209, l. 13: **before they came**, which was added, is deleted after **rewritten**

P. 209, l. 16: **crevices**, which Hemingway crossed out and replaced by **crevasses**, is reinstated

P. 209, l. 19: **every day a** is deleted before **fiesta**

P. 209, l. 21: **bastards**, which Hemingway crossed out and replaced by **people** in File 126-1, is reinstated

P. 209, l. 22: **were** is replaced by **had been** before **functioning**

P. 209, ll. 22–23: **though** is replaced by **although** after **professional**

P. 209, l. 23: the sentence fragment in File 126-1 reads: **functioning as** *ruthlessly as* **a professional** *should,* **I would** (italicized words added in pencil but deleted by the editors)

P. 209, l. 25: the first sentence of the paragraph is dropped: **That was a horror winter.**

P. 209, l. 26: **probably that** is deleted before **there is**

P. 209, l. 26: **This is when** is replaced by **It is that**

P. 209, l. 28: **comes to live** is changed to **goes to live**

P. 210, l. 1: **on a book** is deleted after **work**

P. 210, l. 6: the last sentence of the paragraph is deleted: **Then the one who is relentless wins.**

P. 210, l. 7: three paragraphs are deleted: 1) the first paragraph, beginning **It sounds very simple,** which was typed in at Hemingway's request in File 123 (see chapter 7), is dropped by his editors; 2) the second paragraph, beginning **So that was the sort of winter,** was crossed out by Hemingway in File 126-1; 3) the third paragraph is dropped by the editors. It indicates that the husband and the wife are never bored together and have something that seems unbreakable. They love their child, various places, and their work, **and she has sacrificed hers to his and never mentioned it.**

P. 210, l. 8: **wonderful** is changed to **stimulating**

P. 210, l. 9: **to be** is deleted before **truly wicked**

P. 210, l. 9: **must** is deleted before **start**

P. 210, l. 11: **you,** added in pencil by Hemingway in File 126-1, is deleted before **hate**

P. 210, l. 12: a sentence fragment is deleted after **dangerous,** which says that you work harder and that, when you come out from your work, you know that what is happening is impossible. The last three sentences of the paragraph, according to which he loved them both and everything was split inside of him, are deleted. Moreover, the next four paragraphs (see *MM*, pp. 178–79) are also deleted from the published version: 1) a paragraph about loving them both; 2) a paragraph about Pauline becoming unhappy with the situation and making up her mind to marry Hemingway; 3) a sentence about the winter of the avalanches being a happy winter compared to this preceding winter; 4) a paragraph about Pauline's underrating the power of remorse.

P. 210, l. 14: **to straighten out who I was publishing with after the first book of stories** is changed to **to rearrange publishers**

P. 210, l. 14: the next sentence, which says that it was a bitter winter on the North Atlantic and that there was snow knee-deep in New York when the ship docked, is deleted.

P. 210, l. 17: a long sentence is deleted after **But the girl I was in love with was in Paris.** It mentions that Pauline was still writing to his wife and talks about their treachery, selfishness, and happiness and his black remorse. A new sentence and a new paragraph are created with the last section of the sentence, which reads: *only that* when I saw my wife *who I loved* standing by the tracks as the train came in (I.W.D.F.P.T.). The ending of the published sentence, **and I did not take the first train, or the second or the third,** is added by the editors

P. 210, l. 28: **wonderful** is changed to **fine** before **successful**

P. 210, last line: **when I saw her**, which had been added by hand in File 126-1 after **no one else**, is deleted

P. 210, last line: **wonderful** is changed to **magic** after **lovely**

P. 211, l. 2: **and I thought we were invulnerable again,** is added; it is culled from a passage deleted later

P. 211, l. 4: the end of the paragraph after **started again.** and the remainder of the typescript are deleted, except for the sentences that form paragraph two on page 211. There is both an original and a carbon copy for the last two pages of the text of File 126-1. The carbon is corrected in blue ink by Hemingway, mostly with paragraphing deleted. The original is corrected in pencil and the corrections consist mostly of additions. The deleted text includes:

1) a sentence about remorse being **a fine good thing** that might have saved him instead of being his **true and constant companion for the next three years** (see *MM*, p. 179)

2) a long paragraph about the rich (see *MM*, pp. 179–80)

3) a paragraph about how terrible it was for Pauline to deceive Hadley and how Hemingway accepted all the blame for it (see *MM*, p. 178)

4) a paragraph about the remorse never being away until Hadley had married a much better man than Hemingway, and about Hemingway's happiness with Pauline for many years (see *MM*, p. 179)

5) a paragraph about Hemingway's happiness with Hadley in Schruns before he knew he would **ever get back into the bad-**

ness (see *MM*, page 180). A portion of that paragraph was used to make up the second paragraph on page 211. *But we were not invulnerable and that* **was the end of the first part of Paris. Paris was never to be the same again although it was always Paris and you changed as it changed.** *And we* **never went back to the** *Voralberg* **and neither did the rich.** (I.W.D.F.P.T.) Hemingway then continued, writing that he did not think even the pilot fish went back. He had new places to pilot the rich to and, finally, he became a rich man himself. **But he had his bad luck** *first and it was worst than anyone's* (italicized words crossed out on carbon and replaced by **too**)

6) another paragraph saying that nobody climbs on skis now, that almost everybody breaks their legs, and that maybe it is easier in the end to break your legs than to break your heart, **although they say** *that everything breaks now and* (italicized words crossed out on carbon) **that sometimes afterwards, many are stronger at the broken places.** Hemingway does not remember about that, although he remembers who said it. The last portion of the sentence was used on page 211: **but this is how Paris was in the early days when we were very poor and very happy.** Hemingway adds by hand that there were very many other things to say about Paris, but that maybe this was enough for one book. **There is another book written about the parts that are missing, and there are always the stories that were lost.**

P. 211, last paragraph: except for the last sentence, the last paragraph is not taken from this manuscript. It was culled from File 124, which includes many pencil and ink drafts of the ending. As evidenced by an annotation in her hand, Mary Hemingway was not sure whether to use that passage at the end or in the introduction: "**Put in Last Intro?**" The paragraph was edited for publication and reads in File 124 as follows: **There is never any ending to Paris and the memory of each person who has lived in it differs from that of any other. We always returned to it no matter who we were** *nor* **how it was changed** *nor* **with what difficulties** *nor what* **ease it could be reached** [or approached crossed out by Hemingway]. *It* **was always worth it and** [you crossed out] *we* **received** *a* **return for whatever** [you crossed out] *we* **brought to it** (I.W.D.F.P.T.).

APPENDIX

Street Maps of Paris circa 1923

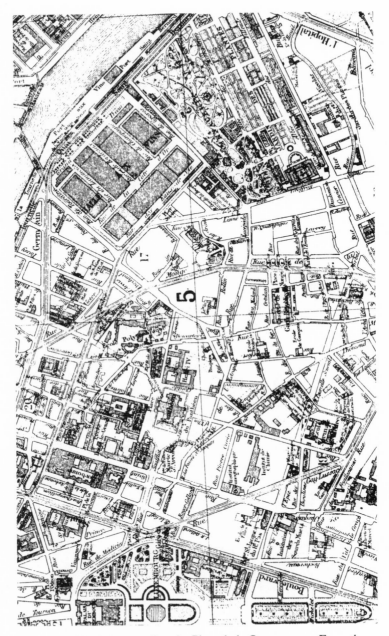

The area of Paris surrounding the Place de la Contrescarpe. From the "Plan Général de la Ville de Paris et de ses environs," 1/10.000, 1923, from the Bibliothèque Historique de Paris.

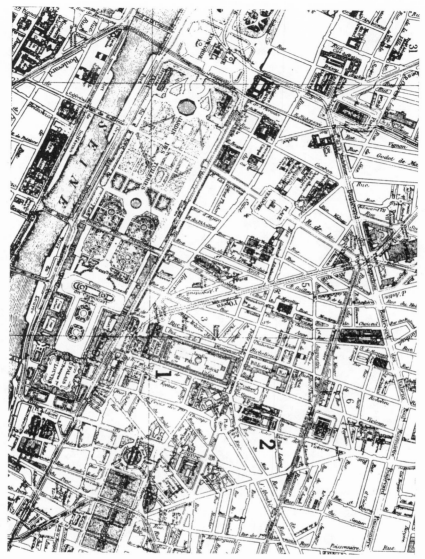

The area of Paris surrounding the Opéra. From the "Plan Général de la Ville de Paris et de ses environs," 1/10.000, 1923, from the Bibliothèque Historique de Paris.

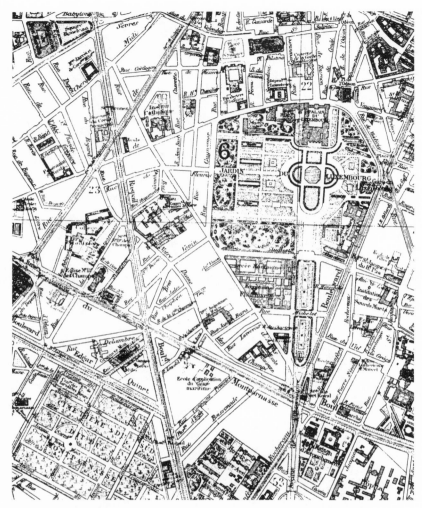

The area of Paris surrounding the Rue Notre-Dame-des-Champs. From the "Plan Général de la Ville de Paris et de ses environs," 1/10.000, 1923, from the Bibliothèque Historique de Paris.

NOTES

1. Leonard Lyons wrote on 11 December 1957:

> During his last trip to Paris the manager of the Ritz found some old trunks
> Hemingway had stored in the basement 25 years ago—It was a treasure
> trove, containing his original manuscript of "A Farewell to Arms," short
> stories and notebooks he'd kept in those years. "It would take six secretaries
> working the year round to transcribe them all.
>
> "Reading those notebooks unlocked in my mind so many details of that
> period of my life. No, I don't just take notes," he said. "If it's good, its
> engraved on my mind; if it's not good it erases itself." The books supplied
> the key to memories of people and events of his Paris years.

Aside from the fact that Hemingway offered to give the manuscript of *A Farewell
to Arms* to Gus Pfeiffer with great flourish on 17 March 1930 (see letter to Gus
Pfeiffer and Pfeiffer's letter of acceptance of 24 March 1930), one might note that
Lyons refers to an unspecified number of trunks. It was only in 1964 that the
number of trunks was narrowed down to two by Mary Hemingway. Clearly, there
could not have been enough manuscripts in the trunks for six secretaries to work
the year round, if one takes into account the fact that Hadley lost most of her
husband's manuscripts, typescripts, and carbon copies in December 1922, Hemingway's own very controlled productivity in those years, as well as the fact that
he had not stored *all* of his old manuscripts at the Ritz or anywhere else. There is
at least one major inaccuracy in Lyons's reporting, which leaves the reader to
wonder who is at fault. Interestingly, on 5 January 1964 Lyons dates the event
January 1957, which is clearly impossible, as the internal logic of his column
itself acknowledges.

2. See Lewis Galantière, "There Is Never Any End to Paris," and Mary Hemingway, "The Making of the Book: A Chronicle and a Memoir," *New York Times
Book Review*, 10 May 1964; Mildred L. Carr, "The Young Hemingway Looks At

Paris, A 'Moveable Feast,' " *Greensboro Daily News*, 10 May 1964; Reece Stuart, "Young Hungry Hemingway Found Paris a 'Feast,' " *Des Moines Register*, 10 May 1964, and George P. Hunt, "Editor's Note," *Life*, 10 April 1964. George P. Hunt's description is somewhat adventurous:

> Hemingway took his trunks. They contained a litter of Paris relics, among them a pile of blue-covered notebooks in which the struggling young author used to pencil his short stories while sitting at a table in the homey Closerie des Lilas. Some of the stories had been sent to publishers and rejected. Some had been published. Others the young Hemingway had judged not worth submitting.

Hunt probably got his information from Mary Hemingway rather than from Lyons's column, since he gives details Lyons never provided.

3. See, for instance, Frederick Shroyer's review "Hemingway's Paris Feast," *Los Angeles Examiner*, 24 May 1964, in which he writes: "While in Paris in the first half of the Twenties, Hemingway kept a number of notebooks in which he jotted the incidents and the meetings he thought he would one day want to remember."

4. Carlos Baker corrected Mary's faulty date in *Ernest Hemingway: A Life Story* (New York: Bantam, 1970), p. 679; hereafter referred to as *A Life Story*.

5. Among the most recent, one might mention Anthony Burgess, who describes *A Moveable Feast* as the "reworked Paris notebooks" and the Ritz Hotel papers as the foundation for the book: ". . . it was a book whose foundations had been laid, and stylistic felicities achieved, in the old days of struggle." *Ernest Hemingway and his World* (London: Thames and Hudson, 1978), p. 107. See also, somewhat surprisingly: Peter Griffin, *Along With Youth: Hemingway, The Early Years* (Oxford University Press, 1985).

6. A. E. Hotchner, *Papa Hemingway* (New York: Random House, 1955), p. 297.

7. See Carlos Baker, *Ernest Hemingway: Selected Letters* (New York: Scribner's, 1981), p. 902; hereafter referred to as *Letters*.

8. She now recalls, for instance, that the baggage men made a very formal speech to Hemingway, to the effect that "it was now thirty years or more since monsieur had left with them two pieces of luggage . . . enjoining them to care for them well since they contained important papers. In their opinion it was now time to relieve them of the responsibility." *How It Was* (New York: Alfred A. Knopf, 1976), p. 440. They apparently no longer threatened to send the trunks to the incinerator, as she said they had in the 1964 account.

9. *Letters*, p. 411. For a good summary of the Hemingway-Seldes quarrel, see Carlos Baker, *A Life Story*, pp. 816–17, and Hemingway's attack on Gilbert Seldes in "Notes on Life and Letters," *Esquire* 3 (January 1935):21.

10. *Letters*, p. 657. Carlos Baker suggests that the "someone" is Pauline. See

also, for instance, Hemingway to Charles Scribner, 29 October 1947, in *Letters*, p. 630. About lost manuscripts, see Hemingway's preface to Lee Samuel's *A Hemingway Check List* (New York: Scribner's, 1951).

11. Mary Hemingway to Mr. Mourelet, 24 April 1950; see also Mary to Mourelet, 15 August 1950, and Mourelet to Hemingway, 4 April 1950. There is also at the Kennedy Library a letter from the Continental Express Co. to Pitt & Scott Ltd. dated 8 November 1950 concerning the shipping of these very cases and trunk on the S.S. *Saint Lô.* I was unable to verify what happened exactly, since the archives of Pitt & Scott have been destroyed and the person who was in charge of import/export is deceased.

12. Letter to the author by Frank Klein, managing director of the Ritz, 27 May 1980: "Malgré tout notre désir de vous être agréable, les livres de mise en garde de 1926 et 1928 ayant été détruits, nous ne pouvons vous renseigner. Les vieux employés se souviennent que Monsieur Hemingway laissait toujours des réserves entre ses voyages mais aucun d'eux ne se rappelle qu'il y ait laissé des objets pendant trente ans." ("Despite our desire to be helpful, we are unable to give you the information you requested since the books indicating items left for storage for the years 1926 and 1928 have been destroyed. Old employees of the Ritz recall that Mr. Hemingway often left things at the hotel between trips, but no one remembers that he left anything for thirty years.")

13. Arthur Mizener, "F. Scott Fitzgerald's Tormented Paradise," *Life*, vol. 30, 15 January 1951, pp. 82–88, 91–94, 96–99.

14. He refers again to that problem in violent terms in his 6 February letter to Mizener, and on 19 April he writes to Malcolm Cowley that Mizener had deceived him completely in his letters, that he had thought Mizener was a straight guy until he published that "unspeakable piece of grave robbery" in *Life*, and that it seems to him hardly a Christian act to hand "a heritage of insanity" to Fitzgerald's daughter.

15. Letter to Harvey Breit, 16 June 1957.

16. See Alice Hunt Sokoloff, *Hadley, The First Mrs. Hemingway* (New York: Dodd, Mead, 1973), p. 101: "The last time that Hadley had heard from Ernest Hemingway was in March, 1961. . . . He wanted to ask her if she could recall the name of someone in Paris during their years together, someone who had not treated the younger writers as he should."

17. *Letters*, p. 411. He also wrote to Charles Scribner on 19 August 1949 that he liked Gertrude Stein very much and never counterattacked her, even when she attacked him after she had learned to write dialogue from him (see *Letters*, p. 664). Hemingway seldom resisted the temptation to attack Stein, whether in *Green Hills of Africa*, in his introduction to James Charters's autobiography, or, particularly, in *Death in the Afternoon*.

18. For letters to Janet Flanner and Maxwell Perkins, see *Letters*, pp. 388,

396. About writing a life story, see also Hemingway to Charles A. Fenton, 18 June and 29 July 1952, in *Letters*, pp. 764–65, 776; and 29 December 1954, in which he asks Fenton whether he thinks it might be useful if he "wrote truly and censoring nothing" about the writers that he has known well, such as Joyce, Pound, Anderson, Stein, Larbaud, Fargue, Gide, Malraux, Sartre, and so on. See also Hemingway to Harvey Breit, 1. 9. 1950, in which he comments that it is too early to write a definitive life story, since all the women are still alive, and he could not write what he knows. He wants to live in his work forever, and he will if he can make it good enough, but if he started writing about himself, he might choke up on everything.

19. Disturbingly, there is no such letter from Ernest Walsh to Hemingway in the collection at the Kennedy Library, the Beinecke, or Princeton University Library.

20. In a letter to Hemingway dated 13 December 1929, Gus Pfeiffer advises him to keep the apartment even though the rent has increased. However, on 8 January 1930 Pfeiffer writes: "I hope that you convinced the new tenants your improvements were worth a lot. . . . Pauline was a wonder to manage the moving so well—especially with Ernest's help. " One wonders a little how Hemingway presented the situation to Gus Pfeiffer, since it appears the Hemingways were not really given a choice—unless they simply refused to pay the rent increase. In any case, the receipts at the Kennedy Library dated 31 December 1927, 1 April 1928, and 30 January 1930 are all for the same amount of 9000 francs per year. Other letters evidence the fact that Hemingway was bitter about the loss of the apartment. Hadley wrote to him on 26 January 1930, "I am so sorry about the tremendous loss on the apartment," suggesting Hemingway had gotten no money from the new tenants, or not enough. In his letter of 3 April 1929 to Maxwell Perkins, Hemingway writes that it was the best home he ever had. See also Hemingway to Perkins, 31 October 1929, in *Letters*, p. 311. For a probable date of departure, see letter from Mary Pfeiffer, 20 January 1930: "We received your letter [Ernest and Pauline's] written on the 4th of January in the midst of packing."

21. Carlos Baker indicates that Pauline was preparing in Paris to send her furniture to Key West in the spring of 1931 (*A Life Story*, p. 284).

22. Hemingway and Pauline stayed at hotels such as the Hôtel Foyot, 33 Rue de Tournon (sample dates: 7 to 10 May 1927), the Crystal Hôtel, 24 Rue St. Benoit (sample dates: 12 to 23 September 1931, 23 September 1933), and, in particular, the Hôtel Paris-Dinard (sample dates: May 1931 and 18 October 1933 [Pauline alone], 15 to 21 October 1933). In fact, in a letter to Adriana Ivancich dated 8 May 1952, Hemingway indicates that it is only as of 1944 that he stayed nowhere but at the Ritz when he was in Paris.

23. These notebooks were first described by Philip Young and Charles Mann, who were the first to see and inventory the Hemingway manuscripts, in *The Hemingway Manuscripts: An Inventory* (University Park: Pennsylvania State Univer-

sity Press, 1969), and later by Jo August in her guide to the Hemingway papers at the Kennedy Library. However, neither provides a complete and detailed description of the notebooks. The three notebooks containing the ending of *A Farewell to Arms* are not described here, since they could not possibly have been in the trunks. I will not describe the notebooks containing the first draft of *The Sun Also Rises* in detail, since they are described in reasonable detail by Young and Mann and by August. Further information on them is also provided by Frederic Joseph Svoboda in *Hemingway & The Sun Also Rises* (Lawrence: University Press of Kansas, 1983). However, the color of these notebooks will be pointed out, for they are not blue as indicated by Young and Mann. In fact, there is not a single blue notebook among the *Sun*'s notebooks. Twenty-eight notebooks are described here, whereas Mary Hemingway mentions only "a dozen or more" in *How It Was* (p. 440).

The Sun Also Rises *Notebooks*

1—*French notebook,* labeled "L'Incroyable," *mauve,* typical school notebook, graph paper (File 194)
2, 3, and 4—*Spanish notebooks, yellow,* Papeleria E. Bort, Pellicer/Valencia, ruled paper
5—*French notebook,* "L'Incroyable," *pink*
6—*French notebook,* "L'Incroyable," *pink*
7—*French notebook,* "L'Incroyable," *pink*
8—*French notebook,* "L'Incroyable," *mauve,* only two pages written, the rest blank. Disconnected sentences, probably remembered from Lady Duff Twysden. One of them: "We can't do it. You can't hurt people. It's what we believe in in place of God" (File 202b).

One Brown Notebook (File 202C)

French, "L'Incroyable," contains manuscript of "Ten Indians" (sixteen pages) and the foreword to "The Lost Generation" (three pages written at the end of the notebook). On inside back cover is a list of four titles for *The Sun Also Rises*. The notebook is headed,"Hemingway/Chartres/September 27, 1925."

One Small Notebook (File 727)

Graph paper, looks homemade, plain paper cover, hand-stitched, twenty-eight pages, eight pages of manuscript (loose sheets), draft of "Ten Indians."

One Dark-Blue Notebook (File 203b)

Small, lined paper, hardcover. It contains:
—pencil notes on *Three Stories and Eleven Poems* (one page)
—several pages of notes on Spain and bullfighting, and notes on the dead

—fragment of a typescript of the "six cabinet ministers" stuck on the back cover.

One Light-Blue Notebook *(File 239a)*

Dated 15 June 1925, quite thick, unlined paper, stapled at the top. Three-quarters of the notebook is blank. It contains:
—*Along with Youth* (twenty-seven pages)
—a four-page story fragment beginning, "In Paris there was a revolution being plotted."
—notes on correspondence and stories to be published (four pages). The covers bear, on one side, a list of books "to Schruns" and, on the other, Hemingway's address in the Rue Notre-Dame-des-Champs.

One Blue Notebook *(File 298)*

Same type as above light-blue notebook, all torn, with only five leaves (ten pages of manuscript) left. It contains titled manuscript written in ink about Switzerland, Pound, and Rapallo: "The Bull Ring"; also the note "Mss.—Schruns." Before they were torn out, the two following manuscripts also belonged to that notebook:
—manuscript fragment: "Boxing is funny that way . . ." (nine pages)
—part of "A Lack of Passion"; the beginning of the story (pp. 1 to 36) was not written in the notebook. The notebook picks up the story on page 37: pages 37–45 (see also Files 291 and 538).

One Blue Notebook *(File 328a)*

Decayed and yellowed, "L'Incroyable," graph paper (twenty-three pages written on rectos only); it contains:
—manuscript of "Chi Ti Dice La Patria"
—"Italy 1927" (titled)
—"After the Rain" (untitled)
—"A Meal in Spezia" (titled).
Three pages titled "Italy 1927" were probably torn out of that notebook; at the end Hemingway wrote the following instruction: "go on in other book page 3." These three pages represent the beginning of the story (File 517).

One Notebook *(File 734)*

Torn, the cover has disappeared, lined paper; different type of notebook altogether, twice as broad as it is high. It contains:
—manuscript fragment, "In those days everyone was very fond of my father . . ." (story)
—other stories about Nick and Robert Thompson (File 513—twelve pages)

—pencil manuscript of a short story on the war in Austria and Eldred Johnstone: "This is the story of the death of Eldred Johnstone . . ." preceded by false start: "Then it was early June . . ."

—note about Robert Warren and the *Forum*: "Two thousand words is the desired length . . ."

—seven blank pages.

One Blue Notebook (File 596)

French, "L'Incroyable," (bought at the "Papeterie Saint Louis, 48 Boulevard St. Michel). Not much left of it: half of the cover plus three leaves. Bears address of the Rue Notre-Dame-des-Champs. It contains a manuscript fragment: "Nacional II was a bullfighter . . ." (six pages). On the inside cover is an outline for a second book of short stories titled "They Never Come Back."

One Small Red Notebook (File 597b)

Hardcover, bearing address of Rue Notre-Dame-des-Champs, in good shape, mostly blank, six pages of manuscript. It contains:

—untitled pencil draft of the "Neothomist Poem" and several workings of it

—notes on finances, stories, names and addresses, and a draft of a letter to P. Chautard

—one date: 11 May 1926.

One Green Notebook (File 597c)

French (bought at L'Etoile d'Or, 155 Boulevard St. Germain), bears Rue Froidevaux address, hardcover, in good shape, larger than above red notebook, mostly blank. It contains:

—untitled manuscript: "The Lord is my Shepherd I shall not want . . ." (one page)

—one page of sentences about the dust and the dew in the dark in Italy

—one sentence on women and menstruation

—manuscript of a poem, "And everything the author knows" (three pages)

—manuscript of a poem, "The poems that I have never written"

—a sentence on "the proper response when one is called a son of a bitch" (one page).

Four Notebooks (File 790)

Octavo booklets plus loose sheets. The booklets seem homemade, unlined, cheap paper (the type used for carbon copies); the pages seem hand-cut and hand-stitched. The first three have thirty-two pages of manuscript each, the last one has twenty-eight pages. They contain the manuscript of "The Undefeated."

Three Notebooks (File 64)

A type of notebook meant for letter writing, "Old Irish Linen," white and green, rough size 8 × 10 inches, some pages have been torn out. They contain the conclusion of *A Farewell to Arms* and were given to Gus Pfeiffer.

One Light-Blue Notebook (File 553b)

Unlined paper (same type as 239a and 298), labeled "Private." It contains:
—untitled manuscript of a sketch beginning, "Lloyd was a fat girl who came to Paris to study music . . ." (pages 1–9)
—manuscript of a story fragment titled "Gusta," beginning, "Gusta met Bertram at a pension in Munich . . ." (seven pages)
—financial figuring, bearing Rue Notre-Dame-des-Champs address. One bank balance is dated 17 December 1924.

One Very Small Black Notebook

German, leather, about 4 × 2½ inches. It contains a casual diary of his preparations for marrying Pauline, such as getting the wedding ring, making the religious arrangements, and so on.

One Small Black Notebook

Spanish, leather, a little larger than the above. It contains a list of paintings bought, with prices, and a furniture inventory with estimated values in French francs. It must be the inventory of the furniture at the Rue Férou apartment. Total values indicated are as follows:
—furniture: 58,946
—pictures: 75,000
—books: 25,000
Between the pages of this notebook was slipped a visiting card for a "maison particulière."

CHAPTER TWO

1. This was clearly in reply to Hemingway's letter of 16 January 1961, in which he wrote that he wanted to get the Paris book out first despite the financial advantages of giving the bullfight book priority in publication.

2. This particular collection is at Princeton and is officially "restricted." I was unable to obtain access to it.

3. Mary Hemingway, "The Making of the Book: A Chronicle and a Memoir."

In February the Hemingways were back in Cuba after returning from France, with a two-day stopover in New York and, finally, a cruise for Hemingway and a short trip to Minneapolis for Mary. In October they were back in Cuba after a holiday trip to New York.

4. See *A Life Story*, p. 927.

5. According to Carlos Baker, he had written 400 pages of *The Garden of Eden* by mid-February 1946, 700 by the end of April, and 1000 by mid-July. By early 1947, apparently, 100 pages had been typed. See *A Life Story*, pp. 577–78, 583. It seems, however, that Hemingway had gotten back to it some time in early 1956, as he wrote Ezra Pound on 25 May 1956 that he had been writing very well and had 856 pages done on a book which he thought might have amused Pound, and that he hoped to be back on it soon. This would tally with Mary Hemingway's comment in her review of *A Moveable Feast*.

6. Hemingway sent the *Atlantic* "A Man of the World," which he had completed by mid-June 1957, and "Get Yourself a Seeing-Eyed Dog," which, according to Baker, he had written during the summer of 1956 (*A Life Story*, p. 926). Both stories were published in vol. 200 (November 1957):64–68.

7. Hemingway can only mean July 1957.

8. This comment could also possibly apply to his having finished "A Man of the World," but it applies, more likely, to the first Fitzgerald sketch. It seems that he sent the two stories to the *Atlantic* in late July or early August 1957, since Edward Weeks sent him payment for the stories on August 16—payment Hemingway judged inadequate in his letter of 20 August (*Letters*, p. 880).

9. See *Letters*, p. 874.

10. According to that same letter, his lawyer, Alfred Rice, had misfiled his income tax for years, and the government wanted $41,696.37 from him.

11. See *A Life Story*, pp. 684, 927.

12. On 10 January 1958 he wrote to Bill Seward from the Finca that he had been working "awfully hard since [they] came back which is why [he] had not written."

13. Letter from Mary Hemingway to Bill Seward, 22 August 1958.

14. Hemingway writes to Charles Scribner on 15–18 September 1958 that people who come to Finca Vigía to see him and whom he refuses to see write imaginary interviews; Rice puts words into his mouth, stating the exact opposite of what he believes, seeking personal publicity.

15. Hemingway also thanks Robinson for sending him the clippings with the second story on the Rice-*Esquire* business, for his fairness, accuracy, and courtesy, and gives details about the whole problem. It seems that *Esquire* had asked for permission to reprint three of Hemingway's stories in a book and that Hemingway had refused that permission since they had paid originally only for first U.S. serial rights. Hemingway is quite bitter about how little Arnold Gingrich

paid him for his articles and for the stories he gave to *Esquire* over the years, when he had no time to write the short pieces he had contracted for: "He paid me $150. for an article that could have sold for $1500 and then upped his price to $250., and $350 and so forth. . . . I had to give them The Snows of Kilimanjaro instead of a piece to meet a deadline when they had my name printed on the cover and Gingrich pried $1000. out of [David] Smart for it (he said)." They had promised him stock as compensation, for which he waited for years, and, as soon as he had it (500 shares for himself, and 500 shares for his wife), Smart promptly watered it down so that it was worth next to nothing—that is, less than they would have had to pay for "The Snows of Kilimanjaro," according to the rate per word he received for other stories such as "The Short Happy Life of Francis Macomber." Hemingway feels that *Esquire* is ripping him off again, and that it is Rice who gave them the chance to do it, since Rice gave them permission to reprint the three stories they wanted against Hemingway's clear instructions over the telephone. "No one ever mentioned that Gingrich admitted to Rice that he bought only the First U.S. Serial rights and nothing else from me. Nobody mentioned that they had to pay $1000. for the single story when they proposed to steal the three stories for nothing. . . ." Apparently, a lawsuit was settled on the matter, and Rice again disobeyed Hemingway's instructions by filing a "pompous bullshit affidavit" instead of Hemingway's own letter to him.

16. See *A Life Story*, p. 684.

17. For the Evan Shipman visit, see File 124a. The manuscript is dated 1, 2, and 3 April, although there is no way of knowing whether it is 1958 or 1961; 1961 seems more likely, given the style and the tone of the narrative. A note by Mary Hemingway indicates that Shipman's visit took place in Cuba in either 1956 or 1957. For a detailed description of these chapters, see chapter 6.

18. Hemingway refers to George Plimpton's visit in some detail and reminisces about his Paris days in a letter to Archibald MacLeish, in *Letters*, pp. 884–86.

19. Hemingway also wrote to Mr. and Mrs. Horne on 1 July 1958 that he was racing with his book and was uncertain as to what he could do or when. See *Letters*, p. 884.

20. Mary also wrote to Gianfranco Ivancich on 19 September 1958 that Ernest had finished the Paris sketchbook and three-quarters of another. See *A Life Story*, p. 927.

21. Both his letter to Harvey Breit of 21 September 1958 and his letter to Juanito Quintana of 26 June indicate that he worked on many Sundays: ". . . when I got to working so hard on this book I took to writing on Sundays too," and "Pero el peso de trabajar mañana, tarde, y noche y mucheso dominges. . . ."

22. See Hemingway to MacLeish, 15 October 1958, in *Letters*, p. 885.

23. See Hemingway to Patrick Hemingway, 5 November 1958, in *Letters*, p. 887.

24. See Hemingway to Brague, 24 January 1959, in *Letters*, p. 892. See also Hemingway to Zielinski, 12 April 1959, in which he apologizes for not having written sooner, saying he had been working very hard and as soon as he was finished each day, he would get his boots laced up and leave to go shooting. "Then in the evening be tired and try to sleep until [he] started writing again."

25. See *Letters*, pp. 888, 891.

26. See Hemingway to MacLeish, 15 October 1958, in *Letters*, p. 885.

27. See *A Life Story*, p. 688.

28. See *Letters*, p. 893. Hemingway wrote to George U. Allen on 19 April 1959, explaining that he was unable to visit the U.S. exhibition in Moscow during the coming summer because of his work—"I am finishing a novel that I have been working on for nearly two years"—and because he wanted to go to Spain to get material for an appendix to a new edition of *Death in the Afternoon* that he had been working on for a long time. He also wrote to Zielinski on 12 April that he had worked until 15 March: "Worked very well—only three chapters from finishing." The Allen letter probably refers to *A Moveable Feast* and the Zielinski one to *The Garden of Eden*. See also Mary Hemingway, *How It Was*, p. 474.

29. See *A Life Story*, p. 690.

30. See *A Life Story*, pp. 695–96, 931.

31. See Hemingway to Patrick Hemingway, 5 August 1959, in *Letters*, p. 895.

32. See Hemingway to Zielinski, 24 May 1959: he has been working well and traveling very much, and he ought to have two secretaries to handle things right. He has to go over a short story he is sending Scribner's for possible use in a new collection of stories not published before. He has written an introduction to it of 6000 words. "Did that since we got here May 1st." See also *A Life Story*, p. 930, and Mary Hemingway, *How It Was*, p. 469. Mary found the preface "tendentious, truculent and smug." She also indicates that Ernest had worked haphazardly in Spain on the Paris book. It would seem, however, that, with the hectic schedule of the summer, he would have been unable to do any serious work on the book. At most, he might have proofread the typescript.

33. See *A Life Story*, pp. 693–96.

34. See *Letters*, p. 897.

35. Hemingway replied to Hotchner's letter on 16 September 1959 without mentioning the Paris chapters at all.

36. In *How It Was*, Mary writes: "While he made a few tries at showing me sympathy, Ernest behaved in the ensuing weeks as though I had broken the elbow with the explicit purpose of interrupting his work on his Paris book and the piece he had agreed to do for *Life* . . ." (p. 480).

37. See Hemingway to Nathan Davis, 17 January 1960, and Hemingway to Charles Scribner, 16 January 1960, in *Letters*, pp. 897 and 901. See also Hemingway to Hotchner, 16 January: "We are getting off tonight."

38. See Hemingway to Hotchner, 18 February 1960; see also Hemingway to William Lang, 26 February 1960, in which he indicates that the count on the bullfighting piece is 25,243 words written since 25 January; 8693 words written at La Consula. He has worked every day but two in February, including Sundays. He has about one-third more to go and requests a deadline extension until 1 or 7 April: ". . . cannot jam any harder and want piece to be very best possible."

39. See letter to Hotchner, 1 May 1960: the word count on the *mano a mano* article is 92,000 words; "That's much too many but it is a full length book now." He hopes to be finished by 20 May, if not before. See letter to Juan Quintana, 1 June: "Estuve trabajando horrores, llevan mas que 100,000 palabras escrito desde feves de Enero. . . ." Mary and Valerie are typing the manuscript and afterwards he will have to correct the typescript. See, finally, letter to Ed Thompson, 2 June 1960: "Finally finished 108,746 words of first draft on May 28th." The manuscript is being typed and he will start corrections, cutting any necessary rewrite. He has to go to Spain to get what he needs for the end and to check certain things nobody will write or tell him on the telephone. Then he must get to work on the Paris book for Scribner's for 1961. "The present end on the bull piece is O.K. if anything should happen to me as things sometimes do." See *A Life Story*, p. 700, for different figures.

40. See *A Life Story*, p. 700.

41. Hemingway's letter to Bill Lang of 1 March 1960 reveals the difficulties he experienced in writing the *mano a mano* piece: since there had been no deaths or dramatic ending, but rather the "gradual destruction of one person by another with all the things that led up to it and made it," he had to establish the personality and the basic differences between the two great artists and show what happened. So many people had stolen material from him that he had to write something with permanent value. "This is what led inevitably to the length." It was necessary to make the people come alive and show the extraordinary circumstances to "make something which would have some unity and be worth publishing." He can write only one way, the best he can, and he therefore offers to return the advance and call the whole thing off. But he hopes *Life* will be able to fit the piece in and he will go on working as he has since 25 January: "Did 750 words today & felt good about it."

42. See Hotchner, *Papa Hemingway*, pp. 240–47. Hemingway was hoping for $75,000. Hemingway thanked Hotchner for his help in revising the manuscript on 5 July 1960: "You certainly were wonderful down here and very patient. Hope book is fine now. . . ."

43. Hotchner is referring to Alfred Rice, Hemingway's lawyer.

44. See *Letters*, p. 902. See also Hemingway to Nathan Davis, 1 April 1960: "The length this ["The Dangerous Summer"] has gone on puts the Paris book into 1961 but from many standpoints that may be a good thing." Matthew J.

Bruccoli and C. E. Frazer Clark, Jr., comps., *Hemingway at Auction* (Detroit: Gale Research Company, 1973), p. 126.

45. See *Letters*, p. 906. See also Hemingway to Lanham, 16 January 1961; he writes that he was so "damned sick and tired of the egotism of all bull fighters and various aspects of the corrida" that he wanted to publish the Paris book first despite the financial advantages of publishing the bullfight book first, and that Charles Scribner agreed with him.

46. See Bill Seward to Hemingway, 20 February 1960: "I read in the N.Y. Times book section that Scribners expects to bring out a book by you in the fall. Wonderful! I shall look forward to reading it with pleasure, as I am sure I don't have to tell you. If it is a book of memoirs of your early days in Paris, as the piece seems to suggest, it should give the critics a time of it." See also Zielinski to Hemingway, 10 April 1960: "Mr. Papa, I would be so grateful if you could tell me whether it's true what I've read that you are going to publish a new book this fall? Is it still a secret or may I know what it's going to be and when—and its title?"

47. See Hemingway to Lanham, 12 January 1960, in *Letters*, p. 899.

48. See *A Life Story*, p. 933.

49. See *Letters*, p. 910.

50. See *Letters*, p. 912.

51. See *A Life Story*, pp. 707 and 935.

52. See Mary Hemingway to Ellis and Lucy (no last name), 15 March 1961, and postscript by Ernest: "It's hard to work without your library and source books." See also Hemingway to Brague, 6 February 1961, in *Letters*, p. 917.

53. See Hemingway to Brague, 20 January 1961. Both books had been reviewed in the *New York Times* of 25 December 1960 by Morris Gilbert: "These companion volumes engrossingly depict, and also annotate textually, two bravura periods in the life of the world's most vivid capital. . . . They include, in color, excellent reproductions of the masters Manet, Degas, Van Gogh, . . . Toulouse Lautrec, Seurat, Bonnard, Picasso. . . . The pictorial content of the two books makes a rich album of events in Paris in almost any field, at the time concerned. . . ." It is more than likely that Hemingway was hoping to refresh his memories of the past with *Paris in the Twenties*. He was also perhaps curious to see what its author, Armand Lanoux, had written about him. Hemingway and Henry Miller were the only two foreigners named in the book.

54. See *Letters*, p. 916.

55. See Hemingway to David Aldrich, late March 1961: "Appreciate letter but working desperately Make deadline. Book delayed illness obliged decline all invitations . . ." (draft of telegram).

56. See File 122.

57. See File 122.

58. See *Letters*, p. 918.

59. See *Letters*, p. 919.
60. See File 124a.

CHAPTER THREE

1. The following is a list of representative errors in the spelling of French names and words. The file numbers refer to manuscripts where the error first appears.

Correct spelling	Hemingway's spelling
poivrottes	povrottes (128, 129, 130, 188–89)
Montagne Ste. Geneviève	Montaigne Ste. Geneviève (128, 129, 130, 188–89)
rue du Cardinal-Lemoine	rue Cardinale Lemoine (128, 129, 130, 188–89); published as rue Cardinal Lemoine
café	cafè (128, 129, 130)
Place de la Contrescarpe	Place Contrescarpe (128, 129, 130, 188–89, and the published version)
Boutet de Monvel	Bouthal de Montvel (131, 132), Boutel de Monville (133), Boutet de Monville (189)
Jardin du Luxembourg	Jardin de Luxembourg (131, 132, 133, 188–89)
Musée du Luxembourg	Musée de Luxembourg (131, 132, 133, 188–89)
rue [de] Fleurus	rue du Fleurus (131, 132, 133, 188–89)
Boulevard St. Germain	Boulevard St. Germaine (139, 140, 188–89)
Quai des Grands-Augustins	Quai des Grandes Augustins (139, 140, 141, 188–89)
clientèle	clientel (139, 140, 141, 188–89); published as clientele
goujon	gougon (139, 140)
Square du Vert Galant	Place de la Verte Galante (139, 140, 141, 188–89); published as Place du Verte Galente
crabe à la mexicaine, or crabe mexicain	crabe Mexicaine (139, 140, 141, 188–89, and the published version)
St. Germain des Près	St. Germain de pre (142)
Paris Sport Complet	Paris Sport Complét (142)
Square Louvois	Square Lauvoise (145, 146, 147, 188–89)
Bibliothèque Nationale	Bibliothique Nationale (145)
Parc des Princes	Parc du Prince (145, 146, 147, 188–89, and the published version)

Boulevard du Montparnasse   Boulevard Montparnasse (151, 152, 153, 188–89, and the published version)

Blaise Cendrars   Blaise Cendras (151)

pavillon   pavillion (151, 152, 153, 188–89)

Emile   Emil (151, 152, 153, 188–89)

rue des Saints-Pères   rue des Saintes Pères (177, 188–89)

All references to *A Moveable Feast* will be to the Scribner's edition (1964) and included in the text between parentheses.

2. Ernest Hemingway, *The Sun Also Rises* (New York: Scribner's, 1954), p. 77.

3. Richard Le Gallienne, *From a Paris Garret* (New York: Ives Washburn, 1936), p. 275.

4. Le Gallienne, *From a Paris Garret*, p. 275.

5. See *Didot-Botin: Annuaire du Commerce—Paris*, 1921, vol. 2, p. 1319; 1923, vol. 2, p. 1739. The café is listed under the name "Charreyre, bar."

6. According to information provided by Mr. P. Cottray, *épicier* at 12 Rue Mouffetard, the painting of the "Nègre Joyeux" is currently being restored by the French government and will return to its customary place after the work is completed.

7. For the history of Zamor and Madame du Barry see, in particular, G. Lenôtre, "Zamor: le Mauvais Page," *Historia* 147 (February 1959): 196–99. See also the portrait of Zamor by Van Loo, "Le Nègre Zamor," Musée Carnavalet, Paris.

8. *The Sun Also Rises*, p. 77.

9. See Robert Gajdusek, *Ernest Hemingway's Paris* (New York: Scribner's, 1954), p. 111. Gajdusek writes: "All that remains of the Nègre Joyeux Restaurant is its sign." No. 14 Rue Mouffetard is listed as "Leroy, épicier" in *Didot-Botin*, 1921, vol. 2, p. 1583, as "Charrière, épicier," in 1922, vol. 2, p. 1691, and as "Panyet, épicier" in 1923, vol. 2, p. 1739.

10. See Le Gallienne, *From a Paris Garret*, p. 275. Actually, Pascal did not die at 2 Rue Rollin, but at 67 Rue du Cardinal-Lemoine in his brother-in-law's apartment. The confusion comes from the fact that it is well known that Pascal died at his brother-in-law's and that, six weeks after Pascal's death, his brother-in-law moved to 2 Rue Rollin. See J. Hillairet, *Dictionnaire Historique des Rues de Paris* (Paris: Editions de Minuit, 1963), vol. 1, p. 386, and vol. 2, p. 361.

11. Hadley Hemingway to Grace Hall Hemingway, 2 November 1922.

12. During the last years of his life, Verlaine lived there with Eugénie Krantz in a small, two-room apartment with a kitchen, led to by a narrow and steep staircase. See F. A. Cazals and G. Lerouge, *Les derniers jours de Paul Verlaine* (Paris: Mercure de France, 1923), pp. 2–3.

13. The story of Hemingway's room is most confusing, since in *Hadley: The*

First Mrs. Hemingway, p. 48, Alice Hunt Sokoloff, as a result of an interview with Hadley, indicates that Hemingway had a room where he retired to write in the Rue Mouffetard in the hotel where Verlaine had died. In *The Hemingway Women* (New York: W. W. Norton, 1983), pp. 112, 513, Bernice Kert provides similar information, with the added detail that Hemingway paid 60 francs rent for the room. However, she states that Hemingway "worked in *the room* once *occupied* by Paul Verlaine" (italics added). It is indeed confusing, since Verlaine did not die in the Rue Mouffetard or in a hotel. Not having found any concrete substantiation in the Hemingway collection for this story, it is difficult to establish unequivocally whether Hemingway actually had a workroom, whether it was in the house where Verlaine died or in a hotel, and whether it was on the Rue Mouffetard or the Rue Descartes. Concerning hotels on the Rue Descartes, *Didot-Botin* indicates that in 1923 there was the "Select Hôtel" at 41 Rue Descartes (vol. 2, p. 1487), and that in 1921, 1922, and 1923, there was the "Hôtel Descartes" at 42 Rue Descartes (vol. 2, p. 1448, for 1921 and 1922, and vol. 2, p. 1487, for 1923). The Select Hotel would therefore have been next-door to No. 39 and the Hôtel Descartes across the street from it. Hemingway mentions in File 484 a room in the Rue Descartes, but this file is merely a draft of the chapter.

14. See M. Block and H. de Pontich, *Administration de la Ville de Paris et du Département de la Seine* (Paris: Guillaumin, 1884), pp. 502–3, 506–9. According to an "Arrêté" dated 22 August 1867, the "vidange des fosses d'aisance" was to be effected in winter between 11 P.M. and 7:30 A.M., and in summer between 11 P.M. and 6:30 A.M. This law was revised in 1883 because of more advanced equipment, and the hours changed to 10:30 P.M. and 8 A.M. in winter, and 10:30 P.M. and 7 A.M. in summer.

15. See A. Daverton, *Assainissement des Villes* (Paris: Dunod, 1922), p. 407, for the law of 18 July 1894. See also pp. 703–10 for the law of 17 July 1907 ("pour l'écoulement direct des eaux-vannes dans les égouts publics par appareils diviseurs"). The annual fee in 1907 was 30 francs per wastewater pipe. In 1921 it was raised to 90 francs. See also pp. 718–23 for the emptying of the cesspools. The sewer system was 228 kms long in 1860, 620 kms in 1878, and 964 kms in 1894, when the new law of the "tout à l'égout" was passed. As a result, the length of the sewers was doubled in a few years: 1029 kms 593 meters, in 1897, 1946 kms in 1948, and more than 2000 kms now. See Charles Kunstler, *Paris Souterrain* (Paris: Flammarion, 1953), p. 219. See also *Assainissement des Villes*, p. 407, and *Vigilat: Revue Trimestrielle de la Fondation Louis Lépine*, no. 51 (1967), pp. 14–17.

16. For the history of impressionist paintings at the Musée du Luxembourg, see Hélène Adhémar and Anne Dayez, *Musée du Jeu de Paume* (Paris: Editions des Musées Nationaux, 1973), pp. 3–7; Léonce Bénédite, *Le Musée du Luxembourg: les Peintures de l'Ecole Française* (Paris: H. Laurens, 1924), pp. 25–61; Sophie Monneret, *L'Impressionisme et son époque* (Paris: Denoel, 1978), pp. 341–43. See also "Les actualités" at the Bibliothèque Historique de Paris for the Mu-

sée du Luxembourg, in particular the following clippings: "La collection Caille-botte," *Débats*, 22 March 1894; "La collection Caillebotte," *Temps*, 2 March 1894; "Au Musée du Luxembourg," *Feuilleton du Journal des Débats*, 26 February 1929; and "Heureuses améliorations réalisées au Musée du Luxembourg," *Com-oedia*, 17 April 1926. Few were the impressionist paintings purchased by the French government. However, one should note the purchase of Renoir's "Les Jeunes Filles au Piano" in 1892.

17. See Jean Adhémar, Lise Dubief, and Gérard Willemetz, *Apollinaire* (Paris: Bibliothèque Nationale, 1969), p. 160. Two days after Apollinaire's death, his friends could well have heard the crowd cursing "Guillaume" while they were sitting with Apollinaire, since the French custom is to keep bodies at home until the funeral.

18. Sylvia Beach, *Shakespeare & Company* (New York: Harcourt, Brace, 1956), pp. 16–17.

19. See G. Pessard, *Nouveau Dictionnaire Historique de Paris* (1904), p. 690. See also *Dictionnaire Historique des Rues de Paris*, vol. 1, p. 696.

20. Jean Paul Clébert, *Les Rues de Paris: Promenades du marquis de Rochegude à travers tous les arrondissements de Paris parcourus de nouveau par Jean Paul Clébert* (Paris: Denoel, 1966), p. 32.

21. Le Gallienne, *From a Paris Garret*, pp. 238–39.

22. Hemingway's editors and Mary Hemingway in copy editing merely re-placed Hemingway's faulty spelling by more faulty spelling.

23. From *La Seine*; see translation from the French in Arthur K. Griggs, *My Paris* (London: Methuen, 1932), p. 29. For George and Pearl Adam's opinion, see *A Book About Paris* (London: Jonathan Cape 1927), p. 62. They are, however, kinder than Hemingway in their appreciation and merely say that the booksell-ers do not understand the meaning of the books they sell.

24. Robert Robert, *Le Guide du gourmand à Paris* (Paris: Bernard Grasset, 1925), p. 120.

25. See Hemingway to Sherwood Anderson, 9 March 1922, in *Letters*, p. 62.

26. *Le Guide du gourmand à Paris*, p. 98.

27. *Le Guide du gourmand à Paris*, p. 53.

28. See *The Sun Also Rises*, pp. 72–78; see also Le Gallienne, *From a Paris Garret*, p. 32.

29. Le Gallienne, *From a Paris Garret*, pp. 163–64. See also, for instance, George Slocombe, *Paris in Profile* (Boston: Houghton Mifflin, 1929), pp. 71–72.

30. Le Gallienne, *From a Paris Garret*, pp. 123, 164. For other comments on the goats and on the bees, see pp. 125 and 163.

31. See *Ordonnances et Arrêtés du Préfet de Police*, Bibliothèque de l'Hôtel de Ville de Paris. The "Ordonnance sur le bruit, 20 février 1931," Article 2, no. 11, forbids the "Publicité ou réclame par cris ou chants, ou emploi dans un but in-dustriel, commercial ou privé, de phonographes, hauts-parleurs et autres

procédés sonores" (Paris: 1934). The "Ordonnance sur la circulation à pied des troupeaux de bestiaux, 10 juin 1929," Article 1, forbids the circulation of cattle in the streets of Paris ("La circulation des troupeaux de bestiaux et des bestiaux conduits en main est interdite à Paris sauf sur les parcours suivants et sous réserve de l'observation des articles 188, 189 et 190 de l'Ordonnance Générale de Police du 15 mars 1925,") except on the following streets: from the Gare Vaugirard-Marchandises to the Abattoirs de Vaugirard, from the Portes Briançon et Plaisance to the Abattoirs de Vaugirard, from the Marché de La Villette to the Porte Pantin, and from the Porte de La Villette to the Abattoirs de La Villette. It was obviously to allow cattle to get to the slaughter-houses that these few exceptions were made.

32. Henry Miller, *Quiet Days in Clichy* (New York: Grove Press, 1978), p. 38.

33. See *Didot-Botin*, 1923, vol. 2, p. 1487. The *papeterie* is listed under the names of Beillard and Deloep in 1921–22, and then under the name of Beillard only in 1923. It was, however, situated at the intersection of the Rue Descartes and the Rue Thouin. In fact, the Rue Descartes does not intersect at all with the Place de la Contrescarpe.

34. *Didot-Botin* lists the Bains du Cardinal-Lemoine for 1921 and 1922 as run by Mr. Mobré (vol. 2, p. 1260 for 1921, and vol. 2, p. 1359 for 1922), and as run by Mr. Bordier and Mr. Crespin in 1923 (vol. 2, p. 1395). For the Bains de l'Observatoire, see *Didot-Botin*, 1925, vol. 2, p. 1810. The name for each establishment was originally provided by the *Annuaire du Téléphone* in the section "Professions" for the years indicated, under the headings "Bains publiques."

35. The information concerning the bicycle races was provided by Mr. Elie Wermelinger, former manager of the Parc des Princes and in 1983, when I talked to him, head of the "Service de Documentation" of the paper *L'Equipe*, 10 Rue du Faubourg Montmarte, Paris. See also *L'auto*, 11 August 1924, for details of Linart's first world championship. For proof of Hemingway's attendance at the bicycle races, see in the Hemingway collection at the Kennedy Library a program dated 9 May 1926 for the Parc des Princes annotated in Hemingway's hand, and programs dated 5 December 1926 and 16 September 1926 also annotated in Hemingway's hand. See also notes in "Les As du Cyclisme" and "Grand Prix de Toussaint," listing Linart four to one. Sylvia Beach also comments on going to the bicycle races with Hemingway in *Shakespeare & Company*, p. 80.

36. The original sentence read: ". . . Pauline and I saw that great rider Ganay fall . . ." (Files 147-2, 147-3, 188–89).

37. There were four restaurants at the Carrefour de l'Odéon in 1926: the café-hôtel Danton at No. 1; Roques, crémerie-restaurant, at No. 2; Jourdan-Restaurant at No. 4; and Cosy, thé-restaurant, at No. 15. See *Didot-Botin*, 1926, vol. 2, pp. 1874–75. There are no significant differences for the years 1924 and 1925.

38. See *Didot-Botin*, 1926, vol. 2, p. 1875.

39. See *Didot-Botin* under the names of the streets (volume 2 for each year). See also *Dictionnaire Historique des Rues de Paris*, vol. 2, pp. 188–89.

40. For an interesting history of the literary past of the Closerie des Lilas, the Dôme, the Rotonde, and other Parisian cafés, see Gustave Fuss-Amoré and Maurice des Ombiaux, "Montparnasse," *Mercure de France* i.XI (1924):677–712, and i.5, XI (1924):89–123.

41. The evidence concerning the Bal du Printemps is contradictory. Hemingway wrote to John Dos Passos on 16 February 1922 that he had an apartment in Paris at 74 Rue du Cardinal-Lemoine, for which he paid 250 francs a month, on top of a tall hill in the oldest part of Paris and directly above a fine place called the "Bal au printemps," which is a "French Frau Kuntz's." Hemingway continues by saying that the noise from the "accordian" the French dance to can be heard if you listen for it, but it doesn't intrude. While Hemingway often recorded facts creatively, it might have been hard even for him to invent the Bal du Printemps. Moreover, Hadley recalls that the bal musette was on the ground floor in her interview with Carlos Baker (question 12). Its description is taken from Stella Bowen, *Drawn from Life* (Maidstone: George Mann Ltd., 1974), p. 129. For information conflicting with Hemingway's, see *Didot-Botin*, vol. 2, p. 1260 (1921), p. 1359 (1922 and 1923), according to which the ground floor of 74 Rue du Cardinal-Lemoine was shared by a wine salesman and an herbalist until 1923. The herbalist still exists today, and the wine shop was first replaced by the Bal Musette, later by the Théâtre des 400 Coups, and is now a nightclub called Le Rayon Vert.

42. See Gajdusek, *Ernest Hemingway's Paris*, p. 102; see also *Didot-Botin*, 1925, vol. 2, p. 1810, where the bakery is listed under the name of Dupuy.

43. See *Didot-Botin*, 1922, vol. 2, p. 1686; 1923, vol. 2, p. 1733; 1924, vol. 2, p. 1805; 1928, vol. 1, p. 3618; and 1929, vol. 2, p. 1606. The Nègre de Toulouse appears under this name for the first time in the *Annuaire du Téléphone* in 1928, p. 233.

44. Clara E. Laughlin, *So You're Going to Paris* (London: Methuen, 1924), p. 432.

45. See *Dictionnaire Historique des Rues de Paris*, vol. 2, p. 191.

46. See *Didot-Botin* for 1923, 1924, 1925, and 1926; in particular, 1925, vol. 2, p. 1829.

47. See *Didot-Botin*, 1925, vol. 2, p. 1460.

48. See *Vigilat: Revue Trimestrielle de la Fondation Louis Lépine*, no. 51 (1967): 14–17. See also the *Plan Général des égouts de la ville de Paris et de ses environs*, 1903, p. 10, Bibliothèque de l'Hôtel de Ville de Paris. See also *Paris Souterrain*, pp. 228–29.

49. For a lively history of the smuggling, crimes, and other happenings in the

catacombs and sewers of Paris, see Simon Lacordaire, *Histoire Secrète du Paris Souterrain* (Paris: Hachette, 1982), particularly pp. 104–8. See also Emile Gerards, *Les Catacombes de Paris* (Paris: Chamuel, 1892).

50. See *Annuaire du Téléphone* for 1922 to 1929, and *Didot-Botin* for the same years, in particular *Didot-Botin*, 1928, vol. 1, p. 366; 1929, vol. 1, p. 385, and vol. 2, p. 1372.

51. See *A Life Story*, p. 188.

52. Information gathered from Herr Nels, owner of the Taube Hotel and son of the previous owner, who was Hemingway's friend.

53. See, for instance, Hemingway to Sherwood and Tennessee Anderson, 23 December 1921, in *Letters*, p. 59.

54. Mary Hemingway to Ellis and Lucy (no last name), 15 March 1961. See also letter to Harry Brague, 6 February 1961, in *Letters*, p. 917. For book request, see the letter to Brague, 20 January 1961.

55. Hemingway to Maxwell Perkins, in the private collection of Maurice Neville, Santa Barbara, California. Information provided by Professor James Hinkle, San Diego State University.

56. See Gus Pfeiffer to Hemingway, 25 April 1938, in which he writes that Hemingway is "one of the few men who qualify to be called honest."

57. See Hemingway to Maxwell Perkins, 24 July 1926, in *Letters*, p. 211.

CHAPTER FOUR

1. Philip Young, *Ernest Hemingway: A Reconsideration* (University Park: Pennsylvania State University Press, 1966), p. 63.

2. See Robert McAlmon and Kay Boyle, *Being Geniuses Together 1920–1930* (Garden City, N.Y.: Doubleday, 1968), pp. 114–15.

3. See letters to Cowley, 13 May 1951, to Pound, 22 July 1933, and to Perkins, 26 July 1933, quoted in chapter 1.

4. See chapter 7 and Files 122, 124, and 124a.

5. George Wickes, "Sketches of the Author's Life in Paris in the Twenties," in *Hemingway in Our Time*, ed. Richard Astro and Jackson J. Benson (Corvallis: Oregon State University Press, 1974), p. 28.

6. See, for instance, Hemingway to Charles A. Fenton, 29 July 1952: "It is important that I should write about the Paris part as no-one knows the truth about it as I do and it is an interesting time in writing" (*Letters*, p. 776).

7. See Baker, *Letters*, p. xii.

8. Sisley Huddleston, *Back to Montparnasse* (London: George G. Harrap and Co., 1931), p. 110.

9. See, for instance, Hemingway to Robert McAlmon, 15 November 1924, in *Letters*, p. 134, and Hemingway to Allen Tate, 31 August 1943, in *Letters*, p. 550.

10. See Huddleston, *Back to Montparnasse*, p. 108.

11. "That afternoon after Ezra had told me of the poet's sad plight I encountered Hemingway at the Closerie des Lilas with Ford and Williams. Discreetly without mentioning a name, I told them of the need for locating opium. Hemingway looked at me questioningly. 'Hell, Ezra's told you too.' I ejaculated, and we wondered how many others Ezra had let in on the secret." Apparently, a can of opium was delivered to McAlmon, but it was unusable and the poet was taken to the hospital (*McAlmon and the Lost Generation: A Self-Portrait*, ed. Robert E. Knoll [Lincoln: University of Nebraska Press, 1962], pp. 192–93).

12. Harold Loeb, *The Way It Was* (New York: Criterion Books, 1959), p. 203.

13. Bowen, *Drawn from Life*, p. 164.

14. Arthur Mizener, *The Saddest Story: A Biography of Ford Madox Ford* (London: Bodley Head, 1972), p. 208.

15. Samuel Putnam, *Paris Was Our Mistress: Memoirs of a Lost and Found Generation* (New York: Viking, 1947), p. 81. Physically, Crowley was the exact opposite of Belloc, whom Hemingway describes as "gaunt" in the book and as "rather tall, grey lantern-jawed" in the manuscript of *The Sun Also Rises*.

16. See James Charters, *This Must Be the Place* (New York: Lee Furman, 1937), p. 146.

17. Gertrude Stein, *Everybody's Autobiography* (New York: Cooper Square, 1971), p. 52.

18. James Mellow, *Charmed Circle: Gertrude Stein and Company* (New York: Praeger, 1974), p. 272.

19. See "Testimony against Gertrude Stein," *Transition Pamphlet* no. 1 (The Hague: Service Press, February 1935), in which Georges Braque, Eugène Jolas, Maria Jolas, Henri Matisse, André Salmon, and Tristan Tzara take objection to *The Autobiography of Alice B. Toklas*. The general line of their criticism would also apply to *A Moveable Feast*. Stein's being taken in by a joke is narrated by André Salmon, p. 15.

20. See *Letters*, p. 182.

21. Donald Gallup, ed., *The Flowers of Friendship: Letters Written to Gertrude Stein* (New York: Alfred A. Knopf, 1953), p. 174. See also Hemingway to Perkins, 9 June 1925, in *Letters*, pp. 162–63.

22. See *Letters*, p. 339.

23. See *Letters*, p. 238. Fitzgerald (and others) felt that the early section of *The Sun Also Rises* reminded him of Michael Arlen; see Fitzgerald to Hemingway, c. early June 1926, reprinted in Svoboda, *Hemingway & The Sun Also Rises*, p. 138.

24. File 194. This belongs to the deleted Ford episode from *The Sun Also Rises*, a later version of which is reprinted in Svoboda, *Hemingway & The Sun Also Rises*, p. 136.

25. When his landlady wanted to raise Hemingway's rent to 1000 francs per month, he wrote to Pound in 1926 (no date) that if *The Sun Also Rises* sold well, all the money should be devoted to "shoving banderillos de fuego up the ass of

French nation," and concluded, "Jesus how I hate the bastards." For negative references to French writers, see, for instance, his comment that Jean-Paul Sartre is "very honest for a Frenchman" (letter to Charles Scribner, 26 October 1949), that seven concussions in a year is probably more than one should give the average writer, "except perhaps Mr. André Gide" (letter to Paul de Kruif, October 1949). About being kicked out of his apartment to make room for people who could pay more by the "bastardly French" who might not even forward his mail once he was out, see letter to Ernest Walsh, c. August 1925. See also assorted comments about French writers, such as Cocteau, Malraux, and others, particularly the one about placing Radiguet behind Mme. de Lafayette, Cocteau behind Radiguet, and giving Racine the benefit of the doubt (*Letters*, p. 368). See also Hemingway, "And Out of America," *Transatlantic Review* 2, no. 1 (July 1924).

26. See *Letters*, pp. 146–47. The Hemingways took Mathilda back to Paris to continue as a nurse for Bumby. She stayed with them for a year. It is probably to her that Hemingway refers in his letter to Harold Loeb of November 1925, in which he complains of Boni and Liveright's not distributing properly *In Our Time* and of his not receiving royalties as a result. He works all the time, therefore he has to eat all the time. "Also Bumby has an expensive nurse and I've got a wife named Hadley that has got to eat too."

27. See *Letters*, pp. 175, 181–82.

28. *Letters*, pp. 178, 182.

29. Deleted sentence from the manuscript of "Une Génération Perdue." See also *A Moveable Feast*, p. 25.

30. See Hemingway to Grace Hall Hemingway, 14 December 1925 (*Letters*, p. 174), and to Fitzgerald, 24 December (*Letters*, p. 182). Unlike Hemingway, Dos Passos remembered the Schruns visit with pleasure: "Mealtimes we could hardly eat for laughing. Everybody kidded everybody during that week at Schruns. We ate vast quantities of trout and drank the wines and beers and slept like dormice under the great featherbeds. We were all brothers and sisters when we parted company. It was a real shock to hear a few months later that Ernest was walking out on Hadley. When you get fond of a couple you like them to stay hitched" (John Dos Passos, *The Best of Times: An Informal Memoir* [London: Andre Deutsch, 1968], p. 159).

31. *Letters*, p. 176. See also Dos Passos, *The Best of Times*, pp. 157–58. According to Calvin Tompkins, "Gerald found the book in questionable taste . . . and Sara, who had been on the point of going to bed when Hemingway arrived unexpectedly at their apartment with the manuscript, slept through most of it, sitting bolt-upright on the sofa. If Hemingway noticed, he gave no sign" (*Living Well Is the Best Revenge* [New York: Viking, 1971], p. 27). Pound, however, liked it and wrote to Hemingway on 15 February 1927: "The only disserptmnt. I had re/Torrents wuz that you didn't land a few more bots to the Jaw." See Jacqueline Tavernier-Courbin, "Ernest Hemingway and Ezra Pound," in *Ernest Hemingway:*

The Writer in Context, ed. James Nagel (Madison: University of Wisconsin Press, 1984), pp. 179–201.

32. *Letters*, pp. 68–69. The trip described by Hadley preceded by less than a week their settling at Chamby for Christmas. On 23 January she wrote that they were planning on staying until the snow left.

33. See letters to his family, 25 August 1922, to Harriet Monroe, 16 November, and to Hadley Hemingway, 28 November, in *Letters*, pp. 71–74. See also an unpublished letter to Frank Mason, 15 December 1922, in which Hemingway requests reimbursement for various telegrams he sent to Mason, and comments that he has been on twenty-four-hour shifts at $50 a week as a favor to Mason and that the result of his work at Lausanne has been a "net loss" to him of fifteen dollars; see also wires to Hadley dated 24 and 25 November 1922.

34. See letters to Dr. C. E. Hemingway, 24 May 1922, to Stein and Toklas, 11 June, to William D. Horne, 17–18 July 1923, to James Gamble, 12 December, to E. E. (Chink) Dorman-O'Gowan, 2 May 1950 and 23 December 1954, in *Letters*, pp. 68, 69, 85, 106–7, 691, and 844. For the comment on Biffi's, see unpublished manuscripts, File 299. See also *A Life Story*, pp. 121, 741, for the description of Chink's visit and the climb over the St. Bernard.

35. The documentation for these facts is extensive, and the following is merely indicative. For the loss of Hemingway's manuscripts, see in particular Hemingway to Pound, 23 January 1923, and Sokoloff, *Hadley: The First Mrs. Hemingway*, p. 60. For the meeting with O'Brien and his taking "My Old Man" for one of the *Best Short Stories of 1923*, see *A Life Story*, p. 139, Hemingway to Sylvia Beach, 6 November 1923, Hemingway to Edmund Wilson, 25 November 1923, and, of course, Hemingway to O'Brien, 20 November 1923, in *Letters*, pp. 98, 105, and 103. For Hemingway's boxing with Pound, see in particular Wyndham Lewis's account in Noel Stock, *The Life of Ezra Pound* (New York: Pantheon Books, 1960), p. 248, Hemingway to Howell Jenkins, 20 March 1922, and Hemingway to Sherwood Anderson, 9 March 1922, in *Letters*, pp. 62 and 65. For Hemingway's seeing a lot of Gertrude Stein, see in particular Hemingway to Sherwood Anderson, 9 March 1922, in *Letters*, p. 62. For Hemingway's friendship with Sylvia Beach and his borrowing books at Shakespeare and Company, see in particular Noel Riley Fitch, *Sylvia Beach and the Lost Generation: A History of Literary Paris in the Twenties and Thirties* (New York: W. W. Norton, 1983), p. 115, and Beach, *Shakespeare & Company*, chapter 9, "My Best Customer." For Hemingway's helping Stein publish *The Making of Americans*, see Stein, *The Autobiography of Alice B. Toklas*, pp. 214–16; Mellow, *Charmed Circle*, p. 267; Bernard Poli, *Ford Madox Ford and the Transatlantic Review* (Syracuse: Syracuse University Press, 1967), pp. 62–71; Hemingway to Stein, 17 February 1924, in *Letters*, pp. 111–12; and Ford to Stein, c. 18 September 1924, in Gallup, *The Flowers of Friendship*, p. 174 (the conflict of opinions concerning what Hemingway actually did is well documented). For Hemingway's going to the races, see in

particular Dos Passos, *The Best of Times*, pp. 142–44 (Hemingway's "enthusiasm was catching but he tended to make a business of it while I just liked to eat and drink and enjoy the show. Now and then he would remember that I was a rival wordfellow and clam up, or else warn me sharply that I mustn't do any writing about bicycle races," p. 143); Hemingway to Isabel Simmons, 24 June 1923, Hemingway to William Horne, 17–18 July 1923, in *Letters*, pp. 84 and 86, and Beach, *Shakespeare & Company*, p. 88. For Ford's parties at the Bal Musette, see Bowen, *Drawn from Life*, p. 129. For Stein's visiting the Hemingways in their flat, see in particular Stein, *The Autobiography of Alice B. Toklas*, p. 213.

36. See Hemingway to Sherwood Anderson, 9 March 1922, for Joyce's eating at Michaud's, and Hemingway to Edmund Wilson, 25 November 1923, for O'Brien's taking "My Old Man," in *Letters*, pp. 62 and 105. About Scott's turning up drunk at Hemingway's apartment, see Hemingway to Maxwell Perkins, 3 April 1929, in which he asks Perkins not to give Scott his address, as he wants no trouble with the apartment and does not want to get "ousted" from the place because of Scott's behavior.

37. See *Letters*, pp. 794–95.

38. See *Letters*, p. 650.

39. See *Letters*, pp. 736 and 781.

40. See also Stein, *The Autobiography of Alice B. Toklas*, for an account of Stein's visit at Hemingway's flat, p. 213.

41. Hemingway to Pound, 22 July 1933, and to Dos Passos, undated letter of 1933. See also references to Stein's "feathered friends" in a letter to Arnold Gingrich (18 January 1934), and to her losing her judgment during menopause in letters to Arnold Gingrich (3 April 1933 and 16 November 1934), to Perkins (26 July 1933), and to Harvey Breit (3 July 1956) in *Letters*, pp. 403, 384, 411, 395, and 862.

42. *Letters*, pp. 387–88. See also letter to Mizener, 1 June 1950, p. 696.

43. Gertrude Stein to Carl Van Vechten, 29 January 1931, in Edward Burns, ed., *The Letters of Gertrude Stein to Carl Van Vechten 1913–1946* (New York: Columbia University Press, 1986), p. 235. See also Hemingway to W. G. Rogers, 29 July 1948, in *Letters*, p. 650, saying that Picasso thought that they had all been flung into outer darkness because of Alice's jealousy, and to Edmund Wilson, 8 November 1952, in *Letters*, p. 795.

44. Stein to Van Vechten, 7 March 1927, in Burns, *The Letters of Gertrude Stein to Carl Van Vechten*, p. 142.

45. Mellow, *Charmed Circle*, p. 272.

46. Hemingway to Mizener, 22 April 1950, in *Letters*, p. 690.

47. Nancy Milford, *Zelda* (New York: Avon Books, 1971), p. 157.

48. Hemingway to Harvey Breit, 18 August 1954, in *Letters*, pp. 834–36.

49. See Kenneth S. Lynn, *Hemingway* (New York: Simon & Schuster, 1987), pp. 283–84. Lynn details Scott's affairs at Princeton and, in particular, his liaison with Rosalinde Fuller.

50. Hemingway to Maxwell Perkins, 7 September 1935, in *Letters*, p. 423.

51. See Hemingway to Mizener, 6 July 1949, and to Harvey Breit, 18 August 1954, in particular, in *Letters*, pp. 657 and 835.

52. See *Letters*, p. 695.

53. See *Letters*, pp. 796–97.

54. Beach, *Shakespeare & Company*, "Ernest Walsh and *This Quarter*," in chapter 13.

55. Hemingway to Lillian Ross, 2 July 1948, in *Letters*, pp. 644–45.

56. See *A Life Story*, p. 763.

57. See Files 486 and 185a.

58. Concerning Scott's advice about *A Farewell to Arms*, see in particular Hemingway to Fitzgerald, 16 December 1935, to Mizener, 11 January 1951, and to Charles Poore, 23 January 1953, in *Letters*, pp. 425, 719, 800. See also in that last letter Hemingway's comment that Scott had not seen the manuscript of *A Farewell to Arms* until it was "completed as published," and that he had learned not to show manuscripts to Scott a long time before. "Not one suggestion made sense or was useful," implying that Fitzgerald had never made a sensible or useful suggestion to him.

59. For Hemingway's inviting Fitzgerald to read the manuscript, see *Letters*, pp. 199–200, and Hemingway to Perkins, 5 June 1926, in *Letters*, p. 208. See also Hemingway to Fitzgerald, 7 September 1926, in *Letters*, p. 217, in which he tells Fitzgerald what cuts he has made and that he hopes Fitzgerald will like the book.

60. Letters from Hemingway to Perkins, 5 June and 21 August 1926, in *Letters*, pp. 208 and 213.

61. Françoise Féret, unpublished dissertation for the Diplôme d'Etudes Supérieures, La Sorbonne, 1957.

62. William Wasserstrom, "Hemingway, the *Dial*, and Ernest Walsh," *South Atlantic Quarterly* 65 (1966):171–77. See also W. A. Bunnel, "Who Wrote the Paris Idyll? The Place and Function of *A Moveable Feast* in the Writing of Ernest Hemingway," *Arizona Quarterly* 26 (1970):334–36, George Wickes, "Ernest Pays his Debts," *Shenandoah* (Winter 1965):46–54, and "Sketches of the Author's Life in Paris in the Twenties," in Astro and Benson, *Hemingway in Our Time*, pp. 25–38; Andrew Lytle "*A Moveable Feast*: The Going To and Fro," *Sewanee Review* 73, no. 2 (1965):339–43.

63. Carlos Baker suggests another explanation—that Mary Hemingway and L. H. Brague allowed material to be transposed on p. 125. This, however, is not supported by the manuscripts and typescripts. See *A Life Story*, p. 762.

64. Nicholas Joost, *Ernest Hemingway and the Little Magazines: The Paris Years* (Barre, Mass.: Barre Publishers, 1968), p. 149.

65. Ezra Pound to Harriet Monroe, 30 November 1926, in *The Letters of Ezra Pound: 1907–1941*, ed. D. D. Paige (London: Faber and Faber, 1951), p. 278.

66. For Pound's not taking Hemingway's quarrel with Walsh seriously, see the same letter to Harriet Monroe: ". . . he [Walsh] more recently annoyed Mr. Hem-

ingway. . . . I can't take it seriously." Neither did Pound espouse Hemingway's grievance: "Please ACQUIT me of wanting people or anyone to share all my feelings. I did not suggest that you shd. or ought to regret Monsieur Walsh. Alow me to understanding M. Carnevalli's feelings in the matter, however, EHEM!" Pound to Hemingway, 8 or 9 November 1926.

67. See *Letters*, p. 321.

68. The *Dial* rejected "The Undefeated" on 27 March 1925. The very same day, Hemingway sent the manuscript to Walsh with a note saying that it had been turned down by every reputable and disreputable magazine in the United States, which was not true. However, it had apparently also been rejected by *Vanity Fair*, the *Saturday Evening Post*, and by an editor named Spike Hunt (File 239a). It was Alyse Gregory who made the decision to reject the story at the *Dial*.

69. See letter to Ernest Walsh and Miss Moorehead (1925), in which he writes that he is not a rich man and that Hadley and he live on $100 a month. "Last year I made just 1100 Francs writing. I worked hard all year. Made nothing in dollars." He got nothing from McAlmon for the "Three Stories and T. Poems. Nothing from Bird for In Our time"—the last having been out of print for two months, and the first having ten copies left to sell. In another letter to McAlmon from Schruns (late January or early February 1925), however, he claims that 1000 francs was far more than he had made in 1924: ". . . about 400 Francs more than all my writings paid last year so feel good and cheerful." He was delighted by Walsh's comments concerning "The Undefeated": "You certainly can make a man feel good when you write about The Undefeated. Picks me up. Makes me feel it's worth while working" (Hemingway to Walsh, c. March 1925). When Hemingway received the check for "The Undefeated," he wrote Walsh: ". . . I got the splendid check and cashed it. We are going to pay the rent with it. Pay a first installment on a suit of clothes. Buy a lot of groceries and go to the six day bicycle race. I wish you were going along and could help us eat the groceries and sit in the house where the rent is paid" (in Bruccoli and Clark, *Hemingway at Auction: 1930–1973*, p. 191).

70. Hemingway to Charles Scribner, 20 November 1952, in *Letters*, p. 797. For Hemingway to Pound, 2 February 1932, see chapter 1 for more extensive quotation.

71. On 11 April 1930 Hemingway wrote Maxwell Perkins that Walsh had written the attack on "The Torrents in the New Masses—the cheapest book I Ever Read—" after Hemingway had told him that he could not let him serialize it in *This Quarter*, in *Letters*, p. 320. On 6 November 1950 Hemingway recalled the incident differently in a letter to William Sensord: this time he indicates that Walsh wanted to serialize *The Sun Also Rises* in *This Quarter*, and that, after Hemingway's refusal, he reviewed it as "The Cheapest Book I Ever Read."

72. For complaints about money, see, for instance, Hemingway to Pound, 7 October 1925 (he feels that a "lot of fucking, not too much to eat, no smoking,

and drinking only at meals" is good for a man; however, he would still like to get the $2500 award), Hemingway to Walsh, January 1925, 1 and 4 April 1925, and 2 January 1926. In the last letter he explains to Walsh why he is not yet sending him the "fight story" ("Fifty Grand") for publication. It was rejected by Hearst because it had no woman interest, but he wants to try it "on other 3 magazines who pay lots of money" because he cannot pass up a chance of getting $1000 for it. See also Hemingway to Walsh, 8 November 1925, where he claims that they are "about broke," to McAlmon, c. January 1925, to Loeb, c. November 1925, and to William B. Smith, Jr., 6 December 1924, in *Letters*, p. 137. For his sponging off McAlmon, see the trip to Spain of 1923, paid for by McAlmon, in *A Life Story*, pp. 143–46, and McAlmon's recollection of how he came to invite Hemingway, in Sanford J. Smoller, *Adrift Among Geniuses: Robert McAlmon, Writer and Publisher of the Twenties* (University Park: Pennsylvania State University Press, 1975), pp. 93–99. McAlmon even purchased a mantilla for Hemingway to give Hadley. For not paying, even much later, see Fitch, *Sylvia Beach and the Lost Generation*, p. 389.

73. Gus Pfeiffer was clearly affected by Hemingway's description of his poverty, as he wrote to him on 18 October 1927: "I especially enjoyed . . . [your letter] recounting your early struggles, and concerning which I cabled you. . . ." The cable of 17 September read: "Your letter recounting your earlier struggles both gripped me and thrilled me." On 20 November, Pfeiffer returned to the same topic: "You experienced difficulties, some near privations and know what it means to progress by the sweat of your brow. . . . Fortunate are those who must climb and succeed in climbing a narrow path up a steep difficult hill." In a letter of 17 September 1927, Pfeiffer had also expressed admiration for Hemingway's courage in returning a check to Hearst, and not allowing a tempting offer to turn him into a "madame" writer. For Hearst's tempting offer, see Hemingway to Fitzgerald, 15 September 1927, in *Letters*, p. 261.

74. See McAlmon and Boyle, *Being Geniuses Together*, p. 277.

75. See Michael Reynolds, *The Young Hemingway* (Oxford: Basil Blackwell, 1986), pp. 151–55, and 252 for Hadley's income. For the average income of the French and an estimation of the value of Hadley's income in France, research carried out at la Bibliothèque de l'Hôtel de Ville, Paris. For the hourly salary of the maid in 1922 and for the brand new piano, see Hadley to Grace Hall Hemingway, 20 February 1922. One might add that in 1924 their monthly rent was 650 francs, that is, roughly $26, just over one tenth of Hadley's estimated monthly income. The rent receipt from Mr. Chautard is at the Kennedy Library.

76. See *Letters*, p. 133.

77. Morill Cody seems to think that it was Ford who interrupted Hemingway: "I saw him there [at the Closerie des Lilas] many times but never interrupted him as he says Ford did on occasion" (Fitch, *Sylvia Beach and the Lost Generation*, p. 146). Ford, however, was no longer a "young man." For Baker's opinion, see *A*

Life Story, p. 684. Hemingway makes a rather unclear reference to George Horace Lorimer of the *Saturday Evening Post* in a letter to Fitzgerald of 7 September 1926, writing that one day he met Lorimer in the "Petit Chaumiere" and that, from then on, things simply "slipped along," in *Letters*, p. 216. Lorimer seems to have been a habitué of the Petite Chaumière, like Al of "Birth of a New School." Moreover, Lorimer appears to have rejected "The Undefeated" for publication. For Hemingway's submitting the story to Lorimer, see in particular *A Life Story*, p. 760. Michael Reynolds, in conversation, indicated that he thought Al might be Lewis Galantière because of Hemingway's 1924 attacks on him for being a critic in the August number of the *Transatlantic Review*.

78. Hemingway refers to "Major Elliott" in a letter to Gertrude Stein and Alice B. Toklas dated 9 August 1924, in *Letters*, p. 121. See also pp. 701 and 703. Perhaps Hemingway's dislike for Eliot came partly from the fact that Eliot did not believe spontaneously and wholeheartedly in Hemingway's genius, as Hemingway revealed resentfully in a letter to Pound, 8 November 1925: "Eliot doesn't know whether I'm any good or not." He came over and asked Gertrude Stein "if I were serious and worth publishing and Gertrude said it were best to wait and see," that Hemingway was just starting and that "there wasn't any way of knowing yet."

79. For a detailed discussion of Hemingway's relationship with Pound, see Jacqueline Tavernier-Courbin, "Ezra Pound and Ernest Hemingway," in Nagel, *Ernest Hemingway: The Writer in Context*, pp. 179–200.

80. See in particular George Wickes, *The Amazon of Letters* (New York: G. P. Putnam's Sons, 1976), pp. 161–63, 249 (in which Wickes mentions that Hemingway's memoirs are not a source he goes to for information), and p. 267. See also Jean Chalon, *Portrait d'une séductrice* (Paris: Stock, 1976), pp. 234–35.

81. Lewis Galantière wondered that Hemingway found room "for a brief moment with the painter Pascin that tells us nothing" and that he should embalm an encounter with such a "flashy nonentity." See "There Is Never Any End to Paris." I disagree here with Mr. Galantière, for Hemingway does tell us something: that he was a faithful husband even in the face of great temptation. Moreover, Hemingway is rather nice to Pascin in this chapter, and to whom can he ever be nice, except a "nonentity"? For details about Pascin, see McAlmon and Boyle, *Being Geniuses Together*, p. 300.

82. About Hemingway's unfaithfulness to Pauline, see, for instance, Gregory Hemingway, *Papa: A Personal Memoir* (Boston: Houghton Mifflin, 1976), pp. 92–93.

83. For Hemingway's admiration for Shipman's work, see in particular Hemingway to Dos Passos, 12 April 1932, to MacLeish, 27 February 1933, and to Cowley, 17 October and 14 November 1945, in *Letters*, pp. 357, 381, and 605. About Shipman's inheritance, Gertrude Stein writes that he "was an amusing boy who was to inherit a few thousand dollars when he came of age. . . . He was to

buy the Transatlantic Review when he came of age, so Hemingway said. He was to support a surrealist review when he came of age, André Masson said. He was to buy a house in the country when he came of age, Josette Gris said. As a matter of fact when he came of age nobody who had known him then seemed to know what he did with his inheritance," in *The Autobiography of Alice B. Toklas*, p. 219.

84. See Hemingway to Shipman, 25 August 1942, in *Letters*, p. 539.

85. Wyndham Lewis, "Ezra: The Portrait of a Personality," *Quarterly Review of Literature*, December 1949. See also Charles Norman, *Ezra Pound* (New York: Macmillan Co., 1960), pp. 258–59, and Stock, *The Life of Ezra Pound*, p. 248.

86. For an account of the incident, see *A Life Story*, p. 330. Lewis was not alone in criticizing Hemingway's anti-intellectualism; see, for instance, Mac-Leish to Pound, 17 April 1956, in which he writes that he visited Hemingway in Havana—"first view of the precipice in more than twenty yrs. He was off to Pern to catch gigantic marlin for forthcoming film of Old Man and See. . . . No literary conversation which was great relief—a relief which can always be counted on with Pappy."

CHAPTER FIVE

1. Wasserstrom, "Hemingway, the *Dial*, and Ernest Walsh," p. 177.

2. See Gerry Brenner, *Concealments in Hemingway's Works* (Columbus: Ohio State University Press, 1983), p. 218, for a discussion of "by remate."

3. Bunnel, "Who Wrote the Paris Idyll?" p. 339.

4. See, for instance, Hemingway's attempts at a letter in French to Mr. Chautard, June 1926 and late June 1927; see also Hadley's translation of a letter by Hemingway to Chautard written partly in English and partly in French (1926). See also File 409 for Hemingway's comments on how he learned French.

5. See, for instance, McAlmon and Boyle, *Being Geniuses Together*, p. 346.

6. For a parallel view, see Bunnel, "Who Wrote the Paris Idyll?" pp. 344–45.

7. See Brenner, *Concealments in Hemingway's Works*, pp. 225–31.

8. For an interesting discussion of Hemingway's father and of Hemingway's passive/aggressive relationships with women, see Reynolds, *The Young Hemingway*, in particular pp. 134, 171.

9. For an analysis of Hemingway's neurotic competitiveness, see Jacqueline Tavernier-Courbin, "Striving for Power: Hemingway's Neurosis," *Journal of General Education* 30, no. 3 (1978):137–53; reprinted with some changes as " 'Striving for Power': Hemingway's Classical Neurosis and Creative Force," in *MidAmerica V* (East Lansing, Mich.: The Midwestern Press, 1978), pp. 76–95.

10. Anderson agreed with Stein: "I keep wondering why the man [Hemingway] feels life as he does. It is as though he saw it always as rather ugly. 'People have it in for me. All right. I'll go for them.' There is the desire always to kill. Stein says that it is because he cannot bear the thought of any other men as artists,

that he wants to occupy the entire field. Anderson to Laura Lou Copenhaver, 9 November 1937, in *Letters of Sherwood Anderson*, ed. Howard Mumford Jones and Walter B. Rideout (Boston: Little, Brown, 1953), p. 392.

CHAPTER SIX

1. See chapter 1. See also, for instance, Lewis Galantière who wrote in "There Is Never Any End to Paris": "*A Moveable Feast* is composed of 20 sketches, rewritten from Hemingway's notebooks of the years 1921–1926."

2. For the text that was cut from the galleys of *The Sun Also Rises* and for the text of Fitzgerald's letter to Hemingway advising the cuts, see Svoboda, *Hemingway & The Sun Also Rises*, pp. 131–39. See also Hemingway to Maxwell Perkins, 21 August 1926, in which he explains that it would have been pointless, in any case, to publish the first section without Belloc's name, in *Letters*, p. 213.

3. *The Nick Adams Stories* (New York: Scribner's, 1972), pp. 233–41.

4. See Hemingway to McAlmon, in *Letters*, p. 133.

5. Young and Mann, *The Hemingway Manuscripts: An Inventory*, p. 19.

6. Files 593, 593a and 593b. File 593a also bears the beginning of two letters to Hadley, addressed respectively to 35 Rue de Fleurus and to the Hôtel Beauvoir. "My Own Life" was published in *The New Yorker*, 12 February 1927, and re-printed in *The New Yorker Scrapbook* (Garden City, N.Y.: Doubleday, Doran, 1931), pp. 154–58.

7. See Hemingway to Pound, 7 October 1925, 14 October 1925, c. November 1925 (the date is unclear), and c. 1 December 1925. The November 1925 letter seems to be a follow-up to Hemingway's letter to Pound of 8 November 1925.

8. For other information concerning that trip, see *A Life Story*, p. 254. It seems that Hemingway was quite keen on describing this evening with Fitzgerald, since he had indicated his intention in a manuscript note (File 720b) under the heading "Stories to Write." Among these stories were: 1) a Nick Adams story to be entitled "The Blue Heron"; 2) a story about a man who drove to Le Havre to meet a girl he was going to marry after his or her divorce, and about what happened during the drive back to Paris; 3) the Fitzgerald story, described as "Une soiree Chez Monsieur Fitz," which was to feature the ride from the Princeton-Dartmouth game, the Buick, its French chauffeur, and so on; 4) a story about a night of violence—"(last night)"—with the note "write it today. No, the hell with it." The story is most probably the story in File 502 which dramatizes Hemingway breaking up a violent row in the apartment across the hall from his. A man seems to be strangling Mary Tugman, and neither her mother nor her uncle Andy seems to help until Hemingway walks in; 5) three titles, presumably for stories not yet written: "The Time in Casper," "In the Beginning," and "Story of Don Stewart."

9. *Letters*, p. 896.

10. See Hemingway to Perkins, 23 February 1933, and another letter of 1933, date unclear, probably January.

11. See chapter 7, in particular for the Preface and concluding chapter.

12. The idea of having to throw things away or having them stolen recurs often in Hemingway's manuscripts. In particular, note File 632, where he compares the crafts of painting and writing, concluding that a painter, if he has a great name, can sell all his failures, as people want only the signature, while a writer "must throw his failures away or burn them." On days he could not write, he felt it would have been much more pleasant to be a painter.

13. In File 186 Hemingway comments, "They insist that you be solemn. If you make a joke they do not understand it." See also Hemingway to Gingrich, 3 April 1933, quoted in James Hinkle's "What's Funny in *The Sun Also Rises*," *The Hemingway Review* 4, no. 2 (Spring 1985):31. See also Jacqueline Tavernier-Courbin, "Ernest Hemingway's Humor in *The Sun Also Rises*: Difficulties of Translation," *Contrastes*, special number on *Humo(u)r and Translation* (1986): 223–33.

14. File 185a. A handwritten note by Hemingway in the margin indicates that he wants the French corrected.

15. File 179. For other discussions of writing by Hemingway, see in particular File 845, in which he develops the idea that the writer is the mine from which he must extract the ore until the mine is ruined, the mill where the valuable metal is extracted and refined, and the artist who creates the work of art.

16. See *A Life Story*, p. 228.

17. The stationery used here is an uncommon one for Hemingway to use: long and narrow (8 × 13 inches), heavier than usual, with perpendicular lines in the grain. In his attempts at dating Files 648a and 648b, Donald Junkins points to their geographic and tonal intimacy with *A Moveable Feast*. However, he does not mention File 529a, which establishes a tangible link with the book. For the texts of Files 648a and 648b, see "[Philip Haines Was a Writer . . .]" and Donald Junkins, "Hemingway's Paris Short Story: A Study in Revising," *The Hemingway Review* 9, no. 2 (Spring 1990):2–32.

CHAPTER SEVEN

1. See, for instance, Hemingway to Lanham, 18 September 1958, in which he writes that he has the book done, copied by Mary, and ready to be given a final go-over. Mary also indicates that she typed parts of the book in *How It Was* (p. 452, for instance) and in "The Making of the Book: A Chronicle and a Memoir," in which she writes that she "retyped as usual, correcting spelling and punctuation and consulting him about phrases which [she] thought needed reorganization."

2. See chapter 8 for a detailed discussion.

3. See chapter 6 for the notebook of *The Sun Also Rises*, and chapter 4 for details about Hemingway's letter to Pound, and for the narration of the episode at Michaud's.

4. See Files 122 (nine pages), 124 (eighteen pages), and 187 (two pages).

5. In the following discussion of textual changes and revisions the following codes for words usually in bold italics stand for: [A] = words which have been added; [C] = words which have been crossed out; (I.W.D.F.P.T.) = italicized words different from published text; (*MM*)-present study.

6. See, in particular, File 124. About that other book, Hemingway expects that it could be a good book, with remorse, contrition, and unbelievable happiness, as well as the story of his truly good work and his final sorrow. What he wrote about Pauline is all intact. It has the most happiness, and it is also the saddest book he knows.

7. See chapter 8 for the text of that paragraph. Hemingway never rewrote it himself, and his editors made the changes to make it coherent.

8. In this passage there is no discussion of making things as opposed to describing them. While many of the elements of the earlier passage are also present, this particular passage focuses more on the chestnut trees in bloom. "They *were* waxen candelabras," Hadley insists, and she claims that even Dorman-Smith agreed finally.

9. This is a very significant change, since Hemingway acknowledges that writing is now difficult for him, and that he had never dreamt it could be so. This sentence was deleted by his editors; see chapter 8.

10. Many of the pages also bear word counts in Hemingway's hand.

CHAPTER EIGHT

1. See Mary Hemingway, *How It Was*, p. 520.

2. See the tongue-in-cheek article published by Paul Smith and Jacqueline Tavernier-Courbin, " 'Terza Riruce': Hemingway, Dunning, Italian Poetry," *Thalia: Studies in Literary Humor* 5, no. 2 (1982):41–42; reprinted in *The Hemingway Review* 3, no. 2 (1984):50–51. To give credit where it is due, the discovery of the reason for the error was mine, and the humorous work was Professor Smith's. The idea originated on the occasion of a lecture I gave, "The Editing of *A Moveable Feast*," at Trinity College, Hartford, Conn., in March 1982.

3. I cannot agree with Gerry Brenner's opinion that ending the book with "A Matter of Measurements" would have been better, as it would have informed Georges, the barman, about Fitzgerald and made good Hemingway's promise to write about the early days in Paris. It seems that his objection to the last chapter is much less valid than his earlier one concerning the nurturing vs. destructive women pattern and that the only reason for not using "There Is Never Any End

to Paris" as the last chapter, despite its obvious structural and thematic advantages, would have been on the grounds that Hemingway had not intended it as such, which is probably in itself sufficient reason. For Gerry Brenner's discussion of some aspects of the editing of *A Moveable Feast*, see "Are We Going to Hemingway's *Feast?*" *American Literature* 54, no. 4 (1982):528–44.

4. Here I again disagree with Gerry Brenner who believes that Mary was wise to cut explicit references to Pauline from the text. Leaving them in would not have necessitated giving information that Hemingway had not provided; it would have been more specific and would have prevented, for instance, the confusion now present in "The End of an Avocation." See "Are We Going to Hemingway's *Feast?*" 534, 542–43.

5. Quotation originally published in *A Life Story*, p. 773, except for the first sentence. The words in italics followed by [A] were added by Hemingway on the original of the typescript, while the words in italics followed by [C] were crossed out on the same original.

6. Brenner, "Are We Going to Hemingway's *Feast?*" 531.

7. This is perhaps an unfortunate deletion, since it also removes evidence of the feelings Hemingway still had for Hadley, a type of deletion that is repeated time and again throughout the text. However, even before Mary Hemingway's editing, Hadley was never dramatized effectively as the heroine of the book.

8. Indeed, I would now qualify my earlier claim that the editing of the book "was very much of the order described by Mary in 'The Making of the Book,' " in "The Manuscripts of *A Moveable Feast*," *Hemingway Notes* 6, no. 2 (1981): 9–16.

SELECTED BIBLIOGRAPHY

Book-Length Secondary Sources

Acton, Harold. *Memoirs of an Esthete*. London: Methuen, 1948.

Adam, George, and Pearl Adam. *A Book About Paris*. London: Jonathan Cape, 1927.

Adhémar, Hélène. *Musée du Jeu de Paume*. Paris: Editions des Musées Nationaux, 1973.

Anderson, Margaret. *My Thirty Years' War: An Autobiography*. New York: Covici, Friede, 1930.

Antheil, George. *Bad Boy of Music*. New York: Doubleday, Doran, 1945.

Astro, Richard, and Jackson J. Benson, eds. *Hemingway in Our Time*. Corvallis: Oregon State University Press, 1974.

Baker, Carlos. *Ernest Hemingway: A Life Story*. New York: Bantam, 1970.

————, ed. *Ernest Hemingway: Selected Letters, 1917–1961*. New York: Scribner's, 1981.

Beach, Sylvia. *Shakespeare & Company*. New York: Harcourt, Brace, 1956.

Bowen, Stella. *Drawn from Life*. Maidstone: George Mann Ltd., 1974.

Brenner, Gerry. *Concealments in Hemingway's Works*. Columbus: Ohio State University Press, 1983.

Burns, Edward, ed. *The Letters of Gertrude Stein and Carl Van Vechten, 1913–1946*. New York: Columbia University Press, 1986.

Charters, James. *This Must Be the Place*. New York: Lee Furman, 1937.

Clébert, Jean Paul. *Les Rues de Paris: Promenades du marquis de Rochegude à travers tous les arrondissements de Paris parcourus de nouveau par Jean Paul Clébert*. Paris: Denoel, 1966.

Dos Passos, John. *The Best of Times: An Informal Memoir*. London: Andre Deutsch, 1968.

Fitch, Noel Riley. *Sylvia Beach and The Lost Generation: A History of Literary Paris in the Twenties and Thirties*. New York: W. W. Norton, 1983.

Flanner, Janet. *Paris Was Yesterday, 1925–1939*. New York: Viking, 1972.

Ford, Ford Madox. *It Was the Nightingale*. New York: Octagon Books, 1975.

244 / *Selected Bibliography*

Gajdusek, Robert. *Ernest Hemingway's Paris.* New York: Scribner's, 1954.

Gallup, Donald, ed. *The Flowers of Friendship: Letters Written to Gertrude Stein.* New York: Alfred A. Knopf, 1953.

George, André. *Paris.* London: Nicholas Kaye, 1952.

Glassco, John. *Memoirs of Montparnasse.* New York: Viking, 1970.

Hemingway, Gregory. *Papa: A Personal Memoir.* Boston: Houghton Mifflin, 1976.

Hemingway, Mary. *How It Was.* New York: Alfred A. Knopf, 1976.

Hobhouse, Janet. *Everybody Who Was Anybody: A Biography of Gertrude Stein.* New York: G. P. Putnam's Sons, 1975.

Hotchner, A. E. *Papa Hemingway.* New York: Random House, 1955.

Huddleston, Sisley. *Back to Montparnasse.* London: George G. Harrap and Co., 1931.

Imbs, Bravig. *Confessions of Another Young Man.* New York: Kenkle-Yewdale House, 1936.

Joost, Nicholas. *Ernest Hemingway and the Little Magazines: The Paris Years.* Barre, Mass.: Barre Publishers, 1968.

———. *Years of Transition, The Dial 1912–1920.* Barre, Mass.: Barre Publishers, 1964.

Kert, Bernice. *The Hemingway Women.* New York: W. W. Norton, 1983.

Knoll, Robert E., ed. *McAlmon and the Lost Generation: A Self-Portrait.* Lincoln: University of Nebraska Press, 1962.

———. *Robert McAlmon: Expatriate Publisher and Writer.* Lincoln: University of Nebraska Press, 1957.

Laughlin, Clara E. *So You're Going to Paris.* London: Methuen, 1924.

Le Gallienne, Richard. *From a Paris Garret.* New York: Ives Washburn, 1936.

Lewis, Wyndham. *Time and Western Man.* Boston: Beacon Hill Press, 1957.

Loeb, Harold. *The Way It Was.* New York: Criterion Books, 1959.

Lynn, Kenneth S. *Hemingway.* New York: Simon & Schuster, 1987.

McAlmon, Robert, and Kay Boyle. *Being Geniuses Together 1920–1930.* Garden City, N.Y.: Doubleday, 1968.

Mellow, James. *Charmed Circle: Gertrude Stein and Company.* New York: Praeger, 1974.

Milford, Nancy. *Zelda.* New York: Avon Books, 1971.

Mizener, Arthur. *The Saddest Story: A Biography of Ford Madox Ford.* London: Bodley Head, 1972.

Monneret, Sophie. *L'impressionisme et son époque.* Paris: Denoel, 1978.

Nagel, James, ed. *Ernest Hemingway: The Writer in Context.* Madison: University of Wisconsin Press, 1984.

Oldsey, Bernard, ed. *Ernest Hemingway: The Papers of a Writer.* New York: Garland, 1981.

Paige, D. D., ed. *The Letters of Ezra Pound: 1907–1941*. London: Faber and Faber, 1951.

Poli, Bernard. *Ford Madox Ford and the Transatlantic Review*. Syracuse: Syracuse University Press, 1967.

Putnam, Samuel. *Paris Was Our Mistress: Memoirs of a Lost and Found Generation*. New York: Viking, 1947.

Rascoe, Burton. *We Were Interrupted*. Garden City, N.Y.: Doubleday, 1947.

Reynolds, Michael. *The Young Hemingway*. Oxford: Basil Blackwell, 1986.

Robert, Robert. *Le Guide du gourmand à Paris*. Paris: Bernard Grasset, 1925.

Slocombe, George. *Paris in Profile*. Boston: Houghton Mifflin, 1929.

Smoller, Sanford J. *Adrift Among Geniuses: Robert McAlmon, Writer and Publisher of the Twenties*. University Park: Pennsylvania State University Press, 1975.

Sokoloff, Alice Hunt. *Hadley, The First Mrs. Hemingway*. New York: Dodd, Mead, 1973.

Steffens, Joseph Lincoln. *The Autobiography of Lincoln Steffens*. New York: Harcourt, Brace, 1931.

Stein, Gertrude. *The Autobiography of Alice B. Toklas*. New York: Random House, 1960.

———. *Everybody's Autobiography*. New York: Cooper Square, 1937.

Stock, Noel. *The Life of Ezra Pound*. New York: Pantheon Books, 1960.

Svoboda, F. J. *Hemingway & The Sun Also Rises*. Lawrence: University Press of Kansas, 1983.

Toklas, Alice B. *What Is Remembered*. New York: Holt Rinehart and Winston, 1963.

Tompkins, Calvin. *Living Well Is the Best Revenge*. New York: Viking, 1971.

Wickes, George. *The Amazon of Letters*. New York: G. P. Putnam's Sons, 1976.

———. *Americans in Paris*. Garden City, N.Y.: Doubleday, 1969.

Young, Philip. *Ernest Hemingway: A Reconsideration*. University Park: Pennsylvania State University Press, 1966.

Young, Philip, and Charles Mann. *The Hemingway Manuscripts: An Inventory*. University Park: Pennsylvania State University Press, 1969.

INDEX

Bal Musette, 56, 76, 112
Bal du Printemps, 56–57
Banville, Théodore de, 59
Barney, Nathalie, 79, 95
Barret, Peter, 33
Barry, Madame du, 42
bathhouses (Paris), 51–52
Battle of Jutland, 73, 134
Battle of Skaggerack, 73
Battle of Waterloo, 46
Baudelaire, Charles, 55–56
Beach, Sylvia, 97, 104, 124, 189; on breakup of Stein-Hemingway friendship, 79; contrasted with Stein, 175–76; correspondence with Hemingway, 16, 73; friendship with Hemingway, 76; Paris bookshop of, 46, 53, 54; on Walsh's financial difficulties, 82–83
Beatty, Admiral David, 73
Bécu, Jeanne. *See* Barry, Madame du
Beillard and Deloep (*papeterie*), 226n.33
Bel Esprit, 94–95, 104, 138, 155
Belloc, Hilaire, 69–70, 86–87, 111, 112; *Paris*, 43
Béranger, Pierre Jean de, 59
Bernard, Tristan, 52
Best Short Stories of 1923 (O'Brien, ed.), 76
bicycle racing, 52–53, 76, 148, 232n.35
"Big Two-Hearted River" (Hemingway), 89, 94, 111, 114, 128
Bird, Bill, xvi, 146
Bird, Sally, xvi
Black Forest, 75–76
"The Blue Heron" (Hemingway), 238n.8
Boni and Liveright (publishers), 230n.26
Bonnard, Pierre, 221n.53
Book-of-the-Month Club, 174, 175, 183, 197
booksellers (Paris), 48
Boswell, James, 3

Bovary, Madame (Flaubert's character), 127
Bowen, Stella, 69, 117
boxing, 119–21
Braddocks (Hemingway's character), 111
Brague, Harry: copy editing of *Moveable Feast*, 171, 174, 233n.63; correspondence with Hemingway, 22, 24, 27, 33, 34, 38, 63, 138
Braque, Georges, 56, 229n.19
Braun, Mathilda, 62, 73
Breit, Harvey, correspondence with Hemingway, 10, 11–12, 12–13, 21, 23, 24–25, 26, 80, 81–82, 212n.18
Brenner, Gerry: on ending of *Moveable Feast*, 240n.3; on excision of references to Pauline Pfeiffer, 241n.4; on Hemingway's relationship with father, 107; on loss of *Moveable Feast* Preface manuscript, 182
Briggs, Peter, 33–34
broken heart, as theme of Hemingway's writing, 122, 124, 139, 168
Brook, John Wilkes, 115
Brown, George, xxii
Bruce, Betty, 27
Bruce, Otto, 27
bullfighting, Hemingway's sketch on, xx, 27, 28, 29–30, 32
"The Bull Ring" (Hemingway), 214n.23
Bunnell, W. A., 101, 102, 109
Burgess, Anthony, 210n.5

Cabaret de la Pomme de Pin, 43
cafés: des Amateurs, 42, 103, 139; Bidault, 61; Bullier, 59; La Chope, 42; de Cluny, 41; La Contrescarpe, 42; Coupole, 125; Danton, 226n.37; de Deux Magots, 54, 147; du Dôme, 56, 57, 94, 95, 112, 125; Harot, 61; Lipps, 54, 154; Napolitain, 120; de la Paix, 59; Rotonde, 56, 57, 125; Saint Martin, 61; Sélect, 57, 125

craft of writing, 81–82; cutting of Belloc, 111, 112–13; deceptiveness of, 69–70, 116–17; destruction of reputation of, 13, 100, 102; editorship of literary journals, 116, 117; as father figure to Hemingway, 107; as foil for Hemingway's self-dramatization, 108; Hemingway's unpublished profile of, 25, 35, 116–17, 131; interruption of Hemingway's writing by, 235n.77; marriages of, 116–17; parties of, 76; profile in *Moveable Feast*, 24, 26, 29, 35, 66, 70, 76–77, 102, 111–13, 136, 175; profile in *Moveable Feast*—Hemingway's revisions of, 152; profile in *Moveable Feast*—posthumous editing of, 190; treatment in *Sun Also Rises* notebooks, 111–13
Fort, Paul, 55
France, privileges of artists in, 71
French Foreign Legion, 56
French names/words, Hemingway's misspelling of, 39–40, 62–63, 141, 143, 145, 172–73, 222n.1
French Revolution, 42, 60
From a Paris Garret (Le Gallienne), 41–42, 43, 47, 50–51
Fuller, Rosalinde, 232n.49

Gains, Larry, 25, 35, 116, 119–21, 131
Gajdusek, Robert, *Hemingway's Paris*, 43, 57
Galantière, Lewis, 4, 94, 236n.81
Gallup, Donald, 18, 77, 78
Gamble, James, 76
Ganay, (bicyclist), 52, 53, 174
The Garden of Eden (Hemingway), xii, xix, 22, 25, 26, 27, 28, 106, 217n.5
Gare de Lyon, 61
"Get Yourself a Seeing-Eyed Dog" (Hemingway), xix, 217n.6
Gide, André, 56, 138, 156–57, 182, 212n.18, 230n.25
Gilbert, Morris, 221n.53
Gingrich, Arnold: correspondence with

Hemingway, 7–8, 13, 232n.41; payments to Hemingway for short stories, 217n.15
goats, in Paris, 50–51
Grande Chaumière, 59
The Great Gatsby (Fitzgerald), 104, 162
Greco-Turkish war, 76
The Green Hat (Arlen), 72
Green Hills of Africa (Hemingway), 65, 127, 211n.17
Gregory, Alyse, 234n.68
Gris, Josette, 237n.83
Guide du gourmand à Paris, Le (Robert), 48–49, 49–50, 225n.24
Gulf Stream Park, 123
"Gusta" (Hemingway), 216n.23

Hadley: The First Mrs. Hemingway (Sokoloff), 211n.16, 223–24n.13
Haines, Philip (Hemingway's character), 129
Halle aux Vins, 46–47, 115
Hearst, William Randolph, 235nn.72,73
Hemingway, Clarence E., 75, 76, 107
Hemingway, Ernest: alleged poverty of, 90–92, 100, 103; anti-intellectualism of, 97; break with Hadley Richardson, 115, 130–31, 136, 166–68, 170, 177–80, 181; chronology of writing of *Moveable Feast* (1956–61), xix–xxii; on connection between reality and fiction, 97; on craft of writing, 114, 115, 122, 125–28; custodianship of papers of, 9–10; decline of creative powers of, 13–14, 14–15, 103–104, 107–108, 109; destruction of associates' reputations, 100, 101–103, 108; on discovery of Ritz Hotel papers, 3, 6, 10, 17–18; justification of personal attacks on Paris associates, 11, 13–15; life chronology (1921–26), xv–xviii; on location of *Farewell to Arms* manuscript, 3–4; management of family finances, 92–94; marital infidelity of, 96, 100, 129, 166, 167–